Voices of the

CODE
BREAKERS

Personal accounts of the secret heroes of World War II

Voices of the

CODE BREAKERS

Personal accounts of the secret heroes of World War II

Michael Paterson

Foreword by Robert Harris

Greenhill
Books

Voices of the Code Breakers
This edition first published in 2018 by Greenhill Books
c/o Pen & Sword Books Ltd,
47 Church Street, Barnsley,
S. Yorkshire, S70 2AS

Publishing History
First published in the UK by David & Charles in 2007

www.greenhillbooks.com
contact@greenhillbooks.com

ISBN: 978-1-78438-313-8

Front cover image supplied courtesy of Peter D. Greenway
Back cover image A four-rotor Enigma machine in use in the cramped confines of a U-boat

CIP data records for this title are available from the British Library

Typeset in Ehrhardt MT Pro
by Servis Filmsetting Ltd, Stockport, Cheshire

Printed and bound in England by
CPI Group (UK) Ltd, Croydon, CR0 4YY

CONTENTS

Foreword by Robert Harris   6

Introduction   8

1   Codes and War   10

2   Bletchley Park   46

3   1940: A Fatefull Year   78

4   Battle of the Atlantic   100

5   North Africa and Italy   128

6   The Resistance   164

7   Towards Victory in Europe   208

8   War in the Pacific   238

Chronology   278
Bibliography and Sources   280
Index   282
Acknowledgments   288
Picture Credits   288

FOREWORD

George Steiner once hailed the British code breaking effort at Bletchley Park as 'the single greatest achievement of Britain during 1939–45, perhaps during this century as a whole'.

The claim will doubtless strike many as ridiculous. Surely, however precise the information about the enemy which Bletchley provided, it would have been useless without the courage of the sailors, soldiers and airmen who had to act upon it? True; nevertheless, I still think Steiner's dramatic assertion is justified. While all the major combatants in the second world war had navies, armies and airforces often as good as, if not superior, to ours, none had anything to compare with our achievements in intelligence. Bletchley was Britain's singular contribution, not just to victory, but to the development of the modern world.

I met my first pair of Bletchley Park veterans by accident over dinner with a friend's parents in 1980, when I was twenty-three. Typically, they were the daughter of an earl, and a grammar school boy from Keighley, who had gone on to become a famous historian. By the end of the war, he had helped compile a set of records of the Luftwaffe, so voluminous they had to be housed in an aircraft hangar, and which eventually proved to be more detailed than those held by Goering's Air Ministry in Berlin. She had operated a Type-X decryption machine – a simple clerical job – but the nature of her work meant that, at nineteen, she held in her head the greatest British secret of the war: a fact of which she was acutely conscious, she said, every time she ventured out in public.

I listened, enraptured, to their stories, and fifteen years later wrote a novel, *Enigma*, which tried to convey something of the atmosphere of this haunting place, which had cut across the traditional barriers of sex and class. I had the good fortune to conduct my research at a time when some of the key players were still alive and able to answer questions: Sir Stuart Milner-Barry, former junior chess champion of Great Britain, and subsequently head of Bletchley's Hut 6; Sir Harry Hinsley, expert in signals traffic analysis, who later became the official historian of British intelligence in the second world war; and – perhaps the most memorable of them all – Joan Murray, one of Bletchley's few women codebreakers, who had worked on the U-boat ciphers in Hut 8, had been briefly engaged to Alan Turing, and who was now living, widowed and solitary, in a small house in north Oxford.

All these three are now dead; and the sad truth is that within the next decade virtually everyone who played a significant role in Bletchley will have gone, too. Hence the need for this book, which skilfully draws together the voices of the past. The wartime code breakers not only produced the most astonishing cornucopia of intelligence in the history of warfare (at its peak, Bletchley was decrypting 10,000 enemy signals *per day*); they not only pioneered the development of the computer, and so helped give birth to the information age, they also represented the triumph of a peculiarly British blend of genius, discretion, amateurism and eccentricity, which seems to be vanishing with them.

Whenever I think of Bletchley, I think of shift-changes at midnight and chilly wooden huts, of glowing orange valves and clanking electro-magnetic machinery; I think of Alan Turing cycling to work in his gas mask during the hayfever season, and of sunlit games of rounders in front of that hideous Victorian mansion; I think of chess-players, crossword-puzzle addicts, Egyptologists, numismatists, philologists, lexicographers, musicologists – in short, of that particular kind of quiet, self-absorbed, recondite intellect, which is often overlooked or even mildly despised in the modern world, but which, for a few years, came together in a suburban park in the dreary midlands of England, and helped save western civilisation.

Robert Harris

INTRODUCTION

Thirty years after World War II ended, a relaxation of British Government security strictures brought to light one of its most important secrets. It was revealed, to understandable astonishment, that the war had been won not just by military genius or by the dogged courage of the Allied Armed Forces – though both had of course been of vast significance – but by groups of obscure or unknown people who found out in advance what the enemy intended to do, and passed on this knowledge to those who commanded the armies, the fleets and the bomber formations. Vital information that turned the tide of battle in the North African desert or on the Pacific Ocean proved to have been obtained not by the skill and bravery of spies, or by miraculous coincidence, but by the plodding and unglamorous work of operatives who read the enemy's coded messages. The result has been, of necessity, a re-evaluation of reputations and a rewriting of history.

The ability to gain access to the very thought processes of the enemy was a major epic of ingenuity, and a great adventure. What makes it even more remarkable is the fact that the people who carried it out (and there were thousands of them) received no public recognition for their contribution to the war effort, and were forbidden to tell even their families what they had been doing throughout the long years of conflict. Without a single known exception, they faithfully kept this silence until, an entire generation later, they were permitted by the government to admit their involvement. The story of these cryptographers has considerable bearing on our own postwar world, for in the process of breaking the secret codes of Nazi Germany they created the computer as we know it today.

The breaking of German codes began long before the start of war in 1939. For almost a decade, cryptanalysts in Poland had studied and replicated the Enigma machine, which was used by German armies from the 1920s until Hitler's defeat. Thanks to their skill and perseverance the Western democracies, France and Britain, were in possession of working copies of Enigma by the time hostilities began. Though Poland itself was dismembered and conquered, it was thus able to make a contribution to eventual victory that was beyond calculation.

As for the Axis powers, it was fortunate that they took a view of cryptography that was both disdainful and complacent. By tradition, the German military mind did not approve of, or appreciate, such skulduggery. Throughout the war, senior officers therefore sometimes ignored opportunities to make use of intelligence that could have been of value. They also largely took it for granted that their communications were secure, and left it at that.

Their greatest disadvantage of all, however, was the nature of Adolf Hitler. Having grown accustomed to a sense of his own infallibility, the Führer saw no need to waste time or effort on cryptanalysis, and with few exceptions he failed to take it seriously. He had, after all, conquered Europe by relying on his own hunches. Swift and decisive action, not painstaking intelligence gathering, was the key to success. Hitler's entourage, and his General Staff, could not have retained their positions without sharing, at least publicly, this belief in his genius and thus by implication regarding intelligence as unnecessary. The Führer was provided, by several organizations, with a great many decrypted Allied messages. These were often highly informative. Hitler, however, committed a classic error by failing to read them objectively. His mind already made up, he would dismiss data that did not fit with his views. He once scrawled across a dossier dealing with Soviet economic recovery the comment: 'This cannot be.' It probably did not, in any case, help the German cause that Admiral Canaris, the head of the *Abwehr* (the German secret service), was anti-Nazi. The Japanese, a similarly militaristic nation, largely took the same view.

It was fortunate that the Allies – the Poles, the French, the British and the Americans – were untrammelled by such a mindset. They had appreciated all along the value of overheard chatter or routine reports. They had the imagination and the flexibility to assemble, analyse, distribute and act upon signals intelligence, and thus to make their enemies' voices a weapon in their own armoury. Because of an ongoing need for secrecy, the attainments of wartime cryptanalysts could not be recognized. A simple but heartfelt tribute, however, was paid to them by one British general, Lord Gort, who told the head of the Ultra organization:

I think there are many people who would bless your codebreakers if they knew what they had done.

The purpose of this book is to tell you what they did.

1
CODES AND WAR

The ether was open. Into it all nations could discharge messages of
the highest importance. Equally important was the complicating
factor that all nations might, if they wished, receive or stop these
messages. We were all involved in the problem of safeguarding our
own information, of discovering and nullifying that of the enemy.
It was not enough merely to prevent the latter from giving
messages to its own forces and allies. It was vital that we should
receive those messages and turn them to our own purpose.[i]

Parallel with the open conflict that raged between 1939 and 1945 there
were other, hidden wars, and what they all had in common was that they
were wars of communication, in which success depended on a flow of
concealed and closely guarded information. Sometimes this meant a
smuggled written message, at others a secretly transmitted wireless signal,
or weeks and months of eavesdropping on the radio traffic of the enemy.

Many thousands of people took part in these secret wars. Some trained
for long periods to carry out sophisticated campaigns of espionage; others
committed a single impulsive or premeditated act of defiance. One of these
hidden conflicts was the struggle of underground forces against the
occupying Germans or Japanese. Another was the battle to obtain secrets, or
carry out sabotage, by the spies who served both sides. A third was the war
waged by armies of clerks, typists, linguists, analysts and assorted academics
to discover the intentions – and weaknesses – of the enemy by breaking its
codes. In Britain, it was only in 1974 that the publication of Group Captain
FW Winterbotham's book *The Ultra Secret* revealed the huge significance of
this work and the extent to which it had contributed to victory.

The war imposed the necessity of secrecy not just on official and military
personnel but on people who found themselves displaced, imprisoned or in
some way unable to express their feelings freely. One example was the

[i] Hugh Cleland Hoy, *40 OB, or How the War Was Won*

deliberate damaging of Axis war materiel made by forced labour in German-controlled countries. Alfred Spickett, a wireless officer in the British Merchant Navy, recalled an attack on his vessel by enemy aircraft in which little damage was done:

> What none of us realized at the time was that we had in fact been hit by two aerial torpedoes. Very fortunately for us, both had failed to explode.
>
> Anyone reading this might think it odd that both torpedoes had failed to explode. I must admit I did myself. A possible explanation, given later by a naval bomb expert in Rosyth, was that they were getting quite a number of torpedoes and bombs which failed to explode, and they were sure it was due to sabotage in a number of factories in German 'occupied' countries. I remember this same chap telling me that in one of the bombs they had subsequently dismantled (which had been dropped near London) they had found a hand-written note in the front section of the bomb which made it clear that it had been made in the Skoda works in Czechoslovakia. Written in English, the note had gone on to say: 'This is the best we can do to help you.' These particular factory workers were successfully interfering with the mechanism in both bombs and torpedoes, thus preventing them from exploding.

While some put their lives at constant risk in enemy territory, others laboured at routine deskwork, far from scenes of conflict or danger. The most significant of these were the men and women who sought to break the codes and ciphers of the Axis powers.

Communications, whether by radio or letter, had to be shrouded in secrecy, with use of passwords, code words, euphemisms and gibberish to baffle enemy eavesdroppers. This was characteristic of all 'secret wars' and was much in evidence by the start of the conflict in 1939. A story published a year earlier in the United States, when many Americans knew little about the shadow lengthening across Europe, made use of a code as its central theme. *Address Unknown*, a short novel by Katherine Kressman-Taylor, became a bestseller in the US. It greatly increased awareness of the evils of Nazism and has since come to be regarded as a highly important historical document (the Nazis themselves placed it on their list of banned literature).

The book is set in the years in which Hitler consolidated power. A Jewish art dealer in America takes revenge for betrayal on his ex-partner, a German living in Munich. By the simple device of sending frequent letters – knowing that they will be read by the Gestapo – whose meaningless contents suggest a developing plot, the dealer is able to have his former friend ruined and arrested. One of them reads:

February 15, 1934

Dear Martin,
Seven inches of rainfall here in 18 days. What a season! A shipment of 1,500 brushes should reach the Berlin branch of your Young Painters' League by the weekend. This will allow time for practice before the big exhibition. American patrons will help with all the artists' supplies that can be provided, but you must make the final arrangements. We are too far out of touch with the European market and you are in a position to gauge the extent of support such a showing would arouse in Germany. Prepare these for distribution by March 24th: Rubens 12 by 77, blue; Giotto 1 by 317, green and white; Poussin 20 by 90, red and white.
   Young Blum left last Friday with the Picasso specifications. He will leave oils in Hamburg and Leipzig and will then place himself at your disposal.
   Success to you!
   Eisenstein.

Once war began, millions of people made use of personal codes to keep in touch with their friends and relations in circumstances where security considerations, or capture, might rob them of freedom of expression. Lieutenant GP Darling, RN, whose usual form of address in letters to his parents was 'My Dearest Ma & Pa', sent them a set of instructions when he was called to active duty. He was concerned not so much with letting them know he was alive and well as with passing on to his superiors a report of what had happened, plus confirmation that sensitive materials aboard his vessel had been disposed of. After personal news and messages came this:

Now for something serious. I must make provision for being captured by the enemy. As soon as possible I will write to you and the manner of my writing will give you the following information. Forward the decoded version to Vice-Admiral Submarines, Northways, Swiss Cottage, London. If in doubt get in touch with Reggie Drake at Blockhouse.

(1) 'My Dearest Mother & Daddy' = Confidential books and asches[ii] destroyed.

(2) 'My Dearest Mother' = Confidential books destroyed.

(3) 'My Dearest Father' = Asche destroyed.

(4) 'Best Love, Godfrey' = Sunk by depth charges.

(5) 'Love, Godfrey' = Sunk by mine on surface.

(6) 'Best love from your loving son, Godfrey' = Sunk by torpedo on surface.

(7) 'Love from your loving son, Godfrey' = Rammed.

Keep this locked away and keep it to yourselves please.

Understandably, there were cases where cryptic meanings were ascribed to what were actually straightforward words or phrases. One such incident took place in 1943 in Burma, the result of a misunderstood abbreviation. The regional headquarters of OSS (the Office of Strategic Services, which was running clandestine American operations) in India received a radio message asking for supplies from one of its officers, who was in command of a remote unit of guerrillas recruited from the local Kachin people. Included in this were the letters CMA. These baffled the operator on the receiving end, and eventually it was decided that they stood for 'Citation for Military Assistance', presumably suggesting that an award be created to acknowledge the tribesmen's loyalty and support. This was duly done, the result being a silver medal adorned with the American eagle and hung from a green silk ribbon decorated with embroidered peacocks. A number of these were dropped with the rest of the supplies and were handed out to the guerrillas, who greatly appreciated them. Only later did it become clear that CMA had stood for 'comma'.

Commercial radio and BBC services offered possibilities for secret communication. Agents could, for instance, listen for pre-arranged signals in the form of a particular piece of music. It was for this reason that the United States Government forbade radio stations to play any music requested by listeners for the duration of the war. When broadcasting to occupied Europe,

[ii] The meaning of 'asches' has not been identified, and the nearest guess is that it refers to Asdic, the antisubmarine sonar device that was a major Allied secret weapon. Bulky and complex, it would have been necessary to destroy the device physically in situ to prevent it falling into enemy hands.

the BBC made regular use of the first bars from Beethoven's Fifth Symphony as an 'opening theme' to its nightly broadcasts. Initially this habit puzzled both the German security services and the resistance. Since the music was written by one of their country's greatest composers, the Germans could scarcely object to it; they had failed to realize that the first four notes sounded like a Morse code signal: dot-dot-dot-dash, representing the letter V, for victory. It was a subtle indication that, no matter what Axis propaganda was telling the local population, the Allies were winning the war.

The most famous use of radio code words was the communication between the European resistance movements and Britain. Agents in France, the Low Countries and Scandinavia would send wireless signals in code (often at great personal risk, for the Germans used location-finding equipment to track them down) and listen to the nightly broadcasts of the BBC from Bush House in London for a reply. Twice every evening a batch of announcements, disguised as and including personal messages, was broadcast in the appropriate language. Many of these sounded absurd. Some of them were deliberately intended to confuse and irritate listening German counter-intelligence operatives, while others had clear meanings for specific groups. A British officer, CW Kemson, who served with a unit of French *maquisards* in 1944, described what happened when one of its leaders was wounded and required medicines from England:

> His physical state was very poor and it worried them. They could only communicate with London at predetermined times and they had to wait until the 24th to ask for urgent supplies. This took place at 9.30 a.m.
>
> Michel sent the message in the code transcribed, and after 'contact' they were overjoyed when Gineste received confirmation signifying that an important message was to follow. The same day at 7 p.m. and 9 p.m. the BBC sent among the personal messages 'The height is at the corner.' At 11 p.m. a drop was received at Boulieu, and several hours later George was out of danger.
>
> The message to London in code had read as follows:
> Send Boulieu serum anti gangrene and anti tetanus for Maxime and other wounded awaiting medical equipment STOP column of about 270 vehicles transport to Figeac. Remain in contact with HQ STOP.

The information exchanged in these announcements was critical to the success of the D-Day operation. It informed the Allies of the strength of opposition they might expect in Normandy, and enabled the resistance to learn where the attack was coming, so that they could sabotage strategic transport routes or tie down German troops.

Radio could, of course, be used to deceive as well as inform. Hitler and many of his generals believed that an Anglo-American invasion, which they anticipated in April or May 1944, would be launched across the Straits of Dover in the neighbourhood of Calais, since this was the narrowest part of the English Channel, and that an attack anywhere else would merely be a feint to draw the defenders away. The Allies had no intention of assaulting this heavily protected region but, knowing that their radio communications were listened to by the enemy, set out to create an entire phantom army that would be based in south-east England in apparent readiness to make the move that Hitler was expecting.

This meant the invention of fictitious divisions, all with numbers, commanding officers and even specially designed insignia. It also meant the invention of radio call signs for each unit, and regular sending of Morse signals between them, so that enemy listeners could use these to track the 'movements' of the different formations. It required an endless exchange of radio messages between non-existent units – the relaying of orders, the requesting of supplies, the movement of immense columns of vehicles and the creation of camps, supply dumps and headquarters. From October 1943, German listeners began to hear, amid this storm of chatter, references to a body called FUSAG (First United States Army Group) and to the divisions and army groups attached to it. From these they deduced that 34 American divisions were massing in Kent and Essex (in fact 11 of them did not exist) and estimated that a total of 79 Allied divisions would be ranged against them in the invasion. The Allies, in fact, had only 47.

Radio was not the only means of conveying this sense that a mighty army was waiting to strike. Nevertheless nothing breathed life into the ghostly echelons of First Army Group more effectively than its radio traffic. For days and even weeks after the landings in Normandy, the Germans continued to waste time and resources on this force. On 9 June 'Cato,' a trusted (but 'turned') Axis agent, sent a message from England saying:

> The present operation, though a large-scale assault, is
> diversionary in character.

Later in the month a situation report by German Intelligence noted that:

> **Not a single unit of the 1st United States Army Group, which comprises around 25 large formations north and south of the Thames, has so far been committed.**

Clearly, continuous and detailed access to the enemy's communications was a vital factor in winning the war. It not only revealed the intentions, strengths and weaknesses of the Axis powers, but their reaction to Allied measures, initiatives and deceptions. Their communications were, naturally, sent in code for reasons of security, and it was therefore a major task of Allied Intelligence to gain access to these.

***

The reading and interpretation of ciphers and coded intelligence was extremely difficult, for it was not simply a matter of breaking a single code and then sitting back to listen in. While the Germans and Italians used a cipher machine invented in 1918 (and first used for banking security) for sending secret messages, there were many variations of the codes they employed. Germany's army, navy and air force, for instance, as well as its foreign office, each used different configurations. In addition, these were changed at frequent intervals as a matter of routine. It was also necessary that they keep track of a huge flow of signals dealing with every aspect of combat, supply and administration. Group Captain Fred Winterbotham, who coordinated the Special Liaison Units throughout the war, remarked:

> **At the height of the conflict the German war machine was sending well over two thousand signals a day on the air. It will be recognised therefore, that when, from time to time, we were able to intercept a number of signals and break the cipher, their contents covered a very wide field.**

The Allied codebreakers, working in the Government Code and Cipher School at Bletchley Park and at other sites, therefore had constantly to attempt to reopen sources of information that had been closed to them. In some cases, they never succeeded in breaking a code; in most, however, they were able to unravel the mysteries time and again.

Those who worked on the codes might see no more than a single 'piece of the jigsaw' and have no understanding of how the paper in their hand fitted in with overall developments. The information they assembled was code-named Ultra (for ultra-secret). It was analysed and passed to commanders in the field through military personnel called SLUs (Special Liaison Units) who were attached to the various armies and lived with the troops in the theatres of war. Though Ultra was obtained by British intelligence, much of the information was shared with the United States Government, at Churchill's request, even before America entered the conflict. Once the two nations were officially allies, SLUs were attached to US forces and Ultra was made available to senior American officers on exactly the same basis as to British.

For those who were engaged in the cryptographic war at secret locations in Britain, their distance from the fighting and the often numbing monotony of their work did not prevent them from sometimes sharing the triumphs and tragedies of their comrades overseas, for they could be closely following Allied progress through the signals they deciphered. Mrs EJE Openshaw, a member of the British 'Wrens' (WRNS, the Women's Royal Naval Service) who, though based on land, was subject to the shipboard routine of naval 'watches', described the view of the war that she developed through her work:

> My work in Derby House (Liverpool) was in the Communications
> Department, where I worked, with many others, as a Cipher Officer.
> Cipher messages, broadly speaking, were 'Secret' or 'Top Secret', and
> could only be dealt with by officers, and codes were 'Confidential',
> and dealt with by ratings. We were divided into four Watches which
> ran from 0800–1300, 1300–1800, 1800–midnight, midnight–0800.
> This was vital work, as all warships at sea received their orders in
> code or cipher, in Morse Code by wireless telegraphy. It was usually
> very busy on duty, sometimes hectic, during attacks on convoys,
> very exciting, and quite horrifying, as we knew the events at sea as
> they were happening. We knew about the loss of HMS Hood, and
> [that there were] only three survivors. We knew of the hunt for,
> and sinking of, the Bismarck, and were ecstatic. The Bismarck had
> sunk the Hood. When you are in a war for survival, you can only
> rejoice when the enemy suffers losses. You have a totally different
> perspective from pundits writing history years later.

Tension, monotony and occasional euphoria, the characteristic feelings of millions of troops involved in the 'shooting war', were experienced in equal measure by those, at Bletchley and elsewhere, whose contribution to the war effort was to listen to enemy signals. The fact that their role could never be revealed gave them a sense of shared purpose and pride, which perhaps exceeded that of any other unit.

THE BEGINNINGS

Espionage is as old as humankind and it has proved as invaluable a source of information in peace as in war. It was always useful to know the intentions of neighbours and rivals – and never more than amid the tangle of European alliances that preceded the Great War. Diplomatic correspondence, which was normally in some form of secret writing, was therefore subject to scrutiny, and those with an ability to work out its meanings were in demand by both foreign ministries and war offices. Diplomatic messages were usually encoded, then enciphered to provide an additional layer of secrecy, and this practice continued with regard to military communications once World War I began. By 1914 the armies and navies of many nations included intelligence specialists devoted to the deciphering of signals. Hugh Hoy, who was one of these, remarked in his book *40 O.B.* published in 1932:

> Obviously none of the Powers would use the wireless for conveying vitally secret messages without disguising these as cunningly as possible. It was essential then that we should be able to read the enemy codes, constructed of the most baffling combinations of letters and numbers that the wit of man could devise. It was this necessity that led to the formation of a special department at the Admiralty, a department that in many ways may now be considered to have been the hub of the mechanism of the Great War.

As in World War II, the secrecy of this work was so well preserved that many participants never admitted their involvement in it, as Hoy remembered:

> Its existence was not made publicly known until a few years ago. One of our most trusted naval officers who was at the Admiralty

during the whole course of the war, told me that he learned of 40
O.B.'s existence some years after the armistice. One officer who
worked in 40 O.B. carried his secret to the grave with him, and
not very long ago his widow learned from me for the first time of
the responsible work of her husband, whom she had understood
to be doing some vague 'clerking job' at the Admiralty.

Room 40, or '40 O.B.' (Old Building), at the Admiralty in Whitehall, was
an address that became as famous in codebreaking circles as Scotland
Yard in police lore. The Admiralty provided the most effective service of
this sort in Britain, and the cryptographic department of British Naval
Intelligence was directed from Room 40 by Admiral Sir Reginald Hall.
Imaginative, innovative and dynamic, Hall was assisted by the brilliant
codebreaker Sir Alfred Ewing. Together they created a highly efficient
department that was to play a major role in the defeat of the Central
Powers. One of their notions, prompted by a shortage of manpower, was
to employ women as cryptographers. This would not be the only respect
in which the codebreakers of Hitler's war would be following a precedent
set in the previous conflict.

Until the invention of wireless, the major means of international
communication had been the telegraph cable. At the start of World War I
Britain, with control of the seas, lost no time in denying this to the enemy.
Hoy, working in Naval Intelligence, remembered that:

As soon as war was declared in August 1914, there were strange
happenings in the deep waters which the vessels of the British
Fleet rode. From the waves there slowly rose great snake-like
monsters, thick with slime and seaweed growths, responding
reluctantly to the grapnels which dragged them to the surface
and beyond and laid their bulk athwart the deck of a boat, soon to
be returned, severed and useless, to the depths. They were
Germany's cables by which she maintained direct communication
with the rest of the world. Thus the British navy struck the first
blow at the enemy's war machinery. As far as telegraphs were
concerned Germany was now isolated. She had two sources of
communication left to her – cables via neutral countries, and
wireless. Nor could she retaliate, and our British cables
functioned throughout the War with very little interference.

In 1914 wireless had become, for the first time, a weapon of war. As a widely used means of communication that could be listened to by anyone, it offered unprecedented opportunities for learning of the enemy's plans and movements. Within days of the outbreak of World War I, the army had set up a department to monitor foreign telegraph traffic, while the Admiralty established a series of radio listening posts throughout the country. These were administered by the General Post Office (they were, in a sense, a natural outgrowth of the government's centuries-old practice of reading the mail of dubious foreigners) and on their staffs were academics and others with the relevant language abilities. One of them was Alistair Denniston, who would later take charge of the Government Code and Cipher School and would direct the work at Bletchley Park in World War II. Another member of staff, the professorial EWB Gill, remarked on an aspect of the work that would be noticed by codebreakers in both wars: the rigidity of German official thinking – and training – made their procedures and patterns of thought easy to predict and to follow. He said:

> Nobody could desire more admirable opponents than the Germans for this class of work. The orderly Teutonic mind was especially suited for devising schemes which any child could unravel.

Even without access to the secret codes of an enemy, a great deal could be learned from studying his signals. Anyone who tapped out Morse or telegraph messages would have an individual style, known as a 'fist', as distinctive as handwriting. With practice and an attentive ear, it could be identified by listeners, who could trace its place of origin. If it originated from a general's headquarters his movements could then be followed, since his signaller would naturally travel with him. Because units usually gave an individual 'call sign' when sending messages, their positions could also be established.

Admiral Hall's staff concentrated on cracking German codes, but he realized, as would his successors in the next war, that obtaining an enemy code book would save a great deal of time and trouble. He was extremely fortunate: in two incidents he was able to acquire, without effort, precisely what his department needed.

On 20 August 1914 – within weeks of the start of hostilities – the body of a German sailor was washed up on the Gulf of Finland's Russian coast. He was the wireless officer from the cruiser *Magdeburg*, which had been sunk by Russian warships, and in his arms was a code book that revealed the secrets of the High Seas Fleet Naval Code. The Russian navy, lacking a sophisticated intelligence service of its own, passed on this priceless treasure to its British counterpart. The second gift from fate was another code book. This was found in December 1914 in the nets of a British trawler in the North Sea. These books were undeniably useful, but they were not enough. As all the belligerent powers used different codes for each of their armed forces, government departments and diplomats, and as codes were in any case altered continually to protect secrecy, Hall had to seek out information wherever it could be found. One of his great successes was the recovery of a code book left behind by the German Vice-Consul to Persia, who had had to flee when caught attempting to sabotage an oil pipeline. This gave access to important diplomatic codes throughout the Middle East, a vital and sensitive theatre of war.

He was particularly keen to get hold of naval codes, and issued orders that any wrecked enemy craft within reach was to be carefully searched. This produced no immediate result, but he hit upon another idea. He was aware that the German Admiralty had cracked several British codes, and that eavesdroppers were therefore listening to his own radio traffic. They were interested in the signals of British minesweepers, which reported whenever they had cleared a channel through the fields of mines that German submarines had sown. On hearing these reports, a U-boat would be despatched to plant more mines and thus endanger British vessels.

Hall knew that one German boat, *UC44*, was engaged in this activity off Waterford in Ireland. He therefore had a signal sent announcing the sweeping of a channel through the minefield there. *UC44* was immediately ordered by Berlin to return and sow more mines. The trap was then sprung; the boat entered the area (in which no 'sweeping' had taken place), hit one of its own mines and sank. Hall had deliberately engineered this sinking in shallow coastal waters so that he could send down a team of divers, and his ingenuity was handsomely rewarded when they brought up the very prize for which he had been hoping: a copy of a newly introduced naval code book. The seeking of the enemy's secrets from captured or damaged submarines, which was to be vital to the gathering of intelligence in the next war, thus had an important precedent.

Hall's department had realized that the German navy was enciphering its messages as well as coding them, but with the German code books in their hands his staff were soon able to read enemy signals within an average of six to eight hours. Once codebreakers came to understand the mindset of their enemy counterparts, and acquired familiarity with the phrases of greeting, reporting and routine enquiry, they were able to work speedily through encoded radio messages, even when the cipher key was changed every week or, as soon became the case, every day. For more than three years after the finding of the first code book, British Naval Intelligence was able to monitor daily the messages of its German counterpart.

In 1916 Hall's department carried out an act of deceit that, once again, was to set a precedent for a larger-scale operation in World War II; in this case, he provided a forerunner for the creation of First US Army Group and its build-up for an invasion of France. That year had witnessed the hugely costly British offensive on the Somme, while the French had paid dearly in lives for the successful defence of Verdun. Something had to be done to relieve pressure on these Allied armies and Hall decided that, if the Germans could be convinced that a new attack was imminent elsewhere, they would withdraw troops from the trenches of Picardy to meet it.

He had messages transmitted that suggested a gathering of forces in southern England for an attack across the Channel. Much of the British Army was already fighting in France and Flanders, but in their thrust through Belgium in 1914 the Germans had seized and held most of the country's North Sea coast, and it was this that Hall pretended would be the target. He invented a 'North Belgian Front', to which his operators made frequent reference in their signals, but he went even further. He planted stories in the British press that hinted at a forthcoming major operation, and he had British spies throughout the world instructed to drop hints or make throwaway remarks in the restaurants and hotel lobbies of neutral countries with a view to starting a groundswell of rumour.

He succeeded. Though his efforts did not end the stalemate on the Western Front, he did cause sufficient concern among the German High Command to have thousands of soldiers transferred to the Belgian coast to repel an invasion, with the frittering away of manpower and resources that followed the building and equipping of defences.

***

It was the decrypters of Room 40 who read what has become known to history as the 'Zimmermann Telegram'. At the beginning of 1917 the US was still neutral. Germany intended, in February of that year, to begin a policy of 'unrestricted submarine warfare' in the Atlantic, which would seriously threaten this neutrality because it would mean that American ships could become the target of U-boat attacks. Should the US enter the war as a result, Germany sought an ally in the Western Hemisphere that could bring pressure to bear on it. Mexico, which shared a long frontier with the US, offered excellent possibilities, and Germany's foreign minister, Arthur Zimmermann, sent a coded message to his ambassador there. In return for joining the Central Powers, Mexico was to be promised large areas of the south-western US, which it had lost in the 19th century. Zimmermann instructed the ambassador to approach the Mexican president with an offer:

> We make Mexico a proposal of alliance on the following terms:
> Generous financial support and an undertaking on our part
> that Mexico is to reconquer the lost territory in Texas, New
> Mexico and Arizona. You will inform the President of the
> above most secretly as soon as the outbreak of war with USA
> is certain. Please call the President's attention to the fact
> that the ruthless employment of our submarines now offers
> the prospect of compelling England in a few months to
> make peace.

This was sent by Germany's Foreign Office cipher, which had long since been cracked by Hall's staff. Britain had been handed a hugely important opportunity to destroy German credibility, and the Admiral had every intention of using it. Like his successors in the next war, who sought to make use of Ultra information but had to conceal its origin, Hall had to decide how the contents of the telegram could be made public without revealing how they had been obtained. After some consideration, he succeeded in arranging an 'interception' of the cable in the US itself.

Its publication provoked an uproar and, instead of denial, Germany compounded its humiliation by confirming that the message was genuine but arguing that it was justified by circumstances. Two months later, America was at war with the Central Powers. The Zimmermann Telegram was therefore perhaps the most important enemy signal to be decoded in either World War.

***

Germany and her allies were not without able cryptographers of their own, as can be seen from their success in reading British naval signals. They claimed after the war to have comprehensively broken the codes of every country except Britain and America – ironically the two most vital ones. Especially proficient was the Austro-Hungarian Army's cryptographic service, which had been established by an officer called General Andreas Figl.

The end of World War I did not bring an era of peace. The defeated Central Powers were obliged to reduce the size of their armed forces drastically, and their intelligence services were disbanded. Nevertheless, the revolution in Russia now threatened the whole of Europe with Bolshevism. All the Western nations, in a dress rehearsal for the Cold War 25 years later, became concerned with monitoring communications both from and within the Soviet Union. No country, however, succeeded in breaking the USSR's diplomatic code. Britain was able to use the proximity to the Soviet frontier of its Indian Empire to glean information. RT Jenks, an army signaller of a later vintage, recalled:

> I was told by an old and venerable friend that as a young soldier
> in northern India in 1921 they were intercepting Russian traffic,
> which was rushed to civilisation by mule!

Throughout the Great War, Britain's cryptographic and intelligence services had gained a considerable reputation, despite the fact that they had been unable to make a coordinated effort owing to intense rivalry between navy and army. In the interwar era, not only the new balance of power but Britain's expanded responsibilities overseas underlined the need for continued intelligence gathering. There was now a permanent official organization, the Government Code and Cipher School (GC&CS), whose function was to protect the security of codes used by Whitehall departments as well as monitoring those used by other powers. 'Y' Section, the army's specialist unit for telecommunications, was also established at this time. Jenks, as one of its members, described how:

> The basis on which 'Y' Section was formed was defined as:
> 'The craft of estimating enemy strengths, intentions and
> locations from the pattern, volume and nature of his wireless
> communications.' This does not necessarily involve the actual
> content of the traffic, although that would obviously be a bonus.

The 'Y' Service was apparently started in Palestine about 1923. This later became 2 Wireless Regiment and was followed by 1 Wireless Regiment. These have probably the longest continuous histories in the Royal Corps of Signals.

As well as posting specialist military units in Britain's overseas territories, plans began to be formulated for combating wireless espionage at home in the event of a future conflict. Drawing on the experiences of 1914–18, the government set out to establish a network of radio communications centres. Attention was also paid to searching out similar centres used by the enemy through 'direction finding' – the tracking of enemy radio, or radar, signals by using directional antennae. Plans were also made for the recruiting of suitable staff in the event of war. According to Jenks:

> The need for the interception of illicit wireless transmissions was recognised in the late 1920s but came to nothing. However, in 1933 it was agreed that the General Post Office should act as the agent for the War Office for the manning, maintenance and technical operation of the service later to become known as RSS (Radio Security Service). The Postmaster General being the regulating and licensing authority for all wireless telegraphy matters. In December 1937 it was agreed that the GPO should build and equip three fixed Intercept and Direction Finding stations. The first was operational in 1938, and with the clouds of war gathering fast, approval was given for the establishment of a network of fixed and mobile stations, and also of an auxiliary 'observer' corps of licensed amateur radio enthusiasts (hams, as they were known among themselves).

VITAL INTELLIGENCE

While Britain retained its prewar and wartime security organizations, and continued to develop them so that by 1939 it had the largest signals intelligence establishment of any nation in the world, Germany had had to begin again from scratch. Though the army's communications intelligence system had been dismantled, the expertise of some of its members lived on. In Germany a number of private armies, called *Freikorps*, came into being to preserve order amid the chaos of the early Weimar Republic and to prevent the Communists from seizing power. The members of these were almost all ex-soldiers, and of a conservative, authoritarian bent; many thousands of them later joined Hitler's own force, the Sturmabteilung (SA). An intelligence unit was set up within one Berlin Freikorps to monitor and analyse the Communist threat.

When the Nazis came to power in 1933, their desire for communications intelligence became acute. Intent on creating a one-party state, the National Socialists sought to consolidate their position by silencing and eliminating all opposition. This was facilitated by spying on the German people, not least through extensive tapping of telephones. One body that carried out this and other electronic surveillance was called the *Forschungsamt*, or Research Office. It was the brainchild of Gottfried Schapper, a long-time Nazi who during the war had been in charge of the army's General Headquarters Radio Station. He thus brought to the National Socialist Government the expertise of a military communications specialist and cryptographer. Because it was Goering whom he persuaded of the necessity for such a department, it was to Goering's fiefdom, the Luftwaffe, that the Forschungsamt was attached.

The organization consisted of six departments. Those that specialized in foreign relations processed a vast amount of intelligence derived from agents' reports, foreign newspapers and wireless broadcasts, radio traffic 'in clear' and coded messages, of which by the outbreak of war they were handling over 2,000 a month. The department called 'Bureau IV' dealt with all communications in code. The years that followed Hitler's coming to power were characterized by growing assertiveness and steady rearmament. It was highly important for the German Government to know the reactions of its neighbours. Bureau IV therefore concentrated on decrypting diplomatic messages. Its staff of nearly 250 were fairly successful in this, breaking about 70 per cent of the codes used by neighbouring powers, and using this knowledge to tap the phones of embassies, individual diplomats and foreign journalists. Their task was facilitated by Germany's central position in Europe, for many important international telephone lines ran through the country and could be intercepted. During the crisis over Czechoslovakia in 1938, this source gave Hitler invaluable knowledge regarding the extent to which France and Britain were willing to support Czech independence, effectively telling him in advance that he would be allowed to have his way in the negotiations. The following year, Poland was in a similarly vulnerable situation when German demands were discussed between Warsaw and the West. Though the attitude of Britain and France was now more inflexible, Hitler decided to risk invasion.

Like so much else in the Third Reich, intelligence gathering was not carried out by a single, centralized body. While the Forschungsamt worked for the Luftwaffe at decrypting diplomatic signals, the Foreign Office naturally saw itself as more entitled to know what was going on in this field, and maintained its own cryptographic unit to carry out the same type of work. There was also the governmental organization for espionage and intelligence, the Reich Security Service (RSA), and the *Abwehr*, a military secret service headed by the naval officer Admiral Wilhelm Canaris. Though largely efficient in themselves (army signals intelligence units were highly effective and made an important contribution to the success of the *blitzkrieg* campaigns) these organizations suffered from a mutual jealousy and distrust that precluded any pooling of knowledge or coordinated efforts. There had initially been some degree of cooperation, but by 1939 the various bodies had retreated into an atmosphere of petulant reciprocal dislike. This meant, for instance, that the navy and air force refused to share information about Allied radar, and that each service had to repeat the labour, and the mistakes, of the other. Under these conditions, while there would be some major successes, Germany's overall effort was doomed from the beginning.

In terms of cryptography, the RSA did manage to achieve a small victory. One of its higher officials discovered that Andreas Figl, the legendary Austrian codebreaker, had been arrested following Hitler's takeover of his country in 1938. The official had Figl released, brought to Berlin and assigned to the *Schutzstaffel* (the SS) as a cryptography instructor.

THE ART OF CRYPTOGRAPHY

All of these organizations, like any concerned with military, diplomatic or political security, used codes and ciphers to conceal the contents of their signals. The practice of cryptography (the word means literally 'secret writing') is very long-established: Julius Caesar, for example, developed a basic cipher that is still in use. The difference between codes and ciphers was defined in a wartime training manual, as follows:

> **A code is a method of concealing a message in such a way as to make it appear innocent.**

A cipher is a method of converting a message into symbols which do not appear innocent, and which have no meaning to a person not possessing the key.

In a code, words or numbers are substituted for plain language – for example, 'blue' could mean north, '12' could mean an advancing army, 'rainbow' could mean 'this Friday' – and no one can know what these represent unless they have been let into the secret, or have gained access to the necessary code books. Ciphers, on the other hand, involve the repositioning of letters as a means of hiding a message, and the systems by which this is done can be worked out by various means. Indeed for those with the requisite ability, to pit themselves against a difficult one can be an enjoyable challenge.

The simplest cipher, such as Caesar's, substitutes one letter for another by simply moving it one place in the alphabet, so that P becomes Q, and so on. This is called a monoalphabetic cipher. A refinement, developed many centuries later, is the polyalphabetic version. This complicates the cipher considerably by using not one alphabet but 26, in each of which the letters are moved one place to the left and those that have been displaced begin again. For instance, the first alphabet runs from A to Z; the second is B to Z + A, the third is C to Z + A + B, and so on until the last alphabet runs from Z to Y. To add to the perplexity of anyone trying to make sense of it, the letters are split into 'groups' of five or six. This means that no words can be identified by length or shape. To muddy the waters still further, a message may be split in half and the second part of it sent first.

Cryptography is a highly mathematical art. Those with a talent for maths and a feeling for statistics are well equipped to work out its mysteries. In addition, skill in playing chess or doing crosswords (and it is often the same people who have all these abilities) makes for a good cryptanalyst, and explains why mathematicians were in such demand by the GC&CS once World War II began. Gordon Welchman, one of the Bletchley academics, admitted:

For my part, I quite shamelessly recruited friends and former students. Stuart Milner-Barry had been in my year at Trinity College, Cambridge, studying classics while I studied mathematics. He was not enjoying being a stockbroker, and was persuaded to join me at Bletchley Park. Stuart in turn recruited his friend Hugh Alexander, who had been a mathematician at King's College, Cambridge, and was then Director of Research in the John Lewis Partnership, a large group of department stores. They brought us unusual distinction in chess: Alexander was the British Chess Champion, while Milner-Barry had often played for England and was chess correspondent for the Times.

To help them break a cipher, cryptanalysts look for the repetition of letters. Every language contains particular letters that are more common than others, and studying these frequency patterns is the beginning of understanding. There are also configurations of letters that occur often, as well as combinations that are extremely rare. When dealing with a particular language, 'frequency tables' compiled by language scholars will indicate what these are. Those attempting to read enciphered military messages know that there are types of phrase, known as 'probable words', that are highly likely to be used: greetings, ways of reporting, or of referring to units, or of signing off. The carelessness of operators who neglect standard security procedures, or otherwise take shortcuts in their haste to deliver a message, enable a listening enemy to work out code words. Furthermore, vital words can be worked out where the contents of a signal can be guessed at – for example, if the enemy is short of men and ammunition it can be assumed that they will be sending requests for them. In both World Wars, Allied analysts found that rigidly structured and inflexible German military thinking made it easier to guess the content of messages.

***

In the 19th century a simple 'machine' for enciphering was invented by Commandant Bazeries, a French army officer. The device he created was easily carried and assembled. It consisted of a wooden frame over which were fitted a series of discs (he used 20), so that they formed a cylinder. Each disc was numbered on its side, and its rim was inscribed with 26 letters. They were arranged on the frame in a particular order chosen by the sender, and the result looked much like a rolling pin covered in lines of letters. The message was spelled out and then the discs were spun until the message was concealed. The receiver would also rotate the discs until he found the message, identifiable as being the only set of letters that spelled out actual words.

This was the basis for the later cipher machines. Those used in offices became larger, faster and more complex. From the 1890s, when the typewriter was invented, they began to be equipped with keyboards. Ten years later, when electricity had become a common power source for governments and businesses, it enabled them to perform speedy and complicated tasks and thus to render ciphers more difficult to break.

The cylinder with its set of lettered discs remained the basis of cipher machines, but the rotors could now move automatically and at varying speeds. The 'settings' were changed at regular intervals to ensure that outsiders who broke the cipher would not be able to read messages for long. They might be altered once a month, once a week, or once a day. Those who communicated using the cipher needed to know in advance what the settings would be for the coming days and weeks. This information, usually given in code books or other secret documents and closely guarded, became in wartime an important target of espionage or military operations. Such was the value of capturing these documents that considerable resources would be expended on making the attempt – and casualties suffered in the course of these actions were deemed worthwhile.

Another important innovation was the 'one-time pad'. This was invented during World War I by an American army officer, Major Joseph Mauborgne. The principle was that numbers were given to all the letters of the alphabet, which were then put into a random sequence, to which the letters were added. When the message was sent, its recipient also had this random sequence of numbers and deciphered the words by simple subtraction. Once the process had been completed, the operators at both ends disposed of the sequence so that it could never be repeated. This system was extremely secure. Cryptographers were extensively trained in its use throughout World War II, and it was implemented for sending messages of particular importance or sensitivity. It took so long to operate, however, that it was simply not practical for the vast amount of signals traffic generated by an average unit, vessel, office or headquarters. Group Captain Winterbotham explained in more detail how it worked – and admitted its drawbacks:

> In order to make the message secret, additional groups of figures known only to the sender and receiver must be added so as to make the final groups in the signal untranslatable by any of the party.

The safest way to do this is for both the sender and receiver to have a sort of tear-off writing pad, on each sheet of which are four columns of four digits printed absolutely at random.

The sender indicates the page, the column and the line where the message is to start in the first group of the signal, thus 1348 would mean page 13, column 4, line 8. Now if the next three groups on the pad are 4431, 7628 and 5016 and these are added to the ones already quoted, we find that the message reads 1348, 9904, 8470, 9609 which means 'To the Commanding Officer, the Division will move on Monday.'

Once used the whole page of the pad is torn off and destroyed. This is known as the one-time pad system and was at that time the only known absolutely safe cipher. If, for instance, the cipher groups are in a non-destructible book form and are used over and over again, in time an enemy will work out where the groups occur in the book and be able to read the signals. This unfortunately occurred in our own naval ciphers during the war.

The one-time pad method is, however, a long and very cumbersome method to use on any very large scale. All the printing presses in Germany could hardly have coped with the numbers of tear-off pads required. It was therefore likely that Germany would turn to a mechanical system which could be quick and easy to operate, a system of so changing the letters of the words in the signal by progressive proliferation that only the receiver who knew the key to the system could set his own machine to unscramble the letters back to their original meaning.

INSIDE ENIGMA

The Enigma was to become the world's best-known cipher machine. It was invented in Germany in 1918 but did not initially appeal to any of the usual governmental or military bodies. It was intended for banks, as a means of keeping secure the details of monetary transactions, and there was initially nothing secret about its existence or its use. It is sometimes suggested that in this role the machine was not successful and that it passed out of use before being rediscovered by the army. In fact, Enigma machines remained important in the financial professions, and not just in Germany. Years later, once World War II had begun and the Bletchley codebreakers were at work, one of them, IJ Good, found that an acquaintance of his was perfectly familiar with Enigma:

> Although I did not know it at first, the original Enigma was an unclassified machine (for enciphering plain language). It had been used by banks. Curiously enough I first learned this when I was billeted close to Bletchley. There was a retired banker living in the hotel, and once he startled me by describing the Enigma which he had used in his bank. I probably said 'fascinating' and raised one eyebrow. Of course, I told him nothing of the work I was doing at the office!

Enigma machines could actually be purchased in the 1920s and Dillwyn ('Dilly') Knox, another Cambridge academic who was later to be one of Bletchley's luminaries, bought one in Vienna. It was examined by the Government Code and Cipher School, in the shape of Hugh Foss (who was also to play a major role at 'BP'), but it was decided that Enigma was not especially difficult to break, and the system was therefore not considered worth using. It was adopted, however, by the Germans, whose navy acquired it in 1926, followed by the army in 1928. The military authorities in Berlin also deemed it too easy to decipher, so the machines went through a series of modifications over the next few years – the last of them in 1937, after which the Germans considered it as secure as a bank vault. Electromagnetically operated, the machine was designed for enciphering radio messages, and it threw out seemingly random groups of numbers; it had the considerable advantage that, if one of these were intercepted, it could not be decrypted unless the interceptor had an identical machine. Germany's opponents knew this as a result of information from a German civil servant, Hans Thilo Schmidt, and it became their primary objective either to steal an adapted military Enigma machine or to build an exact copy of it.

In size and shape the Enigma machine resembled a typewriter and was housed in an unprepossessing, square wooden box. It had a typewriter keyboard but above this, on another board, was a set of lights corresponding with the letters of the alphabet. Inside there were three wheels, each of which had the alphabet marked on it twice – on the inside and on the outside, and each outside letter was electronically linked to an inside one. Pressing a key lit up a bulb on the board as that letter was enciphered, and turned the first of the wheels by one position. After a set number of turns of the first wheel, the second would move by one position, then the third. IJ Good described how the basic Enigma worked:

> The main ingredient of the Enigma machine is a so-called rotor or hebern wheel. It is capable of rotating and it is wired so that the input alphabet is permuted [arranged] to give an output alphabet. The original Enigma machine had three rotors in it together with a reflector so that the plain language letter would come through three rotors, and then get reflected and come back through the same three rotors by a different route. Thus, for any fixed position of the rotors the original input alphabet would go through a succession of seven simple substitutions. Hence no letter could be enciphered as itself. But the whole effect of the machine was not merely a simple substitution since the wheels stopped in a certain way each time a letter was enciphered.

The German military versions were more complicated, for they used different internal wiring, plus the addition of a 'steckerboard'. This, like the rest of the machine, was ugly and unimpressive to look at. It was a plugboard with holes into which an operator could put jack plugs to connect yet more pairs of letters. This provided a further layer of encipherment, increasing the range of possible settings from merely several million to nearly 160 trillion. Once this level of security had been attained, a certain complacency set in among German military and governmental circles.

***

Work on deciphering Enigma began in 1929, when Poland, a country that had good reason to be concerned with German military plans, assigned cryptanalysts to work in on it in earnest. A machine had arrived in Warsaw at that time, sent by accident from Germany and held by Polish Customs. The German Embassy urgently requested that it be returned whence it came, and the Polish authorities complied – after secretly opening the box and having experts examine the contents. Polish Intelligence later made attempts to read Enigma messages, but failed because they had seen only the civilian and not the military machine.

Poland was, during the interwar period, a close ally of France, and it was through the Deuxième Bureau, the French secret service, that the next step forward was made. In 1931 it was approached by German civil servant Hans Thilo Schmidt with an offer to sell some important documents. Schmidt was an official in the Cipher Office of the Defence Ministry in Berlin and was motivated by a simple desire to make money. He sold the French two documents which, it transpired, related to Enigma. They showed how to encipher, though not how to *decipher*. Nevertheless, they offered a beginning. Photographs of the documents, shown to the Polish experts, confirmed that the machine they had seen was in military use. Further settings were provided after subsequent meetings with Schmidt, but the best way of understanding the machine was to build a prototype. Marian Rejewski, one of the ablest of the engineers working on the project, was eventually able to do this after receiving the settings for September and October 1932. Having discovered the layout of the wiring that controlled two of the wheels, he was able to calculate the workings of the third.

Once they were listening to Enigma, they made a welcome discovery. German operators of the military version were instructed that, when sending signals, they must twice encipher the 'message setting' (the position of the wheels when the first letter was enciphered) and then send it. This made it easy for Polish Intelligence to break the code on a continuing basis. Rejewski and his colleagues were also able to arrange a set of six Enigmas that operated in concert, wired together. A group of this sort became known as a *Bomba*. With one for each of the six existing wheel orders, they could often work fast enough to discover the day's settings within about a hundred minutes.

***

For the remainder of the 1930s, and throughout the war years, the German operators of Enigma and their enemies engaged in a battle of wits. As methods were devised for making the machines more secure, the Polish codebreakers found new ways of breaking them. The Germans had originally altered their wheel order every three months, but from 1936 this was done monthly and then daily. The Bomba was rendered considerably less effective when more holes were introduced to the plugboards on Enigma, allowing far more jack plugs to be used and thus increasing the number of possible settings. A subsequent introduction of two further wheels expanded its capabilities yet further. A significant victory for the Poles, however, was their development of 'perforated sheets'.

Rejewski's colleague Henryk Zygalski had noticed that the indicators (the six-letter groups tapped out twice by the message sender) had some similarities. The groups had certain letters continually in common: the first and fourth, second and fifth or third and sixth. These were dubbed 'females'. Since they could not be produced by the German senders, each one represented a setting (and altogether these were to account for nearly 40 per cent of the total) that could not be used and could therefore be eliminated from calculations.

Holes were punched in cards in places where a 'female' was expected to occur. When a whole series of cards had been treated in this way, they were piled on a glass table that was lit from below. Wherever a space showed through the entire stack, it indicated the wheel positions and wheel orders for that day. They would then be manually tested for confirmation. This practice was effective but laborious and therefore very slow, and it fell seriously behind when the Germans began using more wheels.

Most of this work was concealed from their allies by Polish Intelligence, and only in 1939 did they admit to the French and British that Enigma traffic had been read so extensively and for so long. The news caused a good deal of annoyance, not least because Schmidt, the German traitor, had gone on providing Enigma settings over the years at some risk to himself and to those dealing with him. Nevertheless, Polish expertise with the machine was invaluable, and both Paris and London were keen to add as quickly as possible to their own knowledge. 'Dilly' Knox went to Warsaw in the summer and obtained details of the machine's wiring.

Another source had become available through Poland and this was to be of considerable significance. Group Captain Winterbotham, who would be in charge of disseminating 'Ultra' information during the coming war, recalled the chain of events that brought further secrets to the West:

> In 1938 a young Polish mechanic had been employed in a factory
> in eastern Germany which was making what he rightly judged to
> be some sort of secret signalling machine. As a Pole, he was not
> very fond of the Germans anyway and, being an intelligent
> observer, he took careful note of the various parts that he and
> his fellow workmen were making. I expect it was after one of the

security checks which were made by the Gestapo on all high security factories that they discovered his nationality. He was sacked and sent back to Poland. His keen observation had done him some good, and he got in touch with our man in Warsaw.

In due course the young Pole was persuaded to leave Warsaw and was secretly smuggled out under a false passport with the help of the British Secret Service; he was then installed in Paris, where he was given a workshop. With the help of a carpenter, he began to make a wooden mock-up of the machine he had been working on in Germany.

Because Enigma had been available for two decades, it was quickly recognized by specialists:

There had been a number of cipher machines invented over the years and our own backroom boys had records of most of them. It didn't take them long to identify the mock-up as some sort of improved mechanical cipher machine called Enigma. The name Enigma had been given to the machine by the German manufacturers. The Pole had been told not to attempt to make his wooden model to scale. In fact, the bigger the better, because he could then more easily incorporate any details he could remember.

The result was rather like the top half of an upright piano, but it was big enough to tell us that it would be essential to get hold of an actual machine if we were to stand any chance of trying to break into its method of operation. We set about working out a scheme with our friends in Poland. We knew where the factory was and all about its security methods, and there were still some Poles working there under German names. However, the Polish Secret service thought the scheme might well stand a better chance of success if we gave them the money and they did the job. They knew the terrain and the people much better than we did, so we gladly agreed. It was [Commander Alistair] Denniston himself who went to Poland and, triumphantly, but in the utmost secrecy, brought back the complete, new, electronically operated Enigma cipher machine which we knew was being produced in its thousands and was destined to carry all the signal traffic of the great war machine.

Sir John Slessor, Marshal of the Royal Air Force, was later to comment on the immeasurable benefits of this act of larceny:

> There was nothing very remarkable about the act of cracking enemy ciphers as such, but with the secret abstraction from Poland of the theoretically unbreakable German cipher machine, which gave birth to Ultra, that art took on a completely new dimension; and surely no other act in the history of officially sponsored skulduggery ever had comparably fruitful results.

By the time Hitler's troops invaded Poland, the French and British each had two Enigma machines. The race to break the German codes had been won, but only just in time.

HOW ENIGMA WORKED

In the event, Enigma was not as formidable in the eyes of Germany's rivals as might have been expected, and by the outbreak of war in 1939 a good deal of progress had been made toward understanding it. Alan Turing, a young Cambridge student of mathematics and the most powerful of the great minds that set about understanding Enigma, wrote a treatise on the machine. He described the early work in creating methods for decipherment:

> The Poles found the keys for the 8th of May 1937, and as they found that the wheel order and the turnovers were the same as for the end of April they rightly assumed that the wheel order and Ringstellung [ring position] had remained the same during the end of April and the beginning of May. This made it easier for them to find the keys for other days at the beginning of May and they actually found the Stecker [plug] for the 2nd, 3rd, 4th, 5th and 8th, and read about 100 messages. The indicators and window positions of four messages for the 5th were:

Indicator		Window start
K F J X	E W T W	P C V
S Y L G	E W T W	B Z V
J M H O	U V Q G	M E M
J M F E	F E V C	M Y K

The repetition of the EW combined with the repetition of V suggests that the fifth and sixth letters describe the third letter of the window position, and similarly one is led to believe that the first two letters of the indicator represent the second. Presumably this effect is somehow produced by means of a table of bigramme equivalents of letters, but it cannot be done simply by replacing the letters of the window position with one of their bigramme equivalents, and then putting in a dummy bigramme, for in this case the window position corresponding to JMFE FEVC would have to be say MYY instead of MYK. Probably some encipherment is involved somewhere. The two most natural alternatives are i) The letters of the window position are replaced by some bigramme equivalents and then the whole enciphered at some 'Grundstellung' [initial position], or ii) The window position is enciphered at the Grundstellung, and the resulting letters replaced by bigramme equivalents. The second of these alternatives was made far more probable by the following indicators occurring on the 2nd May:

E X D P	I V J O	V C P
X X E X	J L W A	N U M
R C X X	J L W A	N U M

With this second alternative we can deduce from the first two indicators that the bigrammes EX and XX have the same value, and this is confirmed from the second and third, where XX and EX occur in the second position instead of the first.

It so happened that the change of indicating system had not been very well made, and a certain torpedo boat, with the call-sign AFA, had not yet been provided with the bigramme tables. This boat sent a message in another cipher explaining this on the 1st May, and it was arranged that traffic with AFA was to take place according to the old system until May 4, when the bigramme tables would be supplied. Sufficient traffic passed on May 2, 3 to and from AFA for the Grunstellung used to be found, the Stecker having already been found from the ... messages. It was natural to assume that the Grundstellung used by AFA was the Grundstellung to be used with the correct method of indication, and as soon as we noticed the two indicators mentioned above we tried this out and found it to be the case.

There actually turned out to be some more complications. There were two Grunstellungen at least instead of one. One of them was called the Allgemeine [general] and the other the Offiziere [officer] Grunstellung. This made it extremely difficult to find either Grundstellung. The Poles pointed out another possibility, viz. that the trigrammes were still probably not chosen at random. They suggested that probably the window positions enciphered at the Grunstellung, rather than the window positions themselves, were taken off the restricted list.

In Nov. 1939 a prisoner told us that the ... digits of the numbers were [now] spelt out in full [by the German navy]. When we heard this we examined the messages toward the end of 1937 which we expected to be continuations and wrote the expected beginnings under them. The proportion of 'crashes', i.e. of letters apparently left unaltered by encipherment, then shows how nearly correct our guesses were. Assuming that the change mentioned by the prisoner had already taken place we found that about 70 per cent of these cribs must have been right.

Gordon Welchman explained how the Germans used the machine and safeguarded its security with regard to their compatriots as well as their enemies. His analysis provides a detailed picture of what Allied codebreakers were up against:

The Germans had adopted the principle that the security of their communications must rest not on the machine itself, but rather on a 'key' that would determine how the machine was to be set up for a particular purpose. Moreover, they were concerned with both external and internal security. They wanted to prevent their enemies from reading their messages and also to prevent their own units from reading messages that were not intended for them. For example, three of the many different types of Enigma traffic were messages between operational units of the regular army and air force; messages between units of Hitler's private army, the SS or Schutzstaffel; and messages involved in the training exercises of new signals battalions. All three kinds of messages were enciphered on identical Enigma machines, but the regular army and air force units were not to be allowed to read the text of SS messages. Nor were the trainees to be permitted to read the texts of the other two types of traffic. Consequently, different keys were issued for different types of traffic. This, however, did not quite solve the problem, because messages of different types were often transmitted on the same radio net. It was therefore necessary to provide means by which a receiving unit's operator would know what type of clear text was hidden behind the enciphered text, and whether he had the necessary key to read it.

The Germans chose to solve this problem by using a three-letter 'discriminant' transmitted in the unenciphered message preamble. This discriminant was not part of a key. Its purpose was simply to indicate which of many keys was being used. A cipher clerk would examine the discriminant of each incoming message to determine whether he had been issued the key used for its text encipherment. If he did have the key, he could set up his Enigma and decode the message. If not, he couldn't.

The particular needs of the Wehrmacht (the Nazi armed forces) led them to develop a sophisticated form of communications network:

The Germans, in their concept of a blitzkrieg, reckoned that many groups of fast-moving fighting, command, support, and staff elements would need effective communication among themselves wherever they might be, and furthermore that the activities of these groups would have to be tied in the higher command system. The elements of each cooperating group were to be served by signals detachments operating a 'radio net' on an assigned radio frequency. Under ideal conditions any message transmitted by any radio station operating in the net on the assigned frequency would be heard by all the other stations. One station of the net would act as control, to ensure that no two stations would cause interference by transmitting at the same time. There were to be many such nets, and a station could operate in two or more nets, so that messages originating at any point could be relayed to any other point.

The call signs were simply the means of identifying the individual elements that were participating in this overall radio communication system. When passages were passing between elements within a single radio net, the preamble would contain the call signs of the originator and intended recipient(s) of each message. When a message was to be forwarded to other elements, their identifying call signs would also be included in the message preamble. Thus, by studying call signs, we had an opportunity to learn something about the structure of the enemy's forces. As the call signs were changed every day, however, the detective work had to begin anew every twenty-four hours.

Our intercept operators listened to the Enigma messages and their preambles, writing them out by hand on standard message forms. The main part of the form was used for the succession of five-letter groups, or 'words,' which constituted the indicator and text of a message enciphered on an Enigma machine. At the top of the form was a space in which the intercept operator entered the preamble that the German radio operator had transmitted ahead of the message. Indeed the form used by our intercept operators must have been very similar to the form used by the German cipher clerks. The intercept operator, however, also entered the radio frequency on which he was listening and the time of intercept.

THE COMPUTER AGE

The beginning of the codebreakers' war is seen as the dawn of the computer age. The mathematical endeavour needed to keep pace with the increasing complexity of Axis cryptographic communications gave an enormous spur to the development of what would later be called computer science, though its story was by that time over a century old.

The computer was an outgrowth of the calculating machine, and that boasted a long and illustrious pedigree. The word 'calculate' stems from the Greek for pebble, and for most of history the task of adding figures was assisted by such basic objects. Leonardo da Vinci conceived the notion of a machine that would carry out calculations, though he simply described the scheme in his notebooks and it was never built. Worked by a handle, it was to consist of 13 wheels, each cogged and able to turn individually. In 1642 a similar machine was, quite independently, devised in France by the 19-year-old Blaise Pascal, to assist his father, who was a tax-collector. This would have swiftly performed addition and subtraction and saved a good deal of labour, had it been possible to build it. Like da Vinci's concept, however, it was beyond the reach of contemporary technology. Just over 50 years later a machine designed by the German Gottfried Leibniz established basic principles that would remain unchanged until the 20th century.

The development of the computer itself began in 1821, when Charles Babbage, a mathematics professor at Cambridge, wondered if he could avoid repeating tedious calculations by creating a machine to perform the task. He set out to take Leibniz's ideas further by building a bigger and better cog-wheeled structure. The result, which he called a 'Difference Engine', was in fact a series of calculating machines working in unison. These were able to perform a number of mathematical tasks, and produced calculations that were often more accurate than those resulting from unassisted brainpower. Having a degree of engineering skill, Babbage was able to work on the parts himself, and he received funding from the Royal Society. He moved on to a more advanced concept: the Analytical Engine. This had a much wider range of functions, including basic versions of all the elements of a present-day computer: a memory, a control unit, and input and output mechanisms. He had the notion of a machine's operating instructions as something that could be manipulated, and thus conceived the 'computer programme'. He made use of punched cards to input data and give instructions to the machine, which would then complete the work without further human involvement – a concept borrowed from the French textile manufacturer Joseph Jacquard, who used such a system (he called them 'operation cards') to control the patterns in his weaving looms.

Contemporary with Babbage was another brilliant theorist: Ada, Countess Lovelace. She studied his work, adding to and improving the concepts of programming with cards and of solving mathematical problems by having the machine deconstruct them. Though all this proved, once again, beyond the capabilities of technology, it established the concept that in future would define what a 'computer', as opposed to a calculator, actually was. The latter could perform tasks only if constantly attended by an operator. The former could make its own decisions without supervision.

In spite of these discoveries, the development of the computer went no further in the lifetimes of these pioneers. Neither Babbage nor Ada Lovelace was taken seriously by contemporaries, because the equipment they designed or described could not be built. Only near the end of the century, in 1890, did an American statistician pick up the torch. Herman Hollerith was employed by the US Census Bureau, and he invented a tabulating machine that used Jacquard's card system to automate the analysis of census returns. It was not the beginning of the computer age, but neither was it, this time, a false dawn; Hollerith founded a company that, in the next century, would become one of the giants of the communications industry: International Business Machines, now universally known as IBM.

With a new age came the power of electricity and the revolution in communications represented by wireless, and these were ultimately to open new possibilities, as technology at last caught up with the dreams and schemes of inventors. As RB Davison, a writer on computer science, put it:

Up to this point all calculations had been done mechanically, by means of cogged wheels turning numbers in registers. When electricity was used it was simply as a motive power, to drive the wheels more quickly and for longer periods. But with the development of radio and the new science of electronics, a new idea began to emerge – instead of counting by moving cogged wheels, it should be done by electronic impulses.

In 1936 an electronic computer was patented, but not produced. The first to come into use, for performing mathematical calculations, was therefore a model built at the Bell Telephone Laboratories in New York by Dr GR Sterbity in 1939. Parallel with this, and working in complete isolation from other scientists, a young German called Konrad Zuse built another electronic computer at his parents' home in Berlin.

It would be the young Alan Turing, spurred on by the demands of the codebreakers at Bletchley Park, who made the next significant contribution. His wartime colleague, IJ Good, described the moment in which Turing's eyes were opened and his sense of vocation began:

Turing had gone to King's [College, Cambridge] as a mathematical scholar at the age of 19, and was elected to a Fellowship at 23. M.H.A. Newman had been a university lecturer at Cambridge, and it is believed Turing's work was sparked off by one of Newman's lectures. This was a lecture in which Newman discussed Hilbert's [David Hilbert, the German geometrician] view that any mathematical problem can be solved by a fixed and definite process. Turing seized on Newman's phraseology, 'a purely mechanical process,' and interpreted it as something that could be done by an automatic machine. He introduced a simple abstract machine in order to prove that Hilbert was wrong, and in fact showed that there is a 'universal automaton' that can perform any calculation that any automaton can, if first provided with the appropriate instructions to input.

Turing was thus the first to arrive at an understanding of the universal nature of a (conceptual) digital computer that matches and indeed surpasses the philosophic understanding that I believe Babbage had attained, a century earlier, of the universality of the planned (mechanical) Analytical Engine. Central to the Universal Turing Machine is the idea of having data, and input data in particular, represent a programme (called a 'table' in Turing's paper).

Turing carried out further research at the Institute of Advanced Studies at Princeton. Here he was a colleague not only of Albert Einstein but of Alonzo Church – who was doing similar work – and of John von Neumann, who was also his supervisor and whose ideas, running parallel with his, were to create EDVAC (Electronic Discrete Variable Analytic Computer), in June 1945, the first modern computer. Turing was, in other words, in precisely the right place for working with the other major pioneers at a time when their own most important work was being done.

It was while at Princeton that Turing proved his concept was mathematically valid. As computer historian Neil Barrett wrote:

> In a universal Turing machine, we see a mathematical expression of an idealized device that can be programmed with instructions and data to solve any problem that can be solved. The universal Turing machine is the theoretical expression of a 'stored programme, general-purpose computer', the computational model missing from Babbage and Lady Lovelace's earlier work.

Even more important, in view of coming events, was the fact that Turing's machine could be used for analysing ciphers. By this time it was 1938. War was averted in that year, but was a real possibility in the near future.

Turing felt he should return to England, and he was immediately attached to the Foreign Office's Department of Communications as a temporary civil servant. He was, in fact, a member of the Government Code and Cipher School.

The technology necessary for unravelling the mysteries of the formidable Enigma ciphers had not yet been perfected, but the development of the computer had reached a stage at which it could make a unique and effective contribution to the most important event of the century. It was also to initiate, unnoticed by all but the few who had knowledge of it, a new era. One of the Bletchley machines, nicknamed Colossus, was the first-ever programmable electronic computer.

War is often the midwife of scientific progress, and a new era in communications was brought about by the urgent need to know the enemy's thoughts in what was the most scientific conflict yet fought. With foreknowledge of its intentions, it was possible to deploy limited resources to best advantage, to take its forces by surprise or to cut off and destroy its sources of supply. In several instances this information directly affected the outcome of major campaigns. It therefore saved many thousands of lives and hastened the defeat of the Axis. It has been estimated that the work of the codebreakers shortened World War II by between two and three years.

2
BLETCHLEY PARK

Since the restrictions have been lifted I have been so thrilled to think that I was there – I didn't dare think about it before that in case I said something I shouldn't have! I never even told my husband what I was doing at B.P. Now I watch anything connected with it on television and listen to anything on radio.[i]

Station X (Bletchley Park) was known to outstations as the 'Nut House.'[ii]

When its owner died in 1937 Bletchley Park, set in the Buckinghamshire countryside about 50 miles north-west of London, was an unremarkable Victorian country house. Situated at the end of a drive and surrounded by lawns that sloped gently to an ornamental lake, it had been largely rebuilt after 1883 when it had been bought by the financier Sir Herbert Leon. Its red-brick façade boasted neither symmetry nor beauty: it was an eclectic assemblage of gables, crenellations, chimney-stacks and bay windows – perhaps a suitably eccentric setting for the role it was destined soon to play. Tucked behind it were the usual outbuildings: stables, garages, laundry and dairy facilities, and servants' living quarters. Of no historic or architectural importance, it was bought by a local builder for demolition and redevelopment.

Within a year, however, the house had changed hands again. Its new occupant appeared to be a naval or military gentleman, and he was accompanied by a group described as 'Captain Ridley's shooting party'. This term suggested a group of sporting upper-class men in pursuit of local wildlife, yet no gunshots were heard from the grounds. Instead, in the years that followed there would be the sounds of almost constant construction. The mysterious gentlemen were to remain in occupation for almost ten

[i] Mrs FE Clark
[ii] Jean Thompson, WRNS

years, their numbers swelled by over 10,000 more men and women, both military and civilian, and it would be several more decades before local people discovered what they had been doing there.

The house had indeed been bought, for £7,500, by a naval gentleman, though he was not in fact Captain Ridley (who was a real naval officer) but an admiral. Sir Hugh Sinclair was the head of both MI6 and the Government Code and Cipher School. Both had their headquarters in London, and with war looming Sinclair was concerned to find a home for them that would be out of the way of German bombers and Axis spies. He had naturally expected the government to provide the funds for this purchase. In the event, every department he had approached, from the War Office to the Foreign Office, had refused on the grounds that his purposes and organizations came within the jurisdiction of some other body. He therefore paid for Bletchley Park himself. It was to acquire the cloak-and-dagger name 'Station X'. This was not whimsy; the 'X' was in fact the Roman numeral 10, and referred to the fact that nine other sites had also been acquired by MI6 for its wartime needs.

The 'shooting party' arrived in the year that Hitler annexed Austria and seized the Sudetenland. They were the small advance guard of an army that would arrive in increasing numbers from the following summer. They had a vital mission with regard to the inevitable, imminent European war. Their job would be to break the secret codes of the enemy, read its transmissions and pass on its plans to the Allied governments and military commanders. This was a massive and daunting task. It required the mobilization of many of the finest minds to be found in Britain and among its allies, so that as well as creating an effective physical environment for their work, there had to be a search the length and breadth of the country for suitable men and women to carry it out. The 'boffins' – the people of near genius who would be able to work out the nature and content of enemy codes – could be found, without great difficulty, in their natural environment: in learned societies or in university laboratories and common rooms. Those whose age made them liable for military service would have been wasted in the armed forces, and the government was aware of this. Quietly, in the years preceding hostilities, the details had therefore been accumulated of people whose analytical talent could be put to specific use in the intelligence war.

IJ Good was one of these. He suggested that the War Office had learned a lesson from the 1914–18 conflict:

A number of scientists and mathematicians were on the so-called Reserve List and were not called up for military service. Perhaps the authorities remembered the poet Rupert Brooke and the physicist Henry Morley, who were both killed in World War I. I believe the military mind in World War II was more enlightened about the use of trained minds.

STAFF PROCUREMENT

On another level, it was also necessary to find, interview and train the many members of staff whose work would support the codebreakers. Good described the makeup of his own department, providing an example of the numbers of subordinate staff needed to process the work of a single specialist unit:

> The section or department contained about twelve mathematicians, four linguists and a hundred women for mechanical clerical work.

Of these clerical workers much would be expected. They must, whether they were military or civilian personnel, be willing to 'disappear' from the war effort, unable either then or in the future to tell their families and friends what they were doing, and foregoing any public recognition for the vital part they played. Because of this, they were to develop a tremendous esprit de corps. Some came, in any case, from similar backgrounds and had experiences in common, often sharing a lack of practical education. As Felicity Ashbee recalled:

> We clerks 'S/D' [Special Duties] had at least all had some kind of 'further' education (i.e. we had stayed on at some kind of school till 16 or 17), though few if any of us had degrees, or for that matter much in the way of maths or science training. Such refinements were not thought essential for girls of any class; a little biology, or more likely only botany being all that was offered in most girls' schools.
>
> Many of that first intake had been in boarding schools of the 'gentlemen's daughters' kind, so to be back in the 'dorm' at least presented no unaccustomed horrors!

In fact, the 'girls' at Bletchley came from disparate homes and regions, and not everyone fitted this pattern. Those who did not hail from comfortable homes or have a public school education did not share the sense of cosy familiarity. Mrs FE Clark later described her own previous employment:

> I was 'called up' in 1943 having been in a reserved occupation – local borough library assistant. As a young woman from Bow it was quite an eye-opener. I've often wondered how I came to be in the place.

And she was struck not by the similarity in her fellow workers' backgrounds but by the differences:

> We were a very mixed assembly – in the same corridor as me there was a debutante – a titled lady – and two of us from the East End of London.

One of her colleagues, Mrs Ann Harding (née Ann Bruce Low), who came from the less affluent north, was more critical regarding those with whom she was expected to work:

> We worked our first day in Hut 6 and were not happy. It seemed a madhouse, and we were not used to the type of girls from the south of England. Many of the girls recruited early were debs and relations of people in the Foreign Office, War Office and Admiralty etcetera, and all usually by word of mouth and friends of friends. Some were very grand and not at all friendly. Also, they smoked endlessly and often blew it at us. This last is in all my letters home. [I was] horrified by the bright red nails and thick lipstick and the fact that they did not always work but read magazines.

The type of work done by these women was widely varied. They became clerks, typists, secretaries and telephonists. They operated teleprinters and the various mysterious cipher machines. If they had the relevant language skills, they acted as interpreters and cryptanalysts and record officers. The pressure under which they worked was relentless for, in a fast-moving war that involved several major theatres of operations, information had to be decoded, translated, collated and sent onward as fast as possible. They laboured in shifts that covered the whole of the 24 hours.

Though the Park was an uplifting environment in which to work – in good weather its grounds and lake and tennis courts (restored at the direct instigation of Churchill for the benefit of the staff) were a pleasing counterpoint to the gruelling shifts and spartan offices that otherwise filled their horizons – their work required not gracious architecture and spreading lawns but privacy and space for expansion. Within the estate walls, and over a large proportion of the immaculate Victorian gardens, would be built the equivalent of a small town of wooden huts, to provide office and storage space not only for the armies of clerks, cryptanalysts, couriers, telephone operators, catering and security staff but also to accommodate the machinery they would use.

Once a 'key' had been found for a particular code, it might well open others, causing a flood of information. Looking ahead to a time when 'breaks' in enemy codes would be happening frequently, Alan Turing had thought about the settings, staff and equipment that would be needed for the vital work being performed. He saw the necessity of having a decoding room equipped with British cipher machines that would have been adapted to operate as if they were German Enigmas. There must also be a sufficiently large pool of trained decoders that staff could be on duty day and night and at whatever time a breakthrough was made, it could be decrypted, translated, evaluated and passed on to Military Intelligence as soon as possible.

Bletchley was not the only place in the area that took on a new identity as the war began. The Foreign Office bought a nearby country house, Hanslope Park, for use as a radio station; and the Secret Intelligence Service (SIS) took over yet another, Whaddon Hall, to accommodate staff and communications equipment. The neighbourhood was easily reached from London by road and rail, yet was far enough from the capital to allow a degree of privacy. It also lay astride the main GPO telephone cable linking London with the Midlands and the North. As a result, it saw a concentration of secrecy, technology and brain-power that must have been deeply bewildering for the local population. The most conspicuous physical evidence of this – the clutter of radio masts that began to appear around the landscape – came to the notice of Lord Haw-Haw, the voice behind German radio propaganda. He speculated that Bletchley might be the scene of clandestine intelligence activity, and the BBC was obliged to respond by spreading a story that the site was being used for local radio broadcasts.

Most of the staff did not live within the gates of Bletchley Park, but were scattered throughout the surrounding communities. Some lived, en masse, in hostels or country houses, such as Woburn Abbey, that were older and considerably more grand than Bletchley (those occupied by members of the Women's Royal Naval Service were known as 'Wrenneries'). Though these might be highly impressive, the parts of them in which the servicewomen were billeted were often a disappointment. Cynthia Waterhouse recalled her introduction to the area:

> I joined the Wrens and spent a strenuous fortnight learning naval etiquette, squad drill and scrubbing floors. I was then drafted to Stanmore where I was trained for Special Duties X, a category known as P.5 (Pembroke V). Then I went to Wavedon House, near Woburn Sands. The stables had been converted into Wrens' quarters – four Wrens to each stable, meant for one horse!

The majority, however, were billeted with ordinary families, staying in spare bedrooms as compulsory lodgers with hosts who were not allowed to know anything of their day-to-day lives. As well as multitudes of service people, dressed in a range of different uniforms, there were drawling, preoccupied, tweed-clad intellectuals. With all of these, the locals had to share pubs, cafés, cinemas and public transport, but there was little likelihood of satisfying any natural curiosity about them. Such was the all-pervading sense of secrecy at Bletchley that most of the young men and women would have had little to tell, for they knew nothing of what went on outside their own building or department. Good remembered that:

> Owing to the rule of secrecy known as the 'need to know,' which was applied fairly rigorously during the war, there is probably no one person who could give a reasonably comprehensive account of any large project at Bletchley. People who were not at the top did not know much about matters that were not directly of their concern, and the people who were at the top were not fully aware of what was going on because of the complexity of the work, the advanced technology, the ingenuity, the mathematical ideas, and the variety of cliquish technical jargon.

And a young woman who worked as a clerk was later to comment:

> There was so much I never knew about the place in which I spent three years. We were cocooned in our own particular section. The amazing thing was we were handling messages from all over the world, day and night, year in year out and never knew the context of them.

The recruiting of such remarkable people, in the numbers required, was far from being a simple matter. Competence in clerical work, ability to manage complex electronic equipment, skill in the languages of the enemy nations and a gift for quickly solving mental problems of the 'brain-teaser' variety were, naturally, an advantage for those expected to work on enemy codes. The others could be taught the skills they needed, and from them the utmost discretion was all that was initially required.

In the first instance, many were already members of the services as a result of the call-up (men were subject to this from 1939, women from 1941). This was especially true of the women, who formed the bulk – three-quarters, in fact – of the clerical staff. They might be either WRNS (naval) or WAAF (Women's Auxiliary Air Force), though there were also members of the ATS (Auxiliary Territorial Service). In addition there were civil servants, many of them officially employees of the Foreign Office (a total of one-third of the staff were civilians). These bodies, however, could not provide enough staff, and other avenues had to be explored. Banks were trawled, and so were personnel departments. One organization included in the search, through a personal connection with someone at 'BP', was the John Lewis Partnership. In the unrelenting search for brainpower, as well as recommending their own pupils or colleagues – a source that was exhausted fairly quickly – those already working at Bletchley might suggest targeting anyone with the appropriate potential from a particular school, college or university, as happened with, among others, the universities of London, Reading and Manchester. Bletchley was situated roughly halfway between Oxford and Cambridge, which had naturally been seen from the beginning as a fruitful source of recruits with the requisite abilities. Cambridge, which had a reputation for being more science-oriented than its rival institution, was to provide far more mathematicians and cryptanalysts than Oxford, though by no means all the academics dealt in figures; there were 'boffins' at Bletchley who specialized in Egyptian hieroglyphs or ancient Greek.

Ronald Lewin was among this intellectual intake. Referring to the rivers that ran through the two university towns, he wrote:

> It was from the Cam, rather than from the Isis, the men were soon to be drafted, who like that earlier analyst, Daniel, in the end proved able to dissolve doubts, read the writing, and make known the interpretations.

Another possibility was to seek out chess players and those who made a hobby of solving crosswords. The *Daily Telegraph* crossword was famous for attracting regular devotees, and a deliberate attempt to 'trap' recruits was made on 15 January 1942, when a competition was staged in which they were asked to finish the puzzle within 12 minutes. Those who did well were subsequently invited for interview. IJ Good's wartime career began as the result of an interest in chess – and an acquaintance with others who were already involved. He obviously had, unlike most of those who ended up at 'BP', some prior knowledge of what went on there. As he recalled:

> About two weeks before I went to Bletchley I met Milner-Barry at a chess match in London and asked him whether he was at Bletchley Park working on German ciphers. His reply was 'No, my address is Room 47, Foreign Office, Whitehall.' Two weeks later, when I joined Bletchley, I found he was head of a department called Hut 6, sure enough working on German ciphers. At first the official address at Bletchley was indeed Room 47, Foreign Office, Whitehall, London, but it soon became admissible to give one's private Bletchley address.
>
> When I arrived at Bletchley I was met at the station by Hugh Alexander, the British chess champion. On the walk to the office Hugh revealed to me a number of secrets about the Enigma. Of course, we were not really supposed to talk about such things outside the precincts of the office. I shall never forget that sensational conversation.

As occurred throughout the war, recruiting of friends-of-friends was the key to building the specialist teams at Bletchley. Gordon Welchman remembered that a colleague of his introduced a suitable candidate:

Travis produced a scientist, John Colman, to take charge of the Intercept Control Room, which was to maintain close contact with the intercept stations. Colman was soon joined by another scientist, George Crawford, a former schoolmate of mine at Marlborough College. Travis also persuaded London banks to send us some of their brightest young men to handle the continuous interchange of information with intercept stations. Thus, very soon, we had an intercept control team large enough to operate round the clock.

Not all the men interviewed for this type of work were established academics or even undergraduates. Leo Marks had only just left St Paul's School when he was sent to learn cryptography. He described, with a great deal of wit and humour, the process of selecting codebreakers:

I had been accepted as a pupil at a school for cryptographers. My audition took place at a large country house which tried to ramble but hadn't the vitality. Major Masters, the headmaster of the code-breaking school, began the interview by asking what my hobbies were.

'Incunabula and intercourse, sir.'

It slipped out and wasn't even accurate; I'd had little experience of one and couldn't afford the other. I suspected he didn't know what incunabula was and added: 'And chess too, sir – when there's time,' which proved a better gambit. Three weeks later I received his letter of acceptance.

The school for code-breakers was the only one of its kind in England. The course was due to last for eight weeks, at the end of which the students would be graded and sent to Bletchley Park, which was the headquarters of the cryptographic department, known in the trade as MI8.

Fifteen new pupils, including two young women, had been selected for the course and we sat at separate desks in a large, bright room, studying the mating habits of the alphabet, counting the frequency of letters and working our way through exercises which gradually became more difficult until we were ready to tackle codes of military and diplomatic level.

Unfortunately he failed the course, though this was not through lack of ability. He went instead to work for the clandestine organization SOE (Special Operations Executive) and played a significant role in the war, making codes rather than breaking them.

Another 'boffin', Harry Hinsley, had to wait until he was inside before being let in on the secret of his prospective work in 'Hut 3':

> The Security Officer on the gate used his telephone and summoned up a WAAF officer.
>
> She led me across a noble lawn, with on the left a Tudorbethan mansion, on the right a large lake; in front a small office. (It should be noted that the hut numbers not only designated the huts themselves but were also used as cover-names for the work going on in them. When, towards the end of the war, the Hut 3 work was transferred to a brick building, it was still called Hut 3.)
>
> In my initiation stress was laid on the value of work going out from Hut 3. It was 'the heart of the matter' and of immense importance. The Enigma had been mastered. The process up to the production of raw decrypts was carried out in Hut 6 next door. It was the task of Hut 3 to evaluate them and put the intelligence they contained into a form suitable for passing to the competent authorities, be they Ministries or Commands.

THE MYSTERY LOCATION

For outsiders, even if they belonged to the intelligence world, BP had already acquired a reputation as a place of mystery. It had also gained a certain fame for its eccentric civilian staff – some servicemen saw it as a sort of zoo for boffins. Jack Poole, a Flight Sergeant in the RAF, remembered being told what to expect, and suggests how 'top secret' the establishment really was:

> With a number of other RAF sergeants who had been on the cipher course with me I was sent out of town to Bletchley Park. We were accompanied by a British Army Officer who said little except to remark on our arrival, 'Don't be surprised to see people here walking around with beards and red, white and blue umbrellas.' We were billeted in an RAF camp that had plenty of mud and no Sergeants' Mess, because it had just been opened.

Every day we walked through a churchyard to the outbuildings of a vicarage where we learned about 'Ultra' and the operation of Typex coding machines. The church stood between our classrooms and what immediately became to us the 'mysterious' Park. Every time I walked alongside the ivy-covered wall that hid the Park from the pathway to the camp I could not refrain from wondering what was behind it. One night in the Sergeants' Mess one of my companions confided, 'They call this place Station X' and to us, studying on the fringe, that's what the place remained. It was not until I read Group Captain Winterbotham's book 'The Ultra Secret' that I discovered what did, in fact, go on in the Park.

Even those who found themselves working inside the walls shared this sense of mystery. Once assigned to duty there they had first of all to find out where they were going. 'Bletchley' meant nothing to most of them, and only the name of the London terminus from which it was reached offered a clue to its whereabouts. Mrs Clark, the young library assistant from Bow, remembered that:

Some time after the original interview I was sent a ticket to Bletchley, from Euston, and told to send my luggage 'in advance'. Also to take an overnight bag for a couple of days, until said luggage arrived.

The great majority of clerical staff were unaware, on arrival, of the type of work in which they were to be involved, though they were left in no doubt as to its sensitive nature. Their 'joining instructions' often sounded like something out of a spy film. For example:

On arrival at Bletchley [station] you will find a telephone kiosk. Ring this number and await instructions.

Or, equally cryptically:
Take the exit from the arrival platform, go to the station forecourt and report to a hut on the far right hand side marked RTO (Railway Transport Officer) and show him but DO NOT GIVE him your envelope. He will direct you.

When the new recruits reached the Park itself they signed the Official Secrets Act at once. They were then told something of the role they were to play in the defeat of Hitler. For those who had just completed basic training and become used to the structured and smartly uniformed world of a military camp, Bletchley would have been utterly bewildering. Not only were there men and women from all three services, but civilians – often scruffy and dishevelled ones at that – who obviously held positions of authority. Wren Cynthia Waterhouse recalled that:

> The pay was 30 shillings (£1.50) a week and it was never clear who was in charge of us as we were detached from the Navy, working under the Foreign Office.

TASKS AND SKILLS

Many of the skills necessary for the clerical staff could be learned, if they did not already possess them, by quick and concentrated effort. An essential part of the 'Bletchley experience' for many young women was a series of crash courses lasting days or weeks and held in London, Bedford or elsewhere, that taught them the elements of such subjects as speed-typing, telephone operating or Japanese. A background in clerical work, teaching or (since many came direct from school or university) merely a sound education quickly came to be considered sufficient preparation. Many recruits were obtained by word of mouth, summoned to interview because they were friends, relatives, pupils or colleagues of those already involved in the work, who recommended them because they appeared to have the necessary qualities, or simply because their backgrounds could be vouched for. Typical of this intake was Margaret Ward:

> I joined Bletchley Park by chance. I was staying with my godmother in Woburn Sands for a brief rest following the London Blitz, and the question of my 'call up' was mentioned. She mentioned that there was a 'Government department' at Bletchley Park and suggested seeing a friend of hers whose son was 'high up' in the Civil Service, and was working there. I therefore applied and duly received and completed a detailed questionnaire. Shortly afterwards I was summoned to an interview, which took place in what looked like a railway carriage

tucked away behind some bushes near Bletchley railway station. The interview was conducted by two gentlemen – one a retired army colonel, the other a civilian who – I learned later – was a brilliant linguist speaking 16 languages fluently!

Soon after this I received a letter asking me to report at the front gate of B.P. There I was met by the said retired colonel and, following some formalities including receiving an official pass, was then taken to a small room and interviewed by a Don from King's College, Cambridge. Also by a naturalised Russian/German gentleman. Despite the fact that the work they did was completely incomprehensible to me at that time I enjoyed my few weeks with them – such splendid characters, absolutely charming!

Felicity Ashbee set out to find war work that would make use of her flair for languages:

Because I had good German, pretty fair French and a little Russian, the censorship seemed a suitable place to offer my services to. So, I found out where the language exams were being held, chewed the end of my fountain pen over strange texts, and went back home again to Kent to kick my heels impatiently waiting for a verdict.

With these rites of passage behind her, she was mustered into the WAAF. Examining her orders, she was irritated to find she had been assigned a job that seemed to offer no scope for her abilities, and perplexed by a lack of further explanation:

A glance at my curious credentials and I was labelled Clerk.
'Clerk!' I said, chagrined.
'S/D' he added, 'Special Duties.'
Obviously that was the only information we were to get for the time being.

She was to work for RAF Fighter Command, for the radar defences of Britain also required this type of clerk, but she would in due course arrive at BP and find that her skills were not wasted. In the meantime, she and her fellow recruits had to be put at least partly in the picture:

Soon we were summoned to 'report to' a large, shabby house in Leighton Buzzard, whose neglected garden was knee high with uncut grass. We were assembled into what must once have been an impressive drawing room to be given a talk on the elements of Radar (so that was what Special Duties was going to be about!) and a smattering of information, much of it as incomprehensible as it seemed irrelevant, from a fat volume called Air Force Law.

Ann Harding, who clearly possessed a sense of adventure, was looking for an unusual form of war service. She found one:

I thought about going into the WRNS, also the FANYs (First Aid Nursing Yeomanry), which was mostly driving, but also secretly provided suitable girls for dropping into France – not my possibility as they had to be perfect French speakers, bilingual. Then one day a letter came from [my sister] Nancy, at the Foreign Office in London. She asked if [my friend] Jean would like to work in a department of the FO that was badly in need of people, especially German speakers. Jean had just been to Bonn University so spoke very good German. She did not want to go, so I asked if they would see if they would have me. I had had a year's German at school and as Nancy had said this place was not in London, but out in the country, I was allowed to apply, having asked my friend Bunty if she would come with me.

We went off to the Foreign Office in London and were interviewed by a rather terrifying woman, but were both accepted. We were to start at the beginning of May, for which we would get instructions. We were to go to Bletchley in Buckinghamshire. It was a train junction, but that was all we knew.

We were met by a WAAF who took us to a brake with War Department written on it, driven by a very smart chauffeur. Bunty was dropped first, then I was taken to a house by the railway. My landlady was very kind, but her house was not nice with the street on one side and the railway on the other. There was no garden. My room was very small with an iron bedstead, feather mattress and two very thin blankets. There was no bathroom, just a washbowl and cold water on a washstand. The loo was downstairs, through the kitchen (where all the family lived) and outside in the yard.

Miss SM Carman's journey to Bletchley was the result of a quirk of fate – or a disinclination to be stuck at a kitchen sink:

> In November 1943 I joined the WRNS. We had to be slotted into a category and at that time the only ones open were the kitchens or SDX, Special Duties X, which was so secret no-one would tell us what it was. So most of us agreed to the latter, signed the (Official) Secrets Act, and were posted to our various stations for training in our duties.

Doreen Spencer was actively seeking useful war work and already possessed a qualification of interest to recruiters for Bletchley:

> My seventeenth birthday came in January 1941. Many of my friends were joining the Forces as their age groups came up. I was becoming very restless and feeling that, as there was no one else in the family of an age to join the Forces it was up to me to go. In any case I would soon have been called at the age of eighteen to go into a factory or other vital war work and that didn't appeal to me. I was more adventurous than that!
>
> My father was a Signals Officer in the Home Guard and here started my road to Bletchley Park. He was told to learn Morse as part of his duties, and so be totally efficient in any emergency. Pop and I had lots of fun learning Morse together and becoming proficient in handling a Morse key.
>
> As soon as I was seventeen and a half years old, I applied to join the Women's Auxiliary Air Force, the WAAFs. I was told I would be notified in due course. It was an anxious time, waiting for that buff envelope on the doormat.
>
> The tests consisted of general intelligence. We were given various papers containing questions, simple mathematics, relative pictures, drawings and graphs. We had tests for colour blindness. We also had hearing tests. Happily I passed the lot and was told that I would undergo training to become a wireless operator.
>
> Having learned Morse code I now had to build up a speed and send and receive correctly and read what was sent with ease and at an acceptable speed. Most important, how to handle a Morse key with ease and accuracy. I worked hard to be really efficient. Every

word I used, I translated into Morse symbols. Before long Morse is no longer a series of dashes and dots but a rhythmic language. The more experienced one becomes, whole words have a sound of their own, the operator recognises in plain language as opposed to code words like 'and' and 'are', which are in regular use.

She, and others who had been selected, had to acquire further skill before they could begin their work. Their next task:

> ... was to learn touch typing at speed and with great accuracy. The next stage was where our knowledge of Morse was to play an essential part. We were trained to read a Morse slip and type the symbols, translate in other words, the symbols into letters by typing them. All the time the Morse slip would be moving at a reasonable speed.

Having worked up the necessary swiftness and accuracy, they could be posted to their destination.

> We were driven to a stately home and were shown to a series of wooden huts situated under big old broad-leafed trees.
> We were housed in a very nice house at a village called Shenley while a camp was being built next to the Park. When we finally moved into new huts on the camp, Shenley was turned into a rest house for us. We could spend our time off there, staying overnight if we wanted. The camp became RAF Church Green and that became our address, no mention of Bletchley Park.

She recorded her early impressions of the place and of the few parts of the complex that she came to know. Some of her colleagues would not encounter even the small number of other departments that she did:

> Bletchley Park was a series of buildings, as I learned years later, but at the time we were there we only knew of our Block – the Auto Room. I knew of the teleprinter section because I was sent there to work for a couple of days to give me experience.
> I also knew the Cipher Section because that was where all our messages were sent to be decoded, and supposedly that was

where messages came from to be transmitted by us. These were never carried by hand from our department to another but conveyed automatically through a container.

I didn't realise when I first stepped into the Auto Room that I was going to be an integral part of a very secret establishment. In fact I didn't know that until fifty years after the war. My parents were never told of Bletchley Park. My address was Hut Number ? (I can't remember the number), RAF Church Green, Bletchley, Buckinghamshire.

My impressions the first time I went in through those guarded gates were of a grand red brick mansion with a lake in front of it, and a few buildings inside the main gate and the building we worked in.

BILLETS AND HOSTELS

Having taken in their surroundings, the women began to get used to the various premises that would become their homes. A number of them were accommodated in a hostel, as Mrs FE Clark remembered:

Several of us arrived at this time – none of us had ever worked or lived in the same hostel with others. We were met by an estate car – and taken direct to the Park. The driver must have had a pass for us all – otherwise we would never have been allowed past the guard. We went straight to the mansion, for the 'oath of secrecy' and were issued with passes. Thence to the hostel and were allocated a room. One could sit on the bed and touch everything!, but we each had a key, and it was private. Our ration books were handed in and it was some time later when we were allocated a part [of our coupons] to take home on weekend leaves. I think it was every third weekend. I worked 21 days straight off then 2 days off to go home.

There was a bathroom wing, well equipped, with hand basins, WCs and baths. The other two wings were bedrooms – a long corridor with rooms on both sides. There was also a laundry room for our personal washing and ironing, and we were allowed to use the boiler for drying purposes. It all worked very well, later someone acquired a sewing-machine for us – it was kept in the lounge – and was a boon to those of us who made our own clothes (when we could get the material). Also, there was a mini-kitchen with a 'Baby Belling' grill and plate used to make drinks and snacks. This was off the lounge.

We ate in the canteen just inside the gates of the Park, all meals including breakfast. Also we went over later in the evenings for a hot 'night' drink. In our free time we did a lot of walking in the surrounding countryside – or the cinema at Bletchley or Fenny Stratford, or to the little café in the town – usually very crowded.

Mrs LP Holliday recalled that she had been fortunate enough to find convivial lodgings in the nearby town:

I lived in the hostel, outside the main gates, but later was billeted in Bletchley town, with a pleasant homely family consisting of husband and wife and married daughter with husband in the Forces. They were very good to me and I was very happy there.

The commandeering by the authorities of spare bedrooms throughout entire districts sometimes had unexpected results. Ann Harding found that, no matter how distant she might be from where she had formerly lived, she was not, after all, so far from home:

My sister Nancy was sent out to Bletchley from the Foreign Office. She turned up next door to us, the other half of our semi-detached house, No 82, with Mr and Mrs Elson. Mr Elson was an engine driver and Nancy stayed with them for the rest of the war. Her bedroom and our bedroom were next door to each other.

But not all were this fortunate. Felicity Ashbee was to find herself sharing cramped quarters with a larger-than-life room mate:

It transpired that, in the frantic rush on the outbreak of hostilities, the billeting officers had done their fact-finding at the double, and had only asked how many 'bodies' each of the small semi-detached houses along the Elstree Road could take, not how many beds were available to put the bodies into! This meant that I found myself, to the horror of another of my new and rather more clued-up friends, sharing a double bed with a 6-foot lesbian ballet-photographer, who, since her measurements were larger than anything the manufacturers of WAAF uniforms had allowed for, continued for some time to wear her long black cloak and black sombrero.

As it turned out I soon had the bed to myself, for she summoned a lilo from home and inflated it to fill the narrow space between the bed and the wall.

THE UTMOST SECURITY

Before they settled into their work, all members of the Bletchley Park community, whether Oxford don or schoolgirl, who worked with ciphers and intelligence had to learn and abide by a series of strict regulations. Though obviously these rules were formulated before the threat of German invasion receded, the need for security did not change in the least degree throughout the war:

No mention whatsoever may be made either in conversation or correspondence regarding the nature of your work. It is expressly forbidden to bring cameras etc. within the precincts of Bletchley Park (Official Secrets Act).

DO NOT TALK AT MEALS. There are the waitresses and others who may not be in the know regarding your own particular work.

DO NOT TALK TO THE TRANSPORT. There are the drivers who should not be in the know.

DO NOT TALK TRAVELLING. Indiscretions have been overheard on Bletchley platform. They do not grow less serious further off.

DO NOT TALK IN THE BILLET. Why expect your hosts who are not pledged to secrecy to be more discreet than you, who are?

DO NOT TALK BY YOUR OWN FIRESIDE, whether here or on leave. If you are indiscreet and tell your own folks, they may see no reason why they should not do likewise. They are not in a position to know the consequences and have received no guidance. Moreover, if one day invasion came, as it perfectly well may, Nazi brutality might stop at nothing to wring from those that you care for, secrets that you would give anything, then, to have saved them from knowing. Their only safety will lie in utter ignorance of your work.

BE CAREFUL EVEN IN YOUR HUT. Cleaners and maintenance staff have ears, and are human.

These huts were to dominate the memories of those who were stationed at 'BP'. Though they were occupied for the war's whole duration, and underwent a certain amount of modification, they remained as uncomfortable to inhabit as they were unattractive to look at. During the first, stifling summer of the conflict, the staff worked in huts built of pine planks. As construction speeded up under the pressure of events, and more buildings had to be erected, wood increasingly gave way to plasterboard and structures became more draughty and flimsy. Only with the arrival of heavy machinery – the bombe and then the Colossus – was it seen as necessary to create sturdier strcutures of steel and concrete.

Harry Hinsley described the layout of the building in which he worked on naval codes:

> Hut 3 was set up like a miniature factory. At its centre was the Watch Room – in the middle a circular or horseshoe-shaped table, to one side a rectangular table. On the outer rim of the circular table sat the Watch, some half-dozen people. The man in charge, the head of the Watch or Number 1, sat in an obvious directing position at the top of the table. The watchkeepers were a mixture of civilians and serving officers, Army and RAF. At the rectangular table sat serving officers, Army and RAF, one or two of each. These were the Advisers. Behind the head of the Watch was a door communicating with a small room where the Duty Officer sat. Elsewhere in the Hut were one large room housing the Index and a number of small rooms for the various supporting parties, the back rooms.
>
> The processes to which the decrypts were submitted were, consecutively, emendation, translation, evaluation, commenting, and signal drafting. The first two were the responsibility of the Watch, the remainder of the appropriate Adviser.

IJ Good explained how the result of their work might be passed onward, all the way to Downing Street:

When we cryptanalysts broke a message we would not usually read it ourselves, although we would sometimes read the first few letters to make sure there was no mistake. Instead, the keys to the message would be sent to the Intelligence Department, where the message would be deciphered and sometimes translated and where a selection would be made from the various decipherments for transmitting information to Churchill and to the armed forces.

The hours worked by the teams were, in theory, not onerous – though in moments of stress or when a major backlog had developed they might well work whatever hours were necessary. The combination of secrecy, dedication and exhilaration that characterized the better moments at Bletchley is suggested by this account by Ann Harding:

We started off on the 10 a.m. to 6 p.m. shift with a break from 1.00 to 2.30 for lunch in the House after which we used to sit by the lake and often write home. Once inside the hut we were locked in from our side and always had to go and unlock the door if anyone came. We loved our work, but found it very intensive and tiring. We were supposed to have one day off a week, but if we were very busy we often did not take it, but could, with luck, have perhaps two days later. In some cases we were so busy that we could be due six days. Often, we were so fascinated by the work that we didn't want a day off. The town's people were always dying to know what we were doing and called the place the Lunatic Asylum.

ALL ABOUT THE BOMBE

A number of the clerks were to learn the mysteries of the 'Bombe', a machine designed by Alan Turing and built by a local company. A version of this had been used by Polish cryptanalysts the year before the war began, and there were several explanations for its unusual name. One was the loud ticking sound it gave off; another was that the ice cream of that name was being eaten when it was invented. Housed in a bronze cabinet six-and-a-half feet high and seven feet wide, it was an electromechanical device whose rotating wheels ran with a deafening clatter and with the speed of an express train. It could read and analyse vast numbers of

Enigma settings, looking for repetitions. It had 30 drums, or wheels, and each was equivalent to the wheels of ten Enigma machines. To set it to work, the codebreakers first came up with a list, or 'menu', of possible matches between clear and enciphered letters. This was fed into the machine. Once the Bombe had found a connection, an operator using a replica of the Enigma would test it.

The first Bombe, named 'Victory', was ready for use by March 1940. Group Captain Winterbotham went to see it in operation. He remembered the moment that, at a time when German air force traffic had greatly increased, the machine made the vital breakthrough into the code:

> It is no longer a secret that the backroom boys at Bletchley used the science of electronics to help them solve the puzzle of Enigma. I am not of the computer age nor do I attempt to understand them, but early in 1940 I was ushered with great solemnity into the shrine where stood a bronze-coloured column surmounted by a larger circular bronze-coloured face, like some Eastern goddess who was destined to become the oracle of Bletchley, at least when she felt like it. She was an awesome piece of magic.
>
> It must have been about the end of February 1940 that the Luftwaffe had evidently received enough Enigma machines to train their operators sufficiently well for them to start putting some practice messages on the air. The signals were quite short but must have contained the ingredients the bronze goddess had been waiting for. [General Stewart] Menzies had given instructions that any successful results were to be sent immediately to him, and it was just as the bitter cold days of that frozen winter were giving way to the first days of April sunshine that the oracle of Bletchley spoke and Menzies handed me four little slips of paper, each with a Luftwaffe message dealing with personnel postings to units. From the Intelligence point of view they were of little value, except as a small bit of administrative inventory, but to the backroom boys at Bletchley Park and to Menzies, and indeed to me, they were like the magic in the pot of gold at the end of the rainbow. The miracle had arrived.

By August another Bombe was completed, and the number rapidly increased. Teams of Wrens were assigned to operate them, a task that required not only physical stamina but a certain stature, as Cynthia Waterhouse, working at one of Bletchley's outstations, explained:

> The intricate deciphering machines were known as 'bombes.' These unravelled the wheel settings for the Enigma ciphers thought by the Germans to be unbreakable. They were cabinets about eight feet tall and seven feet wide. The front housed rows of coloured circular drums each about five inches in diameter and three inches deep. Inside each was a mass of wire brushes, every one of which had to be meticulously adjusted with tweezers to ensure that the circuits did not short. The letters of the alphabet were painted round the outside of each drum. The back of the machine almost defies description – a mass of dangling plugs on rows of letters and numbers.
>
> We were given a menu which was a complicated drawing of numbers and letters from which we plugged up the back of the machine and set the drums on the front. The menus had a variety of cover names – e.g. silver drums were used for shark and porpoise menus for naval traffic, and phoenix, an army key associated with tank battles at the time of El Alamein.
>
> We only knew the subject of the key and never the contents of the messages. It was quite heavy work and now we understood why we were all of good height and eyesight, as the work had to be done at top speed and 100% accuracy was essential. The 'bombes' made a considerable noise as the drums revolved, and would suddenly stop, and a reading was taken. If the letters matched the menus, the Enigma wheel-setting had been found for that particular key. To make it more difficult the Germans changed the setting every day. The reading was phoned through to the Controller at Bletchley Park where the complete messages were deciphered and translated. The good news would be a call back to say 'Job up, strip machine.'

She also explained the system of shift-work:

> We worked on the 'bombes' in a hut in the grounds and were connected direct to Bletchley Park. The watches were of four weeks' duration, 8–4 first week, 4–12 second week and midnight

to 8 a.m. third, then a hectic 3 days of 8 hours on, 8 hours off, ending with a much-needed 4 days' leave.

The teams laboured day and night to keep up with the flow of traffic. Another Wren, Mrs HB Rance (née Thomson), described their working arrangements, which could involve a certain amount of domestic drudgery as well as the challenge of high technology:

> I think there were 16 bombes at Gayhurst Mannor – 8 in each room. They were named after various scientists: Ampere, Coulombe, Henri, Faraday, Volta, Evershed etc.
>
> There must have been about 34 of us on each Watch as two were Duty Wrens (taken in turns) and they had to clean the cloakrooms as no Wren stewards were allowed in the hut. They also had to make tea twice during the Watch and if it was Night Watch they made the supper – usually bread and cheese I think.
>
> There was a Petty officer in charge of the Watch and she sat in the office and was in touch with B.P. by teleprinter and phone. She issued Menus and settings and would tell us if a job was 'up,' e.g. Successfully completed.

The process began when the women were issued with menus by the non-commissioned officer in charge of their group:

> A Leading Wren sat in each room and issued wheel orders (or woes as we called them).
>
> When you were given a Menu you asked your checker to help you set up. The different coloured drums were on shelves. Each colour represented a number – the naval colours were dark blue, black and silver and were at the bottom of the racks. The drums had 26 wire contacts on their faces and you had to make sure these were all straight. Tweezers were provided. The drums were put on the machines with clips which were quite stiff and we got sore fingers unclipping them.
>
> Menus had a name like Avocet or Jaguar or Leopard for the army and Shark, Dolphin etc. for naval ones. There were three banks on the bombes so we usually ran three wheel orders at a time. At the back of the bombes were three lots of plugs and

leads to correspond with the front settings. We had coupling jacks to join two plugs and there was something called a female. You had to make sure plugs were in properly and not splayed out.

When you had put on the drums and plugged the back you set the drums with the settings given on the Menu. When all were checked you started the bombe. If your bombe stopped quickly your heart sank as it probably meant a wrong stop. You gave the stop to your checker on a small piece of paper. It looked like this:

Ampere (1)

231

NBG/S

The three letters were read from the three master drums on the front and the single letter was read from the input at the side which had three separate banks so you knew which wheel order it was. You couldn't wait for your checker so you continued with the run. If she called out 'wrong stop' you had to see if any of the drums were loose or wrongly set. If you couldn't find any fault you called one of the I/c Watch who were RAF electricians. They usually found out the fault quite quickly although sometimes a bombe would be u/s [unserviceable].

However, if the stop was alright you continued running through the wheel orders. If the stop had some self-steckers e.g. S = S or A = A and some confirmations e.g. E = B and B = E you knew you had probably cracked it so you rushed into the P.O. and she rang through to B.P. Meanwhile you continued in case it wasn't the right one. If it was 'Job up Ampere' or whatever, you stripped the bombe and waited for the next one.

The checking machines were quite small and you could sit down so it was a much less tiring job. Quite often you helped your operator change wheel orders.

THE BIRTH OF COLOSSUS

It was in 1943 that Max Newman, one of the Bletchley mathematicians, decided to develop a machine that would bring to life the ideas proposed by Turing some years earlier. He set out to automate, and thus considerably speed up, the search for Enigma wheel-settings. The device built under his guidance by telecommunications engineers came to be known as the 'Robinson', a reference to the cartoon machinery drawn by the artist William Heath Robinson and thus shorthand for any bewilderingly complicated technology. The Robinson could read a thousand characters per second, but information was fed into it on paper tape and read by another tape. At the necessary speed, the tapes were often torn by the sprockets on the wheels and it was necessary to keep stopping the machine for repairs. Tommy Flowers, a young telephone engineer, became involved in the project at Turing's invitation. He realized that a version built with valves could work even faster, that the cipher text could be read photo-electrically and that it could have smooth instead of sprocketed wheels, which would therefore not tear the tape. It was named 'Colossus'. Flowers explained its object:

> The purpose was to find out what the positions of the code wheels were at the beginning of the message and it did that by trying all the possible combinations and there were billions of them. It tried all the combinations, which processing at 5,000 characters a second could be done in about half an hour. So then having found the starting positions of the cipher wheels you could decode the message.

IJ Good provided a description of its features:

> The machine was programmed largely by plugboards. It read the tape at 5,000 characters per second and, at least in Mark II, the circuits were in quintuplicate so that in a sense the reading speed was 25,000 bits per second. This compares well with the speed of the electronic computers of the early 1950s. The first Colossus had 1,500 valves, which was probably far more than for any electronic machine previously used for any purpose. This was one reason why many people did not expect Colossus to work. But it was installed in December 1943 and began producing results almost immediately. Most of the failures of valves were caused by switching the machine on and off.

With Colossus, Flowers had brought to fruition Turing's concept of a programmable computer, and thus begun a new era in science.

REWARDS FOR MONOTONY

Complex though the equipment was, the technicalities of operating it were quickly mastered, and a sense of downright boredom could assail women who had to stand for hours in front of the wheels and wires, performing a series of deft and automatic movements to keep the machines running and the tapes flowing through. Monotony was made worse by failure to appreciate how this work was helping the war effort, and periodic pep talks were arranged to bolster morale. Cynthia Waterhouse remembered:

> To keep up our morale, we were told that Winston Churchill was constantly on the line 'to his most secret source', and that our work was absolutely vital. We sometimes had news of our involvement in a past achievement such as the hunting and subsequent sinking of the battleship Tirpitz.

As the war continued these triumphs were to multiply, and within the walls of Bletchley there could be private celebrations. The Park received visits from some of those who were directing the war, and who were among the very few people to know the value of what the codebreakers were doing. IJ Good remembered that:

> For the good of our morale, we were given a number of titbits about the results of our work. For example, we were told it had led directly to the sinking of the Bismarck. Also, there were times when Rommel did not receive any supplies in North Africa because all his supply ships were being sunk in consequence of our reading the Mediterranean Enigma. And obviously the reading of the U-boat traffic was tremendously valuable. Also, for the sake of our morale, we were once visited by Churchill, who delivered a pep talk to a little crowd of us gathered around him on the grass. Much later another pep talk was given by Field Marshal Alexander in a hall with an audience of about a thousand. At one point he obtained a laugh by mimicking one of Montgomery's gestures.

And the atmosphere of austerity and purpose in the huts was occasionally lightened by a touch of humour:

I remember towards the end of my time at Gayhurst a new Menu called a Daisy Chain came in and I was given one to do and couldn't understand it. It turned out to be an April Fool!

The eccentricity of the codebreakers became, and has remained, legendary. One common memory was of the regular searches that were necessary through dustbins and waste-paper baskets, because so often a 'boffin' would have absent-mindedly thrown away highly sensitive materials. As Gwen Davies, who worked at BP, remarked:

At least half of the people there were absolutely mad. They were geniuses, no doubt many of them were extremely, extremely clever, but my goodness they were strange in ordinary life.

Another (anonymous) clerk agreed and made an incisive comment on the difficulties of gathering so much genius in one place, dispelling the notion that these exceptional characters invariably worked in harmony:

Their brains were developed to the detriment of their bodies. This led to an atmosphere of egotism, not to mention spitefulness and backbiting. The precept of public service was unknown to them though they would do what they were paid to do, the thought of doing a bit more did not occur to them.

Alan Turing, undoubtedly a hero of the intelligence war, was the outstanding example of this. Though only in his twenties, his nickname, 'Prof', suggested a gravitas and eminence beyond his years, and his role in the development of the computer has gained him admission to the scientific pantheon. Nevertheless he became just as celebrated for his habit of wearing a gas mask when cycling, or for chaining his coffee-mug to a radiator. His colleague IJ Good remembered these peculiarities:

In the first week of June each year he would get a bad attack of hay fever, and he would cycle to the office wearing a service gas mask to keep the pollen off. His bicycle had a fault; the chain would come off at regular intervals. Instead of having it mended he would count the number of times the pedals went round and would get off the bicycle in time to adjust the chain by hand.

Another of his eccentricities was that he chained his mug to the radiator pipes to prevent its being stolen. It was only after the war that we learned he was a homosexual. It was lucky we didn't know about it early on, because if they had known, he might not have obtained clearance and we might have lost the war.

Turing also had his savings converted into silver bars, believing that these would more easily survive postwar economic fluctuations. He buried the bars in a meticulously chosen spot – and was never again able to find it. An incident that is perhaps more illuminating about the nature of genius was recounted by Ann Harding, who found herself one of the staff in his hut:

> One morning I had a bad moment. Prof called me over to his table and handed me a sheet of figures. 'Please could you work these out for me, Ann?' I was appalled. He was so obviously a very brilliant person, a lecturer in mathematics at Cambridge, and maths was not my strong subject. I had a good look and found it was all long division, plenty of it but simple. So I did it all and took it back to him. I said I couldn't understand why he wanted me to do it as I would have thought he would have done it in a flash. He looked rather embarrassed and said, 'Well, you see, I never did simple arithmetic.' At school his maths master realised very quickly that he had a brilliant brain and put him straight onto advanced maths.

It is natural to assume that people of such immense, specialized brainpower have no time or inclination to cultivate other interests, but for all Turing's air of preoccupation, he had a parallel ability that in more favourable circumstances might have brought him renown in a different field. Good remembered that:

> Turing became a first class marathon runner. Unfortunately he developed some leg complaint that prevented his getting into the Olympic Games.

Good considered another boffin to have an even more impressive range of talents:

Shaun Wylie had a very exact logical mind. He was also president of the Bletchley Park Dramatic Club, an international hockey player, a first class teacher and a winner of the unarmed combat competition of the local battalion of the Home Guard. He was a perfect gentleman who never lost his temper except on purpose, and he was an extremely good listener. I used to believe that he wouldn't interrupt a conversation even to mention that the war was over.

In spite of the pressure, and the burden of secrecy, under which the staff worked, there was a lighter side to life at the Park. The tennis courts were much in demand when the weather permitted, and highly competitive games of rounders were played on the lawn between the house and the lake. The mere possibility of strolling in what were, despite wartime development, beautiful gardens gave some a refreshing sense of escape from stern realities:

> After lunch in the summer we used to take our cups of tea or coffee down by the lake in the grounds – the war seemed far away.

In fact, there were most of the makings of a highly successful social environment – a good mix of the sexes, a strong sense of community based on common purpose, and a number of people with a great deal to offer in terms of talent and ability, whether as instructors, designers or performers. To one young woman, the convivial delights that these produced rated almost as highly as the enjoyment of traditional English cuisine:

> Social life at BP was very full – an excellent dramatic society with many professional actors and actresses employed at the Park. There were many concerts and recitals, poetry readings, country dances and language courses. The huge canteen was a meeting place both for meals and functions. The food was really quite good. On Fridays a whole crowd of us used to go to a delightful pub just outside the perimeter of the Park where the publican's wife would use up her weekly jam ration to make a baked jam roll – simply delicious!

There were also ways of striking up friendships in the town without compromising the discretion required by their work. Another young woman recalled that:

> I had several friends among the local people mostly from the Methodist church.

As famous as the rounders matches by the lake was another abiding Bletchley Park passion – Scottish country dancing. This is difficult to do well without a good deal of practice, and the number of sessions engaged in every week by Doreen Spencer suggests how seriously it was taken by the Bletchley staff:

> I learned Scottish dancing – mostly at lunch times – twice a week plus a Friday evening, in the Assembly Hall, with a full-dress dance on St Andrew's nights (30th November). We wore out (Angus) Foss's record of Circassian Circle, and had a collection to buy him a new one. I also went to all performances by the operatic and dramatic groups.

And there were other possibilities beyond the confines of the town of Bletchley. Stratford-on-Avon was a short journey away:

> In the town of Bletchley we had two cinemas, both of which showed good films, so we went when we could. Also visits to Stratford were arranged and we went several times, saw *Hamlet* and *Romeo and Juliet*, but could not afford to go every time, and often we were in the wrong shift to be able to go. To go to Stratford – coach and play – cost 6s 6d (32.5 pence).

Not everyone shared this view. The hours worked by staff could present considerable problems with regard to organizing or participating in activities. A young clerk lamented that:

> It was difficult to have much of a social life, when working a three-shift system all the time.
>   As for entertainment – there was very little, really, mostly dances – put on specially for us – visits to the cinema, and eating out occasionally, plus the odd game of tennis.

She concluded, rather pathetically:

We often went to Bletchley station buffet, just to get a break.

These were the conditions under which the codebreakers waged their war. The combination of the ordinary and the extraordinary, the mundane and the exciting, the regimented and the eccentric was to give them an experience unique in the history of warfare, and one which none of them would ever forget.

3
1940: A FATEFUL YEAR

XILTO SZKAP ACAAP SZBEC SXUYZ (Commence hostilities
at once with Germany). Coded Admiralty signal sent, 'Most
Immediate,' to all Commands, home and abroad. Received at
1121 a.m., 3rd September 1939.[i]

This message, sent using an Admiralty code that had been broken, would
have been intercepted and decrypted by members of German Naval
Intelligence. It made clear that the period of appeasement and diplomatic
nicety through which Europe had passed was over. Hitler's bluff had been
called. His invasion of Poland had exhausted the patience of France and
Britain, whose eagerness to compromise had already enabled the Führer to
dismember Czechoslovakia.

Though Britain and Germany were at war from the beginning of
September 1939, it would be a further seven months before hostilities
actually began in earnest. In the autumn, a British Expeditionary Force
(BEF) arrived in France to assist their allies in what looked like a repeat of
the experience of 1914. It was assumed that a German invasion would soon
be launched, though since the previous war France had created a vast
national defensive barricade, the Maginot Line, that ran for hundreds of
miles along its eastern frontier. A series of bunkers, pillboxes, gun
emplacements and tank traps that took advantage of the terrain, it was
seen as impregnable and was expected to wear out the manpower and
armaments of any attacking German army. It thus permitted the French a
certain confidence.

Since the opening days of the Great War much else had improved. Both
the British and the French had fast-moving armour (though in the event it
would prove far less effective than that of the Wehrmacht) and fighter
squadrons of the Royal Air Force were deployed ready to fly and fight
defensively. The United Kingdom did not yet have the resources in place to

[i] RJ Drury

fight a full-scale war, but its troops were expected to be able to hold the enemy advance and to assist the much larger French army in the coming showdown. This did not materialize, and the winter passed quietly. In the concrete bunkers of the Maginot Line and in the more Spartan defences dug by the Tommies, soldiers waited through long months of inactivity. The French knew this period as the *drole de guerre*, and the British as the 'phoney war' or, more succinctly, the 'bore war'. Their opponents, similarly impatient on their own side of the Franco-German border, called it the *Sitzkrieg* ('sitting war').

One incident during that winter might have given valuable insight to those on the Allied side of the defences – had they taken it seriously. In November a German aircraft lost its way and landed at Mechlin, just over the Belgian frontier. Inside was an officer, who attempted to burn some papers just as a gendarme arrived to investigate. The items were confiscated and proved to be the General Staff plan for the Wehrmacht's westward attack. The information was passed on to the governments of France and Britain, but both assumed the plan to be a bluff and disregarded it. This was the first of numerous occasions in the coming conflict on which the authorities would disdain valuable intelligence on the grounds that they were suspicious of its source.

The 'bore war' ended in April of the following year when, in a sudden but meticulously planned move, German forces struck not westward but north, overrunning Denmark – which had neither the resources nor a suitable terrain for resistance and accepted occupation – and then Norway (the Germans wanted to secure Sweden's iron ore for their war effort), where Anglo-French troops became involved in fighting.

It was at this moment that the codebreakers began the war in earnest, for they decoded the extensive traffic of the German navy as it sailed for Norwegian ports. Ann Harding, a member of the team that worked on these signals at Bletchley, made a comment that was to apply to many situations during the fateful year of 1940: that no matter how detailed and important the information they were able to gather, it was rendered obsolete by the swift movement of events:

Our hut did naval decoding and our first breakthrough was the invasion of Norway by the Germans. It was not a lot of help as they were already invading, but our success was to have broken the code at all.

This seemed very much a sideshow when, the following month, German armies launched the long-expected attack toward the English Channel. The assault followed the classic *blitzkrieg* ('lightning war') tactics that had already proved their worth in Poland: bombers descended on cities and concentrations of troops. They also deliberately targeted columns of fleeing civilians in order to increase panic and clog roads, preventing the movement of their enemy's forces toward the battlefront. Paratroops were dropped to secure strategic points such as bridges and to hold them until they could be reached by swift armoured columns. The Germans cut through Belgium, Luxembourg and the Netherlands, ignoring the Maginot Line by simply going around its northern end and thus rendering useless almost the entire French defensive policy. French armies began to collapse and retreat.

The Netherlands held out for several days, but its defeat was inevitable. Its royal family, members of the government and the nation's gold reserves were evacuated to Britain, but the Hague was captured in a parachute assault and the merciless destruction of one city (Rotterdam) by bombers – with the threat that a similar fate would be visited on others – led to capitulation. In Belgium the fortress of Eben Emael, which was supposedly impregnable, was seized within hours by a team of German commandos who landed by glider on its roof. The Belgian royal family was placed under house arrest at its palace outside Brussels.

DUNKIRK

In less than a month Germany's western campaign was over. Hitler's armies did not follow the route taken by the previous generation – the 'Schlieffen Plan', which had involved a rightward sweep through Belgium to enter France from the north and capture Paris. In 1914 this had been halted at the River Marne and had resulted in a stalemate that lasted for most of the next four years. In 1940 the invaders followed a more difficult, but successful, path. Pushing straight through the densely forested Ardennes, they made for the Channel coast and trapped Anglo-British armies against the sea. Their enemies fought a steady but futile rearguard action, falling back on the few ports not in German hands and abandoning much of their equipment at roadsides and on beaches. While some units defended the perimeter of the town of Dunkirk, the majority of their comrades were lifted from the piers and beaches by a multitude of British ships and boats.

In a triumph of improvisation, the evacuation of over 500,000 troops was carried out in the last days of May and the first days of June. In addition to members of the BEF and RAF, a number of French soldiers and even German prisoners were brought out.

The BEF had survived, but was left demoralized and without the means of fighting on. As the country's new prime minister, Winston Churchill, put it: 'Wars are not won by retreats.' On 18 June (ironically the anniversary of Waterloo) the French government admitted defeat, and Britain was left as Hitler's only remaining opponent. In spite of what was a very decided setback, there was a curious sense of relief among the British population, for whom the survival of the BEF became 'the miracle of Dunkirk'. The comment of Mrs Edith Kup (née Heap), then a young WAAF, reflected a view that was widespread:

> There was no feeling of worry, rather one of relief that, now we were on our own, we would win the war our way and were certain we would win in the end.

Though Bletchley seemed a long way from the evacuation beaches, a sense of catastrophe was much in evidence there. Ann Harding recalled the atmosphere on the day that the news arrived:

> It was after Dunkirk that we went into breakfast one morning and found the French officers sitting with their breakfast in front of them and tears streaming down their faces. They had just heard that France had fallen.

For the staff at Station X, the phoney war had ended as quickly as it had for the fighting troops in Europe: when the German attacks in the west had begun, the volume of Enigma traffic had exploded. Within less than a week of the attack on Scandinavia, Bletchley had broken what its staff had nicknamed the 'yellow' code and was reading German army traffic. They had known, throughout the Wehrmacht's dash for the Channel, where the German forces were going and what difficulties they were encountering. The information had not been of much use, for the collapse and retreat of the Allies had been too swift. Nevertheless, their success gave them extensive knowledge of the enemy which would pay dividends in the months and years ahead.

When messages were received, they were often incomplete because of interference. It was therefore necessary to fill in the gaps by logic or guesswork. The messages would be studied by those with a knowledge not only of German but also of military terminology, slang and profanity – code words could be anything that had occurred to a bored or miserable operator. In order to protect the secrecy of the codebreaking process, the end-products of Bletchley's eavesdropping had to be disguised. The information was presented as having been obtained by spies ('a reliable source' became rather a tired cliché), who would have had to be almost impossibly brave, resourceful and fortunate to have achieved such results. While these supposed qualities impressed many of the military commanders who were given the information, such figures also distrusted material obtained by espionage, and reacted with suspicion or outright disbelief.

So much material came through the huts at Bletchley that the staff had to be urgently increased. Messages were forwarded to MI6 in London each day, and the vast trawl of decoded traffic was divided into four categories. Material considered most urgent, such as that relating to developing situations that could be affected by quick action, was sent direct as soon as it had been deciphered. Items in the second category were sent slightly less urgently, within four to eight hours. In the third category, material was not sent until a regular collection at the end of each day. The fourth category was not sent at all: the 'Quatsch pile' (named after the German word for rubbish) contained all the inconsequential and routine messages that needed no action. It was not disposed of but filed.

With the Channel and North Sea an important field of operations, and a seaborne invasion of Britain likely during the summer of 1940, coastal listening posts called 'Y stations' were set up to monitor the signals of German vessels. Like so much else on the Home Front in the communications war, they were almost entirely staffed by women. The teams in these establishments, usually comprising fewer than a dozen operators, developed a tremendous camaraderie. Lieutenant Commander Leslie ('Freddie') Marshall, one of the male officers involved in processing the information provided by them, described the work of these small but vital outposts in the first years of the war:

> In the acquisition of intelligence before and in the early stages
> of the war it had become known that, included in the equipment
> of the German armed service, there was what was then called a

VH/F transceiver, operating on the 30/50 mc/s band. Transmission and reception were normally very limited as regards range. The limit of audibility was the 'Horizon' range, i.e. the line of sight horizon from the transmitting point.

Essentially the VH/F transceiver was used for short range intercommunications between vessels sailing in company. The motor torpedo boats were the most frequently intercepted naval vessels. Provided the weather was not too rough they would sally forth during the hours of darkness from their bases along the enemy occupied coast and in the narrow waters between these harbours and the British coast they were able to carry out attacks on Allied ships using the convoy routes along the east and south coasts of Britain.

The object of setting up the Wren intercept stations along the coast was to frustrate such attacks by intercepting the signals passed between the units of formation and extracting the maximum amount of operational intelligence from their signals, such as the type and number of units involved, their intentions and their positions.

This intelligence was passed on to the Naval Bases' Operations Rooms via the Intelligence Centres and the speedier this could be done the better were the chances of appropriate action being taken by the Royal Navy.

One of the Y stations was at Dover which, set on the Kent coast only 20 miles from occupied France and soon to be nicknamed 'Hellfire Corner', was the most exposed place in Britain, well within sight – and artillery range – of the enemy. Mrs Daphne Baker (née Humphrys), then a member of the WRNS who was stationed inside the city's clifftop defensive bunkers, recalled life there during one of history's busier moments as a combination of danger and urgency, exhaustion and lightheartedness:

I was lucky enough to be sent to the Casemates in Dover as a cipher officer, sharing a tiny dorm in the Wrennery on Marine Parade, with just the road between us and the harbour. I have to say that the phoney war was enormous fun. I loved the work and friendships, and being able to see old friends on leave, and occasionally my parents 10 miles away at Bishopsbourne. Then suddenly there was Dunkirk, and Dover became the focus of the evacuation – the signals piled up so that we could only deal with the Most Immediate. With difficulty we got permission to work night watches to try to cope. Almost every brass hat in the country was working and sleeping in the Casemates, and we had to pick our way among their sleeping bodies to deliver the signals. There was little sleep even for those not on night watch as every evening the air-raid warning went and everyone was shooed out of the Wrennery to the caves at the bottom of the cliff.

Among all the losses a nice thing happened. We were on night watch and reports of sinkings were pouring in, including the ship of the husband of a fellow cipher officer. We whisked the signal away so that she couldn't see it but were heartbroken for her. Early in the morning there was a sudden scuffle and a figure in a blue French smock burst into the cipher office and clasped this girl to his bosom. I don't know how many times he'd been sunk and picked up that night, but there was her husband, and one happy ending.

From the crowded corridors of the Casemates (a rampart forming part of the defences of Dover Castle and acting as the headquarters for Admiral Sir Bertram Ramsay) she was soon to be posted a few miles north to another clifftop, there to listen for a specific type of traffic. The move resulted from her fluency in German, and her new home was to be a lighthouse:

My orders were to proceed to an empty Trinity House Cottage on South Foreland Cliff, where I would be joined by two German speaking Wren CPOs [Chief Petty Officers] and a couple of radio technicians with a van and VHF sets; our job was to find out whether the German vessels in the Channel were using R/T and if so to establish the frequencies they were using and intercept the signals. The word for which we could be shot was VHF, now a household word, but I still feel guilty in mentioning it.

Our unbelievable cover was that we were factory girls on holiday and no one was to come within two miles of us. So within 24 hours we were up on the cliff. The green van with its tell-tale VHF and DF aerials and VHF sets was parked alongside the three cottages. The charge-hand and his mate showed us how to work the sets, and which bands we were to cover and search. His job was to maintain the sets and take a DF [Direction Finding] bearing on any likely signal that we found. Remember radar was only in its infancy then. The first thing that we picked up was a flood of plain language R/T from the German Army as it moved through France from village to village towards the coast. The naval transmissions from E boats [fast German torpedo boats] or destroyers we were looking for were only expected at night, any movement in the Channel being visible from both sides, so our real job was from dusk to dawn, endlessly sweeping the specified band, pausing on any carrier wave to see if it would turn into a signal, and then on again.

Although radar had reduced the use of R/T, there was still a valuable trickle of signals. If any of us picked something up the other would join her on that frequency and both would try and make sense of the hissing, crackling call-sign and order lasting a few seconds. After about a week a pattern began to emerge of two frequencies used between 40 and 50 megacycles and we developed a sort of shorthand for the executive orders, like Ausfuhrung. It became clear that E boats were using strictly limited R/T and also that if we were to keep our established frequencies covered for a short barked order more sets were needed to continue searching the rest of the band in case the frequency had been changed.

One of the three Trinity House cottages was occupied by a retired lighthouse keeper. We worked in the van, slept when we could in the empty cottages, and his kind wife fed us. The Battle of Britain was beginning overhead and there was a lot of dive-bombing. One morning the lighthouse keeper waylaid me as I came off watch and accused me of murdering his wife. He was convinced that the van was making them a target, and he may have been right – but there was nothing I could do except say I was sorry. In that clear summer weather we could see with the naked eye the transports amassing along the French coast [for an invasion of England]. All British binoculars had been requisitioned early in the war, and we hadn't been re-issued any, being ears not eyes. But they can't have been short of them on the German side, and could well have seen us – but I don't think they identified us as they went on using R/T.

After some weeks, the Wrens were moved again, this time from their lighthouse to a new headquarters in a windmill on a nearby hilltop. They still overlooked the sea, and they were still a conspicuous landmark for those across the Channel. Mrs Baker remembered one occasion on which the girls' understanding of the enemy's language gave them a very unpleasant few moments:

> The only time we ever downed tools for a few minutes was one afternoon, when we were practising by listening to an aircraft, call-sign HABICHT spotting for the German cross-Channel guns. A shell fell into the sea not far from the cliff-edge below our windmill, the spray came up to the top of the cliff, and we heard the spotter say 'Noch ein bischen weiter und Sie haben die Windmuhle' (Just a bit further and you have the windmill). Our scribbling stopped dead and we looked at each other, and I said 'We'd better get under the tables.' So we did, feeling a bit silly, and counting the seconds. We were used to seeing the flash of the guns across the Channel, and you could count up to 120 before the shell arrived. This time it didn't and we got back to work; Habicht had knocked off.

The 'miracle of Dunkirk' was naturally seen in a different light by Hitler, who assumed that, after this ignominious departure from the Continent, Britain's small and ineffectual army was out of the war. Poland, the reason for British involvement in the war, was now firmly under the heel of the conqueror and, with all of Germany's objectives attained in the west, he could think of no reason for fighting to continue. A long-time Anglophile, he stated emphatically that he wished no harm to Britain or its Empire. What he wanted was the economic spoils of Europe – which he now had – and freedom to launch his crusade in the east against Communism without the nuisance of hostile forces behind his back. He made it clear that, in exchange for 'a free hand in Europe', he would leave Britain and its overseas possessions alone.

His generosity was wasted. Britain did not want peace on the terms that Hitler offered, for he had broken too many promises already. Once he realized that there could be no negotiation with this last remaining opponent, he began to plan for the invasion and conquest of Britain, which would take place in the summer of 1940. With immense military triumphs behind him (his armies had accomplished in a matter of weeks what the Kaiser's troops had failed to do in four years) he was understandably confident. He announced that he would accept Britain's surrender on, or about, 15 August.

Group Captain Winterbotham remembered the build-up of indications, evident in Enigma traffic, that an attack was in preparation. In passing this news on to Winston Churchill, he inadvertently inspired one of history's great speeches. Once France had been occupied and fighting had ended, the volume of signals had briefly dropped. However:

> It was not long before the Luftwaffe signals started to increase again, and now it began to look more serious for us. In the middle of July Ultra produced the signal we had all been waiting for. It had evidently been delivered in great secrecy from Hitler's headquarters to the Army, Navy and Air Force commanders-in-chief. Goering, however, then put the gist of it on the air to the generals commanding his air fleets. In his signal he stated that despite her hopeless military situation, England showed no signs of willingness to make peace. Hitler had therefore decided to prepare and, if necessary, to occupy it completely. The operation was to be called Sea Lion. I sent the signal over to the Prime Minister immediately. It was the first time the words Sea Lion had been used and it now made it much easier for us to identify any activities connected with the invasion plan. It was certainly this signal that gave Churchill the idea of making his famous speech telling the Germans that we would fight them on the beaches and everywhere else.

The attack would largely be launched from ports in northern France, and the harbours were quickly filled with hundreds of barges, commandeered from the rivers of Europe, for the conveying of troops. The assault would involve landings on the coasts of Kent and Sussex, between Broadstairs and Eastbourne. Hitler's troops would push across the Home Counties, rolling back resistance and establishing an initial front line between the Solent and the Thames, before continuing their progress northward.

Crucial to this plan was the destruction of the Royal Air Force and the Royal Navy. The first had to be eliminated to allow the Luftwaffe complete air mastery over southern England. The second had then to be kept out of the Channel to provide the invasion force with a clear passage. It was therefore upon the Luftwaffe that the success of the operation depended. Goering had a much larger number of aircraft at his disposal than the British (nearly 2,800, as opposed to 700). He expected to overwhelm the RAF within a matter of days, and its destruction would complete the first phase of Operation Sea Lion. Winterbotham continued:

> In Germany, Goering was the man of the hour and he lost no time in throwing his considerable weight about. One result was that he became prolific in his signals. We soon learned from him that the whole of Luftflotte 2 and Luftflotte 3 were being redeployed right along the Channel coast. Luftflotte 5 was being divided between Norway and Denmark. Ultra was giving us the main framework and, indeed, much of the detail as well. It was possible now to get virtually an exact order of battle of these air fleets, including the aerodromes where their various units were being stationed. They were of course helped by the whole lot of low-level signals sent by the various squadrons from which, now that the units were not far away, we could get cross-bearing fixes on their precise positions. We also knew from Ultra that feverish activities had been made to try and bring the squadrons up to full strength but that due to the poor operation of their repair and supply organization, the numbers of serviceable aircraft were still only about seventy-five per cent of their full strength.

Ultra thus gave the Allies a vital edge – advance knowledge of their opponent's numbers and weaknesses. Combined with shrewd and educated guesswork, it also seems to have given an accurate idea of the German dictator's timetable and intentions:

> It was therefore possible to estimate that although Britain was facing a paper force of nearly three thousand aircraft, some eighteen hundred of which were bombers, probably only three-quarters of this figure would be serviceable at any one time, and if losses exceeded replacements, their serviceability percentage would obviously decrease. From many secret sources of information, it seemed that Hitler would attack Russia in the East in the spring of 1941 and if he wanted the Sea Lion affair

mopped up in time to redeploy his main forces in the East, he must start his invasion by around mid-September at the latest. It didn't give him much time.

Towards the end of July there were signals showing disagreement between the Army and the Navy as to how the vast requirement of ships for the seaborne transport was to be met, but, from the Ultra signals we were now receiving, it was obvious that the main emphasis was still on the operations of the Luftwaffe. We could only guess, from the vast air fleets being ranged against us, and an apparent lack of urgency coupled with the inability of the German Army and Navy to co-operate, that the air battle was going to be the decisive factor. It was a hopeful sign and I think everyone, including the Prime Minister, felt that if we could withstand Goering's efforts to eliminate the Royal Air Force, Hitler would probably give up the idea altogether.

The German air assault began in earnest on 10 July, with attacks by bombers and fighters on RAF stations across south-east England. These continued for weeks but, although they were clearly doing damage, something was wrong. The RAF was supposedly reduced to its last few aircraft, yet there always seemed to be more of them. And these fighters appeared to know exactly where to find the German formations. The British aircraft – Hurricanes and Spitfires – were superb (the latter, particularly, won the ungrudging respect of their enemy) and took a heavy toll among the fleets of bombers. Every day that they defied the Luftwaffe delayed the invasion and made it more unlikely.

The defenders were undoubtedly hard-pressed, but they were not without advantages. The German flyers were operating at the extent of their range: a fighter that had flown from northern France had only ten minutes' fuel left when operating over England. If this ran out, the pilot would have to take to his parachute. As a result, large numbers of German pilots became casualties or prisoners. Their RAF opponents, fighting on their home ground, could if shot down be back in the air in a very short time. The building of fighter aircraft was increased during that summer until it was outstripping losses, and the production of parts was spread across the country to minimize damage when factories were targeted. The training of new pilots was speeded up, and all other types of RAF pilot were retrained in fighters. Thus the supply of men kept pace with the availability of planes. Most significantly, British radar was farther advanced than the German version, and a line of radar stations around the south-east coast could pinpoint the movements of the various *Luftflotten* as they approached. Because the air force Enigma had been broken, British codebreakers were able to learn a good deal about German armament, objectives and losses.

THE AIR BATTLE

The Battle of Britain, as this defensive air campaign came to be known, lasted through the summer and into the autumn. It took on a new dimension when the bombing of cities – 'the Blitz' – began in earnest in September. Hitler had avoided ordering the destruction of large civilian targets because it would increase the population's willingness to fight on, but a Luftwaffe crew accidentally dropped several bombs on London, and Churchill ordered a retaliatory raid on Berlin the following night. This was ineffectual in military terms, but its psychological results were immense. In a paroxysm of rage, Hitler launched a major bombing offensive against Britain. Throughout the autumn and winter of 1940–41, German bombers attacked one city after another. Though this represented the greatest suffering that the country was to experience during the war, it saved the RAF, which by September had been pounded to the verge of exhaustion and could not have held out for more than a few days. By switching its target to Britain's cities at this crucial moment, the Luftwaffe had allowed its opponent a vital breathing-space in which to rebuild, re-equip and retrain. Despite heavy damage and mounting losses, Britain's will to fight was not broken, the RAF was not eliminated and the necessary conditions for an invasion were therefore never achieved. With the arrival of autumn, the ferrying of armies across the Channel was no longer feasible. By the following year, Hitler was preoccupied with another invasion at the opposite end of Europe. He had decided that Britain was defeated and would pose no further threat. For him, it was to be the first of many disastrous mistakes.

For the defenders, the summer of 1940 was a desperate struggle to keep up with the Luftwaffe. In the Operations rooms of the RAF, the swarms of enemy aircraft were plotted as they crossed the Channel and the North Sea, and the dogfights were followed by operators listening to the R/T traffic between the pilots. Edith Kup, the young member of the WAAF who worked in this atmosphere of high tension, recalled her initiation into the work of monitoring the progress of the battle:

A biggish room, with a high balcony where the controller and his minions sat, a big board with a map of south-east England and telephone points all round. We sat down, anywhere, round it and put on our headphones, and were initiated into interpreting the plots and coloured pointers etc. Quite simple, but we needed practice and had lots of dummy runs from the various Observer Corps positions (and offers of dates!). We never used rods, we would reach by hand, four on the bottom and four at the top of the map. Then selection of position was made by the controllers. We could hear open R/T and so the battles were running commentaries to us (with language we had never heard before, and didn't mind, nor understand, for they were anxious occasions).

To us, there was no real start to the Battle. There were skirmishes and fights over the convoys in the Channel.

As she grew in experience, she developed an instinct with regard to the approach of enemy aircraft:

I was in direct touch with the Command teller, and so was the first to hear approaching raids. In fact, I used to say that I could 'hear' the Germans taking off in France, for as soon as they were airborne the radar stations picked them up. Consequently I had a constant amount of plots being told to me, and one kept an almost unconscious track of raids appearing and disappearing out of the sector. The controller would ask 'Anything coming up Edith?' I told him where it all was. He was responsible for sounding the air-raid siren. Sometimes a raid appeared out of the blue, not having been picked up before, especially when some of the radar stations on the coast were bombed out of action for days at a time.

Throughout Britain the sense of imminent danger increased. Beaches were defended with barbed wire and pillboxes. Road signs were removed throughout the country to confuse the invaders. Fields were littered with derelict vehicles and other obstacles to prevent aircraft from landing. Posters illustrated the different uniforms of the German army, and everywhere men and women looked out for the parachutists that were expected to descend from the skies as the harbingers of invasion. Civilian men were encouraged to train in shooting with a view to resisting this assault, and the name 'parashots' was coined for them. At Bletchley Park, Alan Turing and Peter Twinn were among those who took to this activity, though in their own eccentric fashion. As Ann Harding, one of their colleagues, remembered:

> Most of the men had become 'parashots', so called because we were expecting Germany to invade after Dunkirk and were told to watch out day and night for parachutists landing. The 'parashots' were meant to deal with them. One day Prof [Turing] had an awful thought. 'Peter, what do we do if they land in the maze? There would be an awful muddle, Peter, with us and them getting lost.' This was quite a thought as it was a large maze. The threat of invasion was very real. Many people had heavy sticks or, in the case of farms, pitchforks hidden behind their front doors, ready to attack.

Security measures at Bletchley Park were tightened considerably at this time, with precautions that made life in the huts even more uncomfortable, while the sizeable volume of traffic had necessitated the recruitment of more staff. Ann Harding recalled:

> Toward the end of May 1940 we had our first air-raid practice. Each hut had its own shelter and we spent the time writing home, leaning on a box of very precious documents for which we were responsible. The shelters had electric light and hurricane lamps as a backup.
>   Our number of six in the hut increased to 12. As we were now overcrowded in our small hut, a larger hut was being built for us, also at this time, a barbed-wire entanglement was being built all around the Park so that it was impossible to get in except at the entrance. There was no proper guarded gate then and we had no passes until later. They also started building brick walls all around the huts and sandbags between the walls and the huts. The walls were about eight feet high. This meant artificial lights all the time and the windows shut. At blackout time people came round and put up wooden shutters, so there was no air.

Despite the importance of Bletchley and of the work going on there, arrangements for its evacuation in the event of invasion seemed to be of a rather informal nature:

> By mid-June we were having to think of what we would do if the invasion took place. We expected to be sent further west. If Bletchley Park packed up Nancy and I planned to stay together and go west and then north. We all had bicycles and acquired saddlebags so we would go as far as possible that way. Also, we were trying to acquire rucksacks in case we had to walk. At this time, the family made lists of names and addresses of friends to whom we could go and keep in touch with each other by trying all the addresses. We were working overtime, back on the day shift 10–6 p.m., but with our lunch hour cut down and we were also given a war bonus. I was given 15 shillings [75p].
> The grounds were turning into a small fortress, with holes dug all over for men to shoot from and they all had sandbags in front. We were organised ready in case of having to move at very short notice. We had made lists of the essentials to pack quickly if we had to move. We were having a lull in the work, probably because we couldn't crack the codes.

In fact, the civilian male members of the staff had been inducted into the Home Guard, one of the local defence units that were called into being by the government for men aged between 17 and 65. Alan Turing saw the advantages of learning to shoot, and therefore volunteered. He deliberately avoided signing the enlistment document, however, so was able to walk out of the organization as soon as he had gained from it what he wanted.

He was not the only one perfecting his marksmanship. The king and queen both undertook pistol practice, and the prime minister boasted of having a revolver with which to 'take a few with me'. There were contingency plans to evacuate the royal family to Canada, though these were dismissed by the queen with the famous remark: 'The girls will not leave without me, I will not leave without the king and of course the king will never leave.' Churchill, too, refused to consider crossing the Atlantic. At Bletchley, there were similar plans for the evacuation of key personnel to Canada. One of those affected was Phoebe Senyard, who commented on the circumstances:

During the ghastly months of June, July and August when the fear of German invasion was greatest, arrangements were made to organise a mobile section of GC&CS [Government Code and Cipher School]. The air was electric with feeling. Those who had been chosen were photographed and supplied with special passports or identification cards and were in a sense excited by the project. I was surprised by the number of people whose feelings were hurt because they had not been included in the list.

In fact, in September the codebreakers were the first to know that Operation Sea Lion had been put off. A huge army, together with the naval and air force units necessary to transport and protect it, could not be kept in readiness on the coast – or dispersed – without a great deal of signals traffic, and the situation was duly noticed. Hitler had been half-hearted in his desire to invade Britain, and once the impetus had been lost the scheme was allowed to die.

For those with access to German signals, it was quite clear that the German preparations for invasion were not likely to be completed. Winterbotham recalled that:

It was evident from Ultra that the German Army had scant ideas of what was really involved in a large amphibious operation. The German Navy had settled for the great barges which ply the rivers of the Continent, from the big self-propelled ones on the Rhine, right down to the smaller ones usually towed in threes and fours by a powerful tug, mostly on French and Belgian rivers and canals. But they soon found that the barges available were not going to be enough, and Ultra signals revealed a frantic search for ships of all sorts in Germany, Holland, Belgium and France. As the barges began to assemble, it was found that not enough of these were self-propelled, so there was another panic instruction sent out on Ultra to find suitable engines, but these too were evidently scarce, and in some cases aeroplane engines were being fitted. Signals became acrimonious and the whole picture began to show how very hastily the invasion arrangements had been put together. One can imagine that the confusion, which was apparent even to us, must have raised a question in Hitler's mind as to whether his invasion would ever take place.

Hitler was a great deal more determined regarding the bombing of Britain's cities, which he considered a just punishment for the country's refusal to comply with his terms. Early in August, Goering arrived in France to whip up enthusiasm among his aircrews for an intensification of the air assault, which with characteristic bombast he dubbed 'Eagle Day'. Once again, Ultra was able to intercept the vital message and pass it on, as Winterbotham explained:

> On August the eighth Goering issued his order of the day, Operation Eagle. Within an hour it was in the hands of the chiefs of staff and the Prime Minister. Churchill wanted an extra copy and I believe took it over to the Palace. 'From Reich-Marshal Goering to all units of Luftflotte 2,3 and 5. Operation Adler (Eagle). Within a short period you will wipe the British Air Force from the sky. Heil Hitler.'

The decrypted messages that followed over the next few days made it clear that Luftwaffe attacks, which were aimed at targets the whole length of England's east coast, were designed to spread the defences as thin as possible, to keep the RAF's entire fighter strength at full stretch and to keep the defenders guessing as to where the next blow would fall. Unfortunately for Goering, the RAF knew exactly where the raiders would cross the coast and was able to make arrangements accordingly. Waves of German bombers from France and Scandinavia, intending to attack targets at one-hour intervals, were met by concentrations of fighters and suffered heavy losses. Winterbotham described, with a certain nonchalance, the results of this major encounter:

> The first raid by Luftflotte 5, which came from Norway was, thanks to Ultra's early warning and good long-distance radar fixes, intercepted by 13 (Fighter) Group while well out to sea. The formation lost fifteen of their hundred aircraft. The second raid by Luftflotte 5 from Denmark was met by 12 Group; their losses were eight aircraft out of the fifty which came over. After this, with no losses to the RAF, Luftflotte 5 did not try again. In the afternoon it was Luftflotte 2's turn again and two raids within an hour of each other duly came over Essex and Kent. Teatime saw Luftflotte 3 join in. There was a big raid of up to eighty bombers, fully escorted, attacking the south coast west

of Portsmouth, and then, lastly, Luftflotte 2 had another go at around 6.30 p.m, at the Kent airfields. It was a massive effort and quite obviously intended to get as many RAF fighters into the air as possible. Goering wanted a quick kill. If Dowding [C-in-C of Fighter Command] had fallen for the bait, losses on both sides would have been higher than the RAF could afford. Dowding, who was able to recognize Goering's strategy from his Ultra signals, continued to use the minimum of fighters to disrupt and confuse the bomber squadrons to make accurate bombing more difficult. At the same time, since the German fighter escorts dare not leave the massed bomber formations unprotected from above, it was much easier for our small units or even individual fighters to get amongst the bombers.

These tactics were to continue throughout the hectic weeks that followed, and to give the RAF what must have seemed an almost supernatural ability to appear at the precise time and place to meet their opponents. Bletchley staff had broken the 'red' cipher, which allowed them access to Luftwaffe communications, and were aware of potential bombing targets as the Blitz intensified. The Germans used a system of electronic beams to direct their aircraft to the targets, and this was intercepted. Coded signals also indicated the number of aircraft and the route that would be followed. Though this information could not prevent raids, it could naturally be of immense value to the defenders.

The Luftwaffe made use of a very basic code when targeting cities, in that the first letter of the code name and the city's name were the same (Birmingham, for instance, was 'Bild'). In November 1940, when there were indications that a major raid – code named 'Moonlight Sonata – was to take place, no obvious target could be discerned. The code-name for the city was 'Korn'. But the Air Ministry, which was free to interpret as it saw fit the information provided by Bletchley, decided that this was of no particular significance. It was similarly decided that the Luftwaffe's electronic beams, which indicated a concentration on the West Midlands, were simply a test of the system. By the time it was realized that, in German, Coventry is spelled with a K, it was too late. The city had been reduced to rubble in one of the war's severest raids. There was later to be considerable speculation that Churchill had known of the impending attack, but had allowed no warning to be given in case this showed the Germans that Enigma had

Bletchley Park had been the home of Sir Herbert and Lady Leon, who added a host of eclectic embellishments to it in 1882–3. By 1937 it was threatened with demolition and its grounds with redevelopment. Within a year, however, it had been quietly bought and occupied by the Government as its Code and Cipher School.

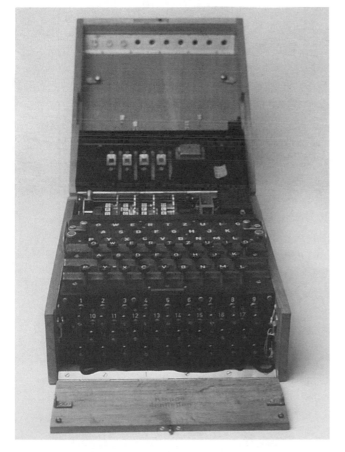

Looking like the ugly sister of a typewriter, the Enigma consisted of a keyboard and plugboard, enclosed in a squat wooden box. Poland's Intelligence Service acquired a German model during the 1930s, and was thus able to pass on its secrets to France and Britain before war broke out. This was perhaps the greatest Polish contribution to the struggle against Hitler.

Alan Turing (1912–54), a brilliantly eccentric mathematician who arrived at Bletchley via Cambridge and Princeton. The epitome of the absent-minded genius (he buried valuables when invasion was expected, but was never able to remember where) he not only helped win the war but arguably did more than any other scientist to develop the modern computer.

The back of a 'Bombe' was, remembered one operator, 'a mass of dangling plugs on rows of letters and numbers'. The machines, invented by Turing, used sets of whirling drums to read Enigma settings at high speed, eliminating billions of options in search of the correct letters. Bombes were so tall that the Wrens who worked on them had to be 5'8" (1.73m) or over.

Wrens operating a Colossus at Bletchley. This machine, the brainchild of telephone engineer T.H. (Tommy) Flowers, was the first ever digital, programmable computer. In place of a microchip it employed valves – 1,500 of them – and was used to decipher enemy teleprinter messages. The Colossus came into use at the beginning of 1944 and immediately improved the speed and accuracy of decoding.

Hut 6, photographed after years of postwar dilapidation. The grounds of Bletchley Park ultimately housed a workforce of 10,000, and the majority of them spent their working hours in buildings of this sort. Often stuffy or freezing, the huts were built and modified by on-site carpenters who were frequently called to erect or demolish partitions or knock doors through walls.

Hut 3 specialised in reading the messages of the German army and air force, but these came in a bewildering variety that included separate ciphers for North Africa, Russia, the Balkans, the Middle East, the railways and the rocket development project at Peenemunde. The resulting vast backlog of work made the lives of translators and analysts highly stressful.

Wrens in a rose garden. Despite wartime building, Bletchley Park retained some touches of its former elegance. Its lawns, ornamental lake and tennis courts could, in good weather, lift the spirits of men and women who had endured gruelling shifts indoors. The gardens were extensively used for games of rounders and for Scottish country dancing practise.

Military and civilian staff in the machine room (top), and the intercept control room (above), at Bletchley in 1943. These images give little indication of the frenetic pace of work as a constant flow of German messages was processed. Each had to be recorded, translated, pieced together (parts were usually sent separately), evaluated and – in urgent cases – dispatched immediately. A weekly summary of traffic also had to be prepared. Decrypters who spent months and even years reading the signals of individual Germans – be they great commanders or humble clerks – came to develop a sense of personal acquaintance.

The War Office Signal Office in Whitehall. Signs above the desks indicate the communications centre or theatre of operations with which the section was concerned. 'Station X' was Bletchley. Urgent material decrypted at 'BP' was sent at once to the War Office or Downing Street, while items of less importance were collected at the end of each day, and more routine material weekly.

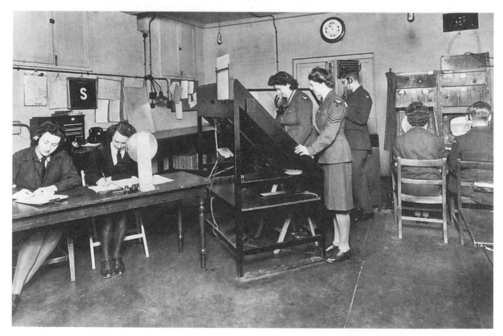

Members of the Women's Auxiliary Air Force at work in the Receiver Room of a radar station during the Battle of Britain. Indicating the strength and direction of attacking formations, radar enabled the RAF's limited resources to be used to greatest effect. Enigma revealed intended targets, but was not foolproof – as would be seen when the Luftwaffe destroyed Coventry.

Aboard a U-boat somewhere in the Atlantic, a coder sits by his Enigma machine. The Allies did not succeed in breaking all of Germany's naval codes, but the capture of codebooks and the interception and deciphering of signals enabled them to re-route many convoys away from U-boat packs, saving both lives and cargoes.

U-116 takes on fuel at sea, photographed from the deck of the supply-vessel U-406. These operations, usually carried out near the Azores (far out in the Atlantic and beyond the range of Allied aircraft) enabled submarines to extend their stay in the hunting-grounds. Enigma informed the Allies of the location of these rendezvous and made possible the sinking of the supply-ships.

An intriguing memento of the Battle of the Atlantic. This picture of members of U-110's crew scraping ice from the deck was found on board at the time of the U-boat's capture (by H. M. Destroyer Bulldog) and the seizure of the first German Naval Enigma Machine and its codebooks.

been broken. The truth was simpler: the bombers' destination had not been worked out in time.

Station X itself did not escape the bombing, though not because the enemy had discovered its secret. An aircraft returning from a raid jettisoned several bombs near the railway junction and five of them landed in and around the Park. There were no casualties, though there was some damage to several buildings – notably the school that housed the Japanese diplomatic section, which was destroyed. Despite the security with which it was surrounded and the unique level of foreknowledge that its inhabitants had of the enemy's operations, Bletchley Park was to share with the rest of the country the rigours of the Blitz.

***

While the air war raged in the skies over southern England and the Home Guard waited behind barbed-wire coastal defences for the expected invasion, there was considerable speculation about the activities of German spies in Britain. A number of them were certainly infiltrated, but it is a matter of record that they failed to accomplish a single act of sabotage or to relay any information of even modest importance. It is believed that, with one possible exception, every spy sent by Germany to the British mainland was caught. The majority were 'turned' by the British authorities and put to work against their former comrades; those who refused were hanged. The level of competence – even the agents' basic knowledge of British geography, language, customs and currency – was ludicrously inadequate. Many of them were put ashore, with radio equipment or other conspicuous accoutrements, on beaches where the presence of any civilian would have raised the alarm. In his book about this period, *Invasion 1940*, Peter Fleming described the combination of rudimentary training and ignorance that caused German espionage in Britain to become a dead letter:

> The spies were to hunt in couples. One pair, after transhipping to
> a dinghy, landed near Hythe in the early hours of 3 September.
> They had a wireless set and an elementary form of cipher, and their
> orders were to send back information of military importance; they
> had been given to understand that an invasion of the Kentish coast
> was imminent. By 5.30 on the same morning both men, although

they separated on landing, had been challenged and made prisoner by sentries of a battalion of the Somerset Light Infantry.

This was hardly surprising. The two men were of Dutch nationality. They were completely untrained for their difficult task; their sole qualification for it seems to have lain in the fact that each, having committed some misdemeanour which was known to the Germans, could be blackmailed into undertaking the enterprise. Neither had more than a smattering of English and one suffered, by virtue of having had a Japanese mother, from the additional hazard of a markedly Oriental appearance; he it was who, when first sighted by an incredulous private of the Somersets in the early dawn, had binoculars and a spare pair of shoes slung around his neck.

Even greater depths of absurdity were plumbed by their colleagues:

The other pair of spies consisted of a German, who spoke excellent French but no English at all, and a man of abstruse origins who claimed to be a Dutchman and who, alone of the four, had a fluent command of English. They landed at Dungeness under cover of darkness on 3 September, and soon after daybreak were suffering acutely from thirst, a fact which lends colour to the theory that on the previous night the whole party had relied on Dutch courage to an unwise extent. The English speaker, pardonably ignorant of British licensing laws, tried to buy cider at breakfast-time in a public house at Lydd. The landlady pointed out that this transaction could not legally take place until ten o'clock and suggested that meanwhile he should go and look at the church. When he returned (for she was a sensible woman) he was arrested.

His companion, the only German in the party, was not caught until the following day. He had rigged up an aerial in a tree and had begun to send messages (in French) to his controllers. Copies of three of these messages survived and were used in evidence against him at his trial. They were short and from an operational point of view worthless; the news (for instance) that 'this is exact position yesterday evening six o'clock three Messerschmitt [*sic*] fired machine guns in my direction three hundred metres south of reservoir painted red' was in no way calculated to facilitate the establishment of a German bridgehead in Kent.

Two men and a woman, who on the night of September 30 were landed from a dinghy on the coast of Banffshire after being flown thither from Norway in a seaplane, had no more luck. They were arrested within a few hours of their arrival. During those hours their conduct had been such as to attract the maximum of suspicion. This – since both men spoke English with a strong foreign accent and the documents of all three were clumsily forged – they were in no position to dispel; and the first of them to be searched by the police was found to have in his possession a wireless set; a loaded Mauser automatic; an electric torch marked 'made in Bohemia'; a list of bomber and fighter stations in East Anglia; £327 in English notes, and a segment of German sausage.

Fleming concluded, 'The receipt, by the *Abwehr*, of any report from an agent in England was a rare and notable event,' and it is obvious that spies, and the signals they might have sent back to occupied Europe, were no significant threat to Britain's security. What knowledge the Germans *did* possess of their enemy's country came from two more formidable sources, as described by Royal Navy historian Captain W Roskill:

> It must be admitted that, during the early months of the war, the procurement by the enemy of intelligence regarding our warship dispositions and movements was superior to our own. It is now plain that the enemy's advantage in this respect was achieved, firstly, through regular air reconnaissance of our bases and, secondly, through the study he had made of our wireless traffic, which could and did reveal to him a great deal.

The Germans' ability to read naval codes more than compensated for the amateurishness of their spies, but this immense advantage came to a sudden end, in August 1940, with the changing of ciphers by the Admiralty. In the war of the codebreakers this occasional action, carried out suddenly as a matter of urgency or periodically as a matter of routine, would often eliminate at a stroke the advantages enjoyed by one side or the other, and start the search for answers all over again.

4

BATTLE OF THE ATLANTIC

The moment England's supply routes are severed, she will be forced to capitulate.[i]

I don't remember ever having decoded a message from start to finish to see what it said. I was much more interested in the methodology for getting German out of a coded message.[ii]

In World War II there was no more vital theatre of conflict than the waters of the Atlantic Ocean, and here, as in every place where the opposing sides sought to outwit each other, the use of codes (and the breaking of enemy codes) was of huge importance to the outcome of the contest. Knowledge of British Admiralty codes initially gave the German U-boats such opportunities for sinking Allied shipping that their crews referred to this period of pre-eminence as 'the happy time'. Subsequent Allied use of signals decrypted from the German naval Enigma turned the tables completely, making the mid-Atlantic a killing ground for submarines. On this vast ocean, so different from other arenas in which the Allies and the Germans fought, Ultra was as vital as ever. Through their incomplete but decisive mastery of German naval signals traffic, the Bletchley staff enabled Allied armies to cross the Atlantic and the English Channel without hindrance and to take the war on to the European mainland.

By the summer of 1940, German armies had overrun northern and western Europe. The only remaining belligerent, Great Britain, was an island that did not have sufficient food or raw materials to sustain an all-out war effort. Its only recourse was to depend on imports, and the majority of these came east across the Atlantic from Canada and the United States or, in the case of oil, from the Caribbean and the Gulf of Mexico. If the transatlantic lifeline could be severed, even temporarily, by sinking enough

[i] Adolf Hitler
[ii] Peter Twinn, Bletchley Park

of the merchant ships that carried these cargoes, Britain would be unable to carry on fighting. The Germans thus possessed, in their submarine fleet, a highly effective means of defeating Britain quickly and without heavy casualties. Lieutenant Commander DE Balme of the Royal Navy, who was to play a heroic part in the battle, recalled that:

> The Germans recognised that the Atlantic was the vital artery for Britain to obtain supplies of food (we had let our agriculture decline between the wars, so that we could only grow about one-third of our food), fuel (we had coal but no oil) and raw materials for our factories. If they could cut that line, they could win the war.

The importance of this supply route remained paramount until the end of the European war. It did not matter that America and Russia had now joined Britain in the fight, or that Allied armies were accumulating victories in North Africa, Italy, Eastern Europe or France. Unless the Atlantic shipping routes were secure, Britain would starve and the men and materiel needed to defeat Hitler would not reach the battlefields. It is small wonder that Churchill was to comment:

> The Battle of the Atlantic was the dominating factor all through the war. Never for one moment could we forget that everything happening elsewhere, on land, at sea or in the air, depended ultimately on its outcome, and amid all other cares we viewed its changing fortunes day by day with hope or apprehension.

He was later to admit:

> The only thing that really frightened me during the war was the U-boat peril.

In this, history was repeating itself. In World War I the enemy's surface fleet had made no lasting contribution, but its submarines had proved a considerable menace. Germany itself had been blockaded by the Royal Navy and its warships had largely been unable to leave the Baltic, but U-boats had had the freedom of the North Sea and the Atlantic. They had set out to strangle Britain by attacking the ships that fed and supplied it. The Allies had responded by introducing the convoy system, in which merchant vessels sailed in batches, guarded by warships. While this undoubtedly saved many lives and cargoes, the German submarines had nevertheless proved effective, for in the course of the war they had sent to the bottom a total of 7,500 vessels, representing 11 million tons of shipping. The price of this success, however, had proved too high. With the approval of the country's parliament, the German High Command had adopted a policy of 'unrestricted submarine warfare', which meant that not only the vessels of belligerent countries but also those of any nation deemed likely to be assisting the enemy could be attacked and sunk without warning or explanation. This tactic had brought Germany immense international odium. It had also brought the United States into the war in 1917, and thus ensured Allied victory.

Following its defeat in World War I Germany had been forbidden, under the terms of the peace treaty, to retain a submarine fleet. Its navy, however, had continued to build and to train in secret. The expertise of German engineers and submariners had been in demand among nations that were developing fleets of their own and so, while fulfilling this consultancy role in Spain, Turkey or Finland, Germany's officers and crews had been able to keep their own skills up to the mark. Meanwhile its U-boats had been built in the yards of these countries. In 1935, with Germany well on the way to resuming Great Power status and with the United Kingdom anxious to appease Hitler, a naval agreement had been signed between the two nations that allowed Germany a submarine fleet 35 per cent the size of Britain's. From that moment, German submariners had begun to train in earnest for the coming war. Like other branches of Hitler's armed forces, they had also acquired useful experience through supporting Franco's cause in the conflict in Spain.

***

The Type VIIC U-boat, developed in 1938, was the world's most advanced submarine. With continuous modification, it was to be the basis of Germany's fleet for most of the war. It displaced 871 tons underwater, carried a crew of 44 and had a top speed when submerged of 7.5 knots, with an operational range of 8,500 miles. It was armed with an 88mm deck gun but its 'teeth' were its 14 torpedoes, fired from four tubes in the bow and one in the stern. Germany had 56 U-boats of this type in service at the start of World War II.

They made an impact at once, for the 'Battle of the Atlantic' began on the day that Britain entered the war. On 3 September 1939, a U-boat sank the liner *Athena*, which was on its way from Canada to England, having mistaken it for a troopship. (The 118 passengers who died included 22 Americans; Hitler, who feared offending the neutral United States, was furious.) A month later *U-47*, commanded by the legendary Günther Prien, torpedoed the battleship HMS *Royal Oak* at its anchorage inside Scapa Flow with a loss of over 800 crew. In the first three months of conflict, despite the introduction of convoys, U-boats accounted for 114 merchant ships. Hitler was convinced by the spectacular success of his submarine fleet that they represented the best means of putting Britain out of the war, though he remained somewhat indecisive about inflicting a crushing defeat on a country that he still hoped would become an ally.

***

The following year brought fresh disaster for the Royal Navy, when the aircraft carrier HMS *Glorious* and two escorting destroyers were sunk in the North Sea by the battleship *Scharnhorst*. What made this event worse was the fact that it could have been avoided. Harry Hinsley, one of the young men working at Bletchley, specialized in naval codes. Though he had no access to naval Enigma messages (that version had not yet been broken), he had studied the volume of signals traffic, and in June 1940 he concluded that German ships were about to leave the Baltic. He warned the Admiralty, in the shape of its OIC (Operational Intelligence Centre), but it took no action. The OIC regarded Bletchley as untested and Hinsley as an amateur, a civilian, and too young to be taken seriously – he still looked every inch the undergraduate that he had recently been. It was only after this sinking, and even then only gradually, that the Admiralty began to accept that the academics at 'BP' might after all have something to offer.

In this first phase of the war, the German navy was the most formidable enemy faced by Britain. The B-Dienst, its intelligence service, had broken the Royal Navy's Number 3 cipher, which was used to organize convoys, and the detailed knowledge of routes, gathering places and sailing times that this offered gave the U-boats a huge advantage in the Atlantic. For long months there was no corresponding British access to German naval codes, which were more complex than those of the other services. At the start of the war there were 13 separate codes and there would ultimately be 40, some of which Bletchley would never succeed in breaking. AEGIR was the code for ships of the surface fleet, HYDRA was for operational U-boats and TETIS for those that were undergoing training in the Baltic. The staff at Bletchley also came up with their own nicknames: 'Dolphin', for instance, was the term for the U-boats' 'home waters' code.

The Enigma machines used by the German navy were more complex than those of the other services. They had up to eight wheels and thus the number of possible wheel-orders was 336. Alan Turing, with the help of Peter Twinn and a staff of Wrens, set up a specialist cryptographic section ('Hut 8') to concentrate energies on this vital area, and Turing managed to break into the cipher, though only for a short time, in April 1940.

IJ Good described the purpose of Hut 8 and the head-spinning complexity of the work they were trying to do:

> Our job was to carry out certain cryptanalytic work and thus to prepare jobs for the machine known as the Bombe, which was housed in another building. The Enigma was used both by the German Navy and the German Army. In Hut 8 we were only concerned with the Naval Enigma. The U-boat version had four rotors after a time instead of only three so it was more difficult to break.
>
> The particular set of rotors in a machine was determined by daily keys. For example, the three rotors for the Mediterranean Enigma were selected from a set of eight, of permanently fixed wiring. Since the order in which they are put in the machine is relevant, the number of possible wheel orders was $8 \times 7 \times 6$. The wheel order was fixed for two days at a time. The number of initial settings was about 26 = 17,576 and moreover there was the additional plugboard which had 26 possible initial states, changed daily. Thus, the number of possible initial states of the machine at the beginning of the message was about 9×10. For the U-boats it was 10.

One means by which the codebreakers tried to crack the naval settings was through the use of what came to be known as 'Banburismus'. This process, invented by Turing, took its name from the long printed sheets – delivered from a printer in Banbury, Oxfordshire – on which the calculations were made. The sheets were almost a foot wide and several feet long. On each one was a series of vertically printed alphabets, with the letters divided by horizontal lines.

Clerks punched holes in these sheets that corresponded with enciphered messages; the first enciphered letter would be punched in the first alphabet column, the second in the second, and so forth. Once a large number of sheets had been prepared in this way, they would be stacked in a pile and examined against a dark background to determine where holes, and therefore letters, were repeated. This enabled the sequences used in signalling to be studied, and similarities to be found in the encoding. Turing's colleague Peter Twinn explained the two alternatives that could be attempted by those working on the complexities of the code:

> **You can either find out the wiring of a brand new wheel or you can work out with a reasonable degree of accuracy what the messages might be saying.**

Though apparently crude and time-consuming, Banburismus enjoyed a degree of success – at any rate until the beginning of February 1941, when the introduction of a fourth wheel to the naval Enigma made the process suddenly redundant.

For all the brilliance of their hunches and deductions, there was no substitute for solid evidence of German encoding practices, and Hut 8 had been able to begin work in earnest because in the same month that Turing first read the cipher (April 1940), there had occurred the first of a series of captures – 'pinches', as they came to be known – that arguably were to make a greater contribution to winning the Battle of the Atlantic than the painstaking work of the mathematicians. Like Admiral Hall in the previous war, the codebreakers knew how much time and trouble could be saved by seizing enemy code books. The importance of these pinches was therefore impressed on the commanders and crews of British vessels. Wherever opportunity offered, boarding parties needed to be ready to clamber on to captured or sinking enemy craft and make straight for the communications equipment. Enigma machines were screwed to tables and so time might not allow them to be dismantled and removed, but failing this any loose parts, together with all possible paperwork, must be gathered up and passed (probably by human chain) to the boat. In these circumstances papers frequently became wet through and largely illegible. Fortunately, one of the Bletchley boffins had previously been on the staff of the Natural History Museum in London, and had considerable expertise in paper restoration. In the first pinch in April 1940, cipher forms picked up aboard a German patrol boat provided the enciphered version of plain text messages. Further pinches, this time from U-boats, produced two of the wheels for the naval Enigma.

Organizing pinches became a preoccupation for one man. Ian Fleming, later to win fame as the author of the James Bond novels, spent the war years working at the Admiralty as an officer in Naval Intelligence. He conceived the notion of 'Operation Ruthless', a highly colourful attempt to steal a code book. Andrew Lycett, a biographer of Fleming, described the plan:

> The Germans had begun operating a new air-sea rescue boat out of Denmark. Ian was convinced this would carry the latest German code books. If he and a few others could don some German uniforms and wait in a boat in the Channel, pretending to have ditched, the rescue boat would come to pick them up. The British could then overpower the Germans and capture the boat and its valuable contents.
>
> Ian suggested the following strategy to secure 'the loot':
> 1. Obtain from the Air Ministry an air-worthy German bomber.
> 2. Pick a tough crew of five, including a pilot, W/T (wireless/ telegraph) operator and word-perfect German speaker. Dress them in German Air Force uniform, add blood and bandages to suit.
> 3. Crash plane in the Channel after making SOS to rescue service in P/L (plain language).
> 4. Once aboard rescue boat, shoot German crew, dump overboard, bring rescue boat back to English port.

The scheme was taken seriously by the OIC and by Turing, who looked forward to the result. A crashed Heinkel bomber was reconditioned and captured Luftwaffe uniforms were provided. Fleming became more ambitious, deciding that the hoax should be played on a Channel minesweeper, since that would offer richer pickings. Having stipulated that the group should be led by a 'tough bachelor, able to swim', he was very keen to go but was forbidden to have any active part in the mission, because his knowledge of secrets made his capture too risky. He therefore became the operation's director rather than its hero – M rather than Bond. It came to nothing, however, because weeks went by and no suitable German vessel appeared; postponement therefore turned to cancellation.

THE U-BOAT ENEMY

After the fall of France in the summer of 1940, the U-boats had access to French ports, such as Lorient and St Nazaire, on the Atlantic coast. This meant they no longer had to make lengthy voyages from the Baltic and could extend their operational range as far as Newfoundland and America's eastern seaboard. With much of Britain's navy and air force kept at home in anticipation of a German invasion, Atlantic shipping became more vulnerable, and that year losses amounted to a massive 3,991,641 tons.

In 1941 the statistics worsened: the year's total would be 4,228,558 tons. Winston Churchill demanded that the Atlantic become an absolute priority in the planning and waging of the war, with top-level conferences held at the Admiralty every week. In some respects, the situation was already improving. Neutral America offered Britain 50 destroyers (a foretaste of the later Lend-Lease agreement) and agreed to provide escorts for convoys as far as Iceland. Britain's own resources once again became available when it was clear that Hitler's invasion plan would not be carried out. Nevertheless, as noted by Commander Balme, the difficulty was in replacing the continuing losses of shipping:

> The Battle of the Atlantic was a 'tonnage war'. Could the U-boats sink ships faster than we could replace them? Happily, a high proportion of our ships' crews were rescued after sinking, but in 1941 we just could not replace them fast enough.

In the event, losses were less crippling than had been predicted. Although U-boats took a heavy toll, large percentages of the merchant fleets of occupied countries remained at large and joined the Allies. This was especially true of Greece, whose sizeable merchant marine became available when that country was overrun in 1941.

The U-boats' method of operation was to sail for a designated area – usually a set of map coordinates in mid-ocean – and to patrol this for a period of weeks, awaiting any shipping that passed through it, while also awaiting orders to assemble en masse or to attack. They would return to port only when their fuel or ammunition ran out. By 1941, their missions could be extended through the presence of fuel tankers nicknamed 'milk cows', which loitered around the Azores (an area too far south to be within range of Allied aircraft). Though they began the war patrolling as single vessels, they developed a trademark tactic that was known as: the 'wolf pack': they would gather in groups of between 10 and 20 in the path of a convoy and then attack it under cover of darkness, with each boat choosing its own target.

On occasions in the 1914–18 war, U-boat commanders had behaved chivalrously. They would attack by surfacing and ordering the crew of the target into the lifeboats, giving them time to get clear before their torpedoes were fired. In the new conflict this practice was seen as sentimental and counter-productive. Hitler and Admiral Karl Dönitz, the commander of the German navy's submarine arm, knew that trained crews were even less easy to replace than ships, and demanded that they share the fate of their vessel. A month after the U-boat campaign began, Dönitz issued this order:

> Rescue no one and take no one with you. Have no care for the ship's boats. Weather conditions or the proximity of land are of no account. Care only for your own boat. We must be hard in this war.

Despite the risks run by ships on the Atlantic routes, life on board was monotonous, and the notoriously rough North Atlantic could be challenging, to say the least. Eric Marshall, who served aboard a naval vessel in these waters, described conditions that would have been extremely common for much of the year:

> We were battered by the seas, many waves sweeping right across us, damaging and carrying away quite heavy gear. Travelling anywhere on deck was hazardous and choosing the right moment to move was not easy, particularly at night. Lifelines were always rigged in these circumstances but I could never make up my mind whether it was better to make a slow crawl using them or a quick dash and get it over as quickly as possible.

Marshall was a Coder and he and his colleagues worked in both Morse and radio. Their equipment included sets of code books, to which they were constantly referring and which they were trained to throw over the side if there were any danger of their vessel being captured. The books were deliberately weighted with lead for this purpose:

> Work in the sea-cabin with heavily weighted code books crashing about was frustrating, and even sitting at the desk having to brace oneself against violent movement was exhausting.

When not engaged in his specialist work Marshall was an ordinary member of the ship's company, taking his turn at other tasks, and was expected to help on the bridge (because it was next to his office) in stressful moments. Recalling the type of quiet interlude that could sometimes be snatched away from his desk, he provided a glimpse of a Coder's life at sea:

> While still dark during either the middle watch (midnight to 4 a.m.) or morning watch (4 a.m. to 8 a.m.) and if W/T traffic allowed, I would go into the wheel-house and have a chat with the helmsman and perhaps have a spell at the wheel, which in our case was not discouraged bearing in mind the duties that a Coder on watch might be required to undertake in an emergency. With one leg drooped over a spoke of the large, fixed wheel, an eye on the compass ahead fastened from the deckhead, one ear for any orders which may come down via the voice pipe from the Bridge and the other for any call from Mac through the door behind me busy with the continuously chattering Morse from his W/T sets, I was able to experience an unusual sense of calm.

His links with the world beyond the ship's bulkheads made him popular with the rest of the crew, for he could provide gossip and diversion:

> As Coders we were generally welcome wherever we went, for we were a useful source of information, not only from the routine less confidential messages we received, but also from the BBC news, which at sea could only be received through the sets in the wireless cabin. One of our official jobs was to prepare a daily news sheet for pinning up in the wheel-house.

Occasional relaxation notwithstanding, the atmosphere aboard an escort vessel was more usually characterized by taut nerves. The ships had to travel at the slow speed of the lumbering freighters. They had to steer an evasive course to present a more difficult target for pursuing submarines. Their crews had to scan the sea day and night for the telltale white wake of a periscope. Commander Balme remembered one such convoy:

> The most tiring time of all was at night (for in the winter months night was 16 hours out of 24). We had 40 to 50 merchant ships and 8 to 10 escort vessels and we would zig-zag night and day at a speed of only 8 knots. On the bridge was an officer of the watch, a signalman and two lookouts.

The enemy was often not far away. Single U-boats might be following a ship or a convoy, but it was also likely that a group of them was gathering.

WORKING IN CONVOY

With its access to British naval code, the B-Dienst was listening to as many as 2,000 Admiralty signals a month during the first half of 1940, and could thus build up a detailed picture of shipping movements in the Atlantic (until the Admiralty changed its code, ending this intensive eavesdropping at a stroke). It would pass on to U-boat commanders by coded Morse radio signals the map references for the route being followed by a convoy. The predators could then decide where to rendezvous and set up an ambush, opting for mid-ocean so that they would be within the 'air gap' beyond the range of either British or Canadian escort aircraft. The horizon would then be searched by the submarine's crew – either with binoculars from its conning tower or through the periscope – for the far-off wisps of smoke that heralded the arrival of its quarry in the hunting ground.

Commonly, a single vessel or a pack of submarines might follow the ships for days, waiting until enough of them had assembled before attacking. In turn the convoy and its escorts would naturally be searching the seas for any sign of the U-boats' presence and so the wolf packs would keep both depth and distance between themselves and their prey, usually waiting until dark before moving in for the kill.

Aboard the convoys, the tension mounted palpably each evening. At dusk the crews of freighters would go to action stations, remaining at their posts until dawn. On a voyage lasting a week or more, they could expect to be attacked on consecutive nights by the same enemy submarines, and though the timing of these incidents might be predictable, nothing could be done except to remain alert and hope that the accompanying naval vessels, with their detection devices and depth charges, would spot them. Danger increased once they reached the air gap. S France remembered the anxiety, and the horror, of those long nights:

> After two days and nights, the aeroplanes and corvettes [reached the limits of their range]. They could go no further so the convoy was left with nothing but the clear blue skies and the rolling waves of the Atlantic.
>
> On the third night at 10.00 p.m. exactly, the U-boats struck among the ships of the convoy. There were loud explosions and the ships were lit up like an inferno. By daybreak there was silence and the damage done was quite visible. There were broken and battered ships scattered about. The ships that were intact kept moving steadily ahead throughout the daytime. They just sailed ahead and, as before, 10.00 p.m., the U-boats struck and again there were explosions.
>
> On the third night at 10.00 p.m. the same destructive chorus opened up with the usual sounds and the heavens blazing red from the fires on the sea. As the stricken ships exploded one ship spilled out liquid all over [the water] and as it became alight the ships were all travelling through waves of flaming fire. The sea was so brilliantly lit that the whole scene was like a well-lit stage. The crew on board a burning ship formed a queue and a priest placed the Holy Sacrament into each man's mouth, made the sign of the cross, then each man, after he had taken the Sacrament, jumped overboard right into the flames. The priest was the last man; he also swallowed the Sacrament, then, clasping his hands together, he too dived into the flames ...

The wolf packs did not have things all their own way, however. Sailing with another North Atlantic convoy, Ordinary Seaman CJ Fairrie, a Bridge lookout aboard the destroyer escort vessel *Bulldog*, witnessed U-boat attacks over a period of three days. He described the ensuing action:

> In the evening about 2100 we received a contact on our ASDIC submarine detecting outfit [an electronic probing device, formulated

by the Anti Submarine Detection Investigation Committee, hence its name], however it was ignored – whales had been in the vicinity all day. At 2115 explosions were heard and two merchant ships in the rear of the convoy were seen to be sinking. The larger of the two, believed to be carrying whisky, was on fire. Small boats and rafts put off from both vessels, and it was later confirmed that no lives were lost.

Meanwhile 'Action Stations' had been sounded (I was Port Action Lookout on the bridge). The *Amazon* and escort vessel *Rochester*, together with *Bulldog*, dropped patterns of depth charges while the other escort vessels proceeded with the convoy. The U-boat encounter was eventually abandoned and the prey believed to be sunk owing to the severity of the attack. However the search went on throughout the night. Praise must be given to the U-boat commander for his daring attack, which was carried out at short range – he had contrived to pierce the defences of the escort vessels and had got among the convoy itself. After the U-boat attack, several contacts were registered – these stopped at 2325. It is said that 130 depth charges were dropped – what underwater craft could survive such a bombardment?!

The following day 1201. Ship noticed to be giving off white clouds of steam. Convoy moves off to port – some ships go to starboard. Smoking vessel settles low in the water – bows and stern seem to be coming up to meet. Another ship – larger than the other (in fact the largest in the convoy) is seen to be dipping her bows among the waves. The silence of the attack is eerie. *Broadway* (destroyer) and *Aubretia* (corvette) counter-attack. Three more ships in the meantime are torpedoed! The *Esmond* (the large merchant packet) is seen to have received a hit beneath the bridge.

The sea is rougher today and soon bobbing black objects are seen among the waves as boats and rafts lay off. One ship blows up amid a huge mass of flame and smoke. It appears that we have run into a nest of U-boats and the convoy is broken up. Armed trawlers stand by to pick up survivors.

Once a vessel had been hit, there was a set of procedures for evacuating those aboard and for destroying any materials that could be of value to the enemy. Captain Eric Monckton of the freighter *Empire Starling*, carrying beef from South America to Britain, remembered vividly his actions after his ship was torpedoed near the 'Serpent's Mouth' off Trinidad:

> After throwing the weighted bag over the side and getting rid of all secret papers, I made for the boat deck and gave orders for the crew to take to the boats and stand by one ship's length astern. On going to the radio room, the Operator informed me that he had got away the SOS twice on the emergency set.
>
> The Chief Officer and Chief Steward informed me that all their staffs were mustered and getting away in the boats. The Radio Operator had thrown the radio codes and secret orders over the side and came to inform me of it.
>
> Before leaving, I went to the crews' quarters and shouted for anyone who might have gone unnoticed in the muster for the lifeboat. There was no response and, all secrets and codes being disposed of, I made my way to the lifeboat.

The attackers too experienced apprehension as they stalked their prey, aimed at the target and then waited for retribution (in the form of depth charges) to descend on them from above, for a horrific fate might await them amid acrid fumes and claustrophobic darkness if their craft went to the bottom. Ironically, and in spite of Dönitz's orders, Captain Monckton was captured by the U-boat that sank his ship and spent weeks aboard the *U163*. He witnessed the moment that this vessel discovered another potential target:

> An American cruiser and an accompanying destroyer were sighted on the bow. The U163 dived hurriedly to periscope depth and closed for action, everyone on board being chased to their attack stations. All electric fans were turned off and amongst the crew there was great tension and excitement. The heat inside the submarine was unbearable and the perspiration just poured off me in streams. All was deathly quiet, except for the occasional sharp orders through the repeaters which were placed in each compartment of the hull.
>
> I heard the torpedo being fired, the hiss caused by the compressed air used to initially send out the torpedo causing a definite pressure on the eardrums. Less than a minute after the

torpedo had been fired, I heard a slight 'ping' as it struck the ship. Later, I learned that two torpedoes had been fired simultaneously.

Later the U163 took on a 'down by the head' position (e.g. with the bow pointing downward) and it was evident that we were going deeper. Some ten minutes after this, I could hear a noise like the rush of an express train and then the explosion of the 'ashcans' raining down and severe shakings of U163. We remained very still for about an hour. After remaining still and quiet for several hours and the hot atmosphere inside the submarine being just unbearable, we rose to periscope depth and after a careful look round through the two periscopes and seeing nothing, we broke surface.

The sending of reports and receiving of orders was, of course, carried out by radio, using the naval settings of the Enigma code. Captain Monckton noticed the regularity with which this was done:

Every night at a certain time, the U163 was in touch with Berlin and other German Base Stations, and if not on the surface could pick up [signals] from periscope depth via the 36-foot retractable tapered receiving mast which was mounted on the deck of the conning tower, and so received orders for her next day's operating area. The charts used on the U163 were all marked out in numbered squares for easy reference purposes.

A GREAT COUP

If Allied Intelligence could break the naval Enigma code and decipher U-boat radio traffic, the onslaught on the Atlantic convoys could be significantly hampered. In the early summer of 1941, Harry Hinsley of the Bletchley staff conceived of a possibility. The enemy was monitoring the weather in the North Atlantic from trawlers that sailed the waters around Iceland. These did not report their findings through Enigma, but they did use it to receive messages from Germany and must therefore have code books aboard. If one of these unprotected vessels could be boarded, the result might be a vital intelligence breakthrough.

The chosen target was the *München*, a trawler that would be at sea during May and June. An armed naval party would board the vessel, but it was highly likely that the crew would dump overboard any materials regarded as secret or sensitive. The Enigma settings were changed every month and the May ones were expected to go over the side. The June settings, however, would be kept somewhere secure and the boarding party would gamble on capturing the boat before the captain could reach them.

The Admiralty approved the plan, and a sizeable force was sent in search of the trawler. Aboard the flagship HMS *Edinburgh* was Colin Kitching, then an Ordinary Seaman. He remembered that:

On May 5th the 18th Cruiser Squadron (HMS *Edinburgh, Manchester* and *Birmingham,* with five destroyers) sailed from Scapa Flow and headed north.

The operation (codenamed EB) had been mounted with the specific aim of intercepting and capturing the *München.* Using surprise and speed, Admiral Holland intended to capture and board the vessel; all being well, an immense prize might be secured – a set of coding tables enabling the enemy's naval cipher system, Enigma, to be read immediately for the first time.

At 1707 on May 7th the *München* was sighted between *Edinburgh* and [the destroyer HMS] *Somali.* The latter fired warning shots which caused most of the *München's* crew to take to the boats. *Somali* closed at speed and boarded the ship. A prize crew and boarding party from HMS *Edinburgh* then went over in a cutter, which also carried a man in civilian clothes.

I made an inconspicuous contribution to the capture of the *München.* I was a member of the *Edinburgh*'s boarding party and escorted the mysterious 'civilian' to the vessel and back again. (Many years later, when this most hush-hush mission was at last declassified, it was revealed that he was Captain J.R.S. Haines, RN, of Naval intelligence.)

For the first time in my life I was equipped with a revolver and we – the boarding party – were under orders to fight our way on board the *München* if necessary. But the *Somali* was alongside and most of the *München*'s crew had quickly abandoned ship, leaving – as I remember – only the captain, another officer and a couple of ratings to receive us, which they did with great courtesy. Indeed one of them kindly helped me over the guardrail. The boarding party had to search the *München* in case the Germans had laid scuttling charges in the bowels of the vessel. I was somewhat handicapped by the fact that I didn't know what a scuttling charge looked like. As it happened, there were none.

The *München's* captain had thrown the Enigma machine and the May coding tables over the side as *Somali* approached, but the settings for June were in his desk; these were duly collected by Captain Haines, who knew exactly what he was looking for. Some of *München*'s crew were taken on board *Edinburgh*. *Somali* escorted the captured vessel to Scapa. HMS *Nestor* took Captain Haines to Scapa at speed; he was flown to London and reached Bletchley Park on May 10th.

At almost exactly the same time another prize was seized by the Royal Navy when a German submarine, *U110*, was boarded in the Atlantic after its crew surrendered. Though the vessel itself was later lost while being towed in rough seas, the finds made on board proved a priceless treasure for the Admiralty and for Naval Intelligence. This was a tremendous coup. The settings were precisely what the Bletchley codebreakers needed, for from the beginning of June they made it possible for the first time to read current U-boat messages within about six hours of receiving them. It had previously taken an average of ten days. As with the *München,* the German authorities had no idea that the Enigma machine with its coding materials had been captured.

The boarding of *U110* became one of the most celebrated events in the intelligence war, for the combination of circumstance and courage made it an exciting story as well as a highly significant achievement. It was seen from the Bridge by Ordinary Seaman CJ Fairrie aboard the destroyer HMS *Bulldog,* which was escorting a convoy. Parts of his account were clearly written with hindsight: few of those who waited aboard, or manoeuvred the ship's whaler through pitching seas toward the U-boat, would have known anything about German code books or realized at the time the importance of the finds. Nevertheless, there is about his memories a breathless immediacy that conveys the excitement of capturing one of these elusive enemy vessels:

About 1230, my opposite number lookout suddenly sights what appears to be a conning tower rising up out of the waves. It is! A surrendering U-boat brought up owing to damage received from *Aubretia*'s depth charges. At first sight I was astonished at what appeared to be a gasometer surfacing, and then the whole structure came into view. The starboard lookout yelled 'U-boat surfacing!' before I could open my mouth!

[The destroyer] *Broadway* swings round and bears down on the U-boat. The latter's crew are pouring out of the conning tower. *Broadway* prepares to ram but at the last minute turns away – but not without damage to herself – a glancing blow on her stern which puts one of her screws out of action. She fires point-blank into the conning tower. *Bulldog* turns, increases speed and prepares to ram. About 40 yards off the captain thought better and the *Bulldog* swung round to starboard. Previously, our 4.7s and 3-inch [guns] had opened up, but our fire fell short. Our pom-poms later sprayed the U-boat decks. Tommy guns, fired from the bridge, also joined in. A man clutched his stomach and fell forward into the water. Another with face covered in blood dived from the U-boat decks – spray and blood mingled together. A third was seen to have stopped a pom-pom bullet which took his head off, and he stood fountaining blood before pitching into the sea. Twice the crew tried to man their forward gun, but were driven back. The after-deck of the U-boat was awash. By now the majority of the crew were floating about in the water. Their facial expressions were inexplicable: no sign of fear. Resigned and unquestioningly calm. One raised an arm and cried 'Kamerad!' This was greeted by jeers and the brandishing of fists. Another Nazi was seen to be supporting a dying companion in his arms.

On the side of the conning tower was a monogram – a leering dog. One ear cocked and the other drooping. Beneath this was a gaping hole in the armour plating. Two officers clung to the conning tower amid a hail of murderous fire. At last they too jumped into the sea. The order 'Cease fire' was given. In spite of my previous humanitarian ideas, I could summon up no feeling for those men in the water. On previous convoys I had witnessed oil tankers hit and the sea on fire, choking and burning survivors, making rescue impossible. U-boats did not wait around to pick up survivors. I remembered the tale of the destroyer captain who, when he received orders to pick up U-boat survivors, raised his glasses to the sky and said 'I can see no survivors' and steamed on.

Previously a man believed to be the captain stood on the U-boat deck and semaphored to our bridge – unintelligible. It is said that he was trying to say that his was the only U-boat operating. What a tale! He was later identified as Fritz-Julius Lemp, who on the first day of the war had torpedoed and sunk the passenger liner *Athena*.

Bulldog lowered a whaler, and with Sub Lieut. Balme in charge, it went alongside the U-boat. They boarded the half-submerged vessel, and signalled to say she was watertight below and could be towed. The *Broadway* and the corvette [*Aubretia*] stood by screening our activities from attack. Meanwhile corvette picks up German survivors. She already had merchant ship survivors on board – a good mixture!

Our whaler buffeted by waves breaking against side of submarine, was damaged, broke loose and sank. *Broadway*'s whaler joins the fellows on the U-boat. Secured for towing about 1530, but had to loose again owing to fouling of screws. Secured again about 1700. Charts, codes, names of spies, U-boat bases, knowledge of movements of our convoys – an enormous coup – turning point in the Battle of the Atlantic! Materials seized from the U-boat [were] passed up from hand to hand. Among them was a wooden box that looked like a typewriter [though he added later: 'At no time were we aware that a German Enigma machine had been captured']. Meanwhile *Amazon* after dropping depth charges sees patches of oil and bubbles – claims another U-boat. A third U-boat is also supposed to have been sunk. The nest is losing its chicks!

We head back for Iceland with U-boat in tow. The disabled *Broadway* is our escort; both almost devoid of depth charges! We are open targets, proceeding at 5 knots! A signal has been sent calling for two tugs but they will not arrive until the following night – maybe later!

A coded signal is sent to HQ: 'Have Primrose in tow, consider petals to be of great value.' The following Thursday an answering signal is received from A.V. Alexander, 1st Lord [of the Admiralty]: 'To Bulldog from Admiralty. Hearty Congratulations The petals of your flower are of rare beauty.'

When towing operation began we were approx. 420 miles from Iceland. No further signals are sent out owing to the possibility of our position being detected (whilst the securing of the U-boat was being done, lookouts reported a periscope on our starboard side – after 5 secs it disappeared and no more was seen of it).

Early next morning a signal came through to say that the convoy had run into another U-boat nest. Imagine our feelings – the seas are getting rougher, our speed is below 5 knots and we are a sitting bull['s eye] to enemy action. It is hard to sleep and everyone is jumpy and nervy – will we get our prize home? If only the tugs would arrive and we could take over the escort duties from the crippled *Broadway*.

Saturday 10th May. Seas choppy, high wind. 1055 U-boat sank. Relief felt, in spite of our losing a grand coup. Wires are cut and we speed at 20 knots back to Iceland.

Another surviving account is that of the man who led the boarding party. Lieutenant (later Commander) Balme had had no preparation for his role in capturing Enigma. He and his shipmates had not practised boarding submarines, or even launching their ship's boat. Balme was the gunnery-control officer aboard HMS *Bulldog* and at the time was concentrating on his task of directing the ship's guns as they raked the submarine. On the bridge of *Bulldog* the Commander of the 3rd Escort Group, Joe Baker-Cresswell, saw the potential of the situation and decided to take immediate action. There was a heart-stopping moment as the destroyer USS *Broadway* appeared to be trying to ram the U-boat and sink it. Baker-Cresswell immediately ordered the nearest available officer to take a party of men and get aboard the U-boat. Balme rose to the challenge. His account began by setting the scene:

On the 9th of May, 1941, we were attacked at noon. I had been on watch from 0400 to 0800, and after a bath and breakfast I was on the bridge. It was a sunny day, moderate wind but the usual Atlantic swell.

Suddenly, at noon, two ships were hit by torpedoes and we went to action stations. We turned the convoy 45 degrees away from the attack and *Bulldog* went full speed to the likely position of the U-boat.

The corvette *Aubretia* gained contact with the U-boat and attacked with depth charges. The U-boat surfaced 400 yards from us and we opened fire with every gun.

The noise was deafening and especially from our Lewis machine-guns which were being fired from the bridge over our heads by anyone who could pick them up. However it was undoubtedly the noise of all the shells and bullets hitting the U-boat which panicked the German crew, who all jumped overboard as fast as they could without successfully scuttling the U-boat. Thus the order went out: 'Away armed boarding party.' The captain ordered me to take the boarding party and get what I could out of the U-boat.

He then described the adventure itself:

The Gunner's Mate was issuing revolvers and ammunition to me and the crew of the seaboat. We were 8 men and the seaboat was the traditional 27 foot wooden whaler pointed at both ends. We got out the oars and began rowing over to the U-boat. As speed was essential, I steered the boat to the nearest side which was to windward with the rollers breaking against the hull.

He ventured along the foredeck and climbed down the ladder inside the conning tower:

There were no Germans on deck or in the conning tower, and surprisingly the watertight hatch was closed. The worst moment was going down the last vertical ladder to the control room. Going down bottom-first, I felt a very vulnerable target to any German still down below.

The most eerie feeling was the complete silence except for an ominous hissing sound which was either from the batteries or a leak in the hull. The secondary lighting gave a rather dim ghostly effect. The U-boat had a 15-degree list to port and there was a plopping noise as she rolled against the Atlantic swell. This swell eventually broke up our whaler and we were then supplied with a motor boat from the destroyer *Broadway*.

I walked forward and aft through the two watertight doors out of the control room and decided that the Germans really had abandoned ship. I called my sailors down and told the signalman to semaphore back to *Bulldog* that she was deserted.

Balme and his men demonstrated immense bravery in searching methodically a vessel that was slowly sinking and whose scuttling-charges could have gone off at any time. Their comrades could do nothing to assist them – except see to it that their problems did not include hunger. The notion of providing snacks for men working in such danger strikes an oddly prosaic note amid the drama:

> Speed in searching the U-boat was now essential, as I felt sure that the scuttling-charges would go off sooner or later, especially as there were continuous explosions around us from our depth charge attacks on other U-boats. This was a most unpleasant and frightening noise. We formed a human chain up the two ladders and began passing up books, charts and wireless equipment.
>
> The great thing was for all the boarding party to be kept busy, passing out the items, including the Enigma cipher machine which was found in the wireless office. It was unscrewed from the table and so began its fateful journey up the conning tower into the motor boat of *Bulldog*. Thence to Iceland, then to Scapa Flow and from there to Bletchley.
>
> Time was marching on. We boarded *U110* at 1230 and were glad to receive sandwiches from *Bulldog* during the afternoon. Throughout these hours our escort vessels were attacking U-boats with depth charges and my fear was that their explosions, which felt very close, would set off the detonating charges.
>
> Having got most of the books, charts and moveable wireless and other instruments out of the U-boat, I now thought I should have an engineer to try and get the engines working. So I semaphored *Bulldog* and in due course our Engineer Officer came over with a few stokers, as they were still called. But with everything written in German and nobody having ever served in submarines, we decided we would do more harm than good by turning the cocks to get her under way.
>
> Meanwhile, on deck, *Bulldog* came in close and we tried to secure a towing wire. The first one parted and then *Bulldog* had to leave to investigate and attack a reported U-boat contact.

This was indeed a desolate and awful moment. There was I, with my boarding party, aboard *U110* in the middle of the Atlantic, alone with no ships in sight and the wind and sea gradually increasing. This must have been about 4 p.m. There were not really any more books or moveable gear we could collect, so I battened down the watertight hatches and we waited. Happily, *Bulldog* returned and we set about securing a tow. This held and thus at about 6.30 p.m. we evacuated the U-boat and returned to *Bulldog*, having spent 6 hours in *U110*.

The findings aboard *U110* were, in intelligence terms, a sort of Tutankhamen's tomb. Together with the Enigma machine there was a stack of code books that gave the key to reading the U-boats' short signals and weather reports. There was a set of bigram tables that confirmed, and expanded, the knowledge of these that Bletchley staff had already attained. Most significantly, perhaps, there were the '*Offizier*' settings for June. These were a means of doubly enciphering particularly important messages. Sensitive material was first encoded using the 'officer' settings, and then again using the general ones. The ability to read this traffic made an immense difference to the Allied war effort, especially since changes to the naval Enigma were often announced via the *Offizier* code.

There were charts among the booty that indicated the positions of German minefields as well as the clear channels within them (this knowledge was to prove invaluable in planning Allied raids at St Nazaire and elsewhere). There were also charts for fixing the positions of U-boats in the Atlantic and indicating the locations of the 'milk cows' that refuelled them, 15 of which were to be sunk in the following weeks (unlike the U-boats themselves, their hulls were not designed for quick submersion).

All those involved in the operation were sworn to secrecy, and without exception kept silence for decades afterwards, but at Bletchley and Whitehall the excitement was intense. The *U110* captures enabled the Hydra code to be read by the Allies almost as swiftly as by the Germans themselves. They were able to build up a detailed knowledge of U-boat tactics, patrol routes, operational routines, supply arrangements, and plans for attacks. From Bletchley the U-boat radio traffic, once deciphered, was forwarded to the Admiralty's Submarine Tracking Room from which the war against the U-boats was organized, and which would now be able to route convoys away from the concentrations of U-boats.

A third coup, this time in the Mediterranean off the coast of Egypt, brought further secrets into the possession of the Allies but at a steep cost. In October 1942 a U-boat was forced to the surface by destroyers. Two members of a three-man boarding party in search of coding materials – Lieutenant Francis Fasson and Able Seaman Colin Grazier – lost their lives and received, posthumously, the George Cross for their bravery. The third member of the party, a 16-year-old canteen boy named Tommy Brown, remained on the U-boat's conning tower to receive the items while the others went aboard. He survived the sinking and was awarded the George Medal. The incident is described, using the words of the citation, in Sir John Smyth's history of the GC. Neither at the time nor when this history was published in 1968 could the nature of the finds or their relevance to the war effort be revealed. Both Fasson and Grazier very nearly received the Victoria Cross, but the Honours and Awards Committee decided, regretfully, that they were not quite eligible because 'the service cannot be held to have been in the face of the enemy'. The George Cross is, nevertheless, evidence of truly outstanding bravery, and its award to men involved in pinches reflects the significance attached to the results of these daring raids·

> The U-boat had been sighted on the surface by a British aircraft on a dawn patrol, which at once alerted the Destroyer Flotilla. After a lengthy search of the area the submarine's approximate position was ascertained. Depth charges were dropped which forced the submarine to the surface, when she was immediately holed by gun fire from the destroyers. The crippled submarine at once surrendered and her crew were taken off. It was however important that the submarine's papers and documents should be recovered, and HMS *Petard* came alongside her for this purpose. Lieutenant Fasson, who had given valuable assistance in tracking down the submarine, at once boarded her, taking with him Able Seaman Grazier. They were both fully aware that in the darkness, with the water rising rapidly in the sinking submarine, time was not on their side. They continued to produce and hand over instruments and papers until the submarine suddenly sank like a stone, taking them both to their death.

It was not always the naval Enigma that enabled the Allies to achieve victories at sea. On one occasion it was the air force version that provided information vital to the snaring of a major prize. In May 1941, the battleship *Bismarck* was heading for the French port of Brest. Bletchley knew that the ship was heading south, but did not know its destination. This was given away when a signal was intercepted from the Luftwaffe Chief of Staff, General Hans Jeschonnek, who wished to know *Bismarck*'s movements because a relation of his was on board. Once this knowledge was passed to the Royal Navy, *Bismarck* was ruthlessly hunted by ships and aircraft. On 26 May it was cornered and its rudder disabled in a bombing attack by planes from HMS *Ark Royal*. It sank shortly afterwards. The news provided an immense boost to morale at Bletchley, where the clerks and codebreakers could appreciate the part they were playing in winning the war.

***

Though findings of German coding materials were of great importance to the Royal Navy, they did not 'turn the tide' in the Battle of the Atlantic. There had been successes before the breakthroughs with the Enigma machine and there were disasters afterwards. One of these, in February 1942, was the replacement of Hydra with a new code (dubbed 'Shark' by the Allies) based on the addition of another wheel to the machine, which caused shipping losses to soar again.

The ability to read German signals was of vast importance to the Allies, but it was only one of a series of factors that brought gradual success. In March 1941 Günther Prien, regarded as Germany's leading U-boat ace since he had sunk the *Royal Oak* in 1939, was lost with his entire crew when *U47* was sunk by a depth charge. Only days later another legend, Karl Schepke, perished with his crew after being rammed by a British ship. A third famous submariner, Otto Kreschmer, was captured after his boat was sunk. Nevertheless, German submarine production was steadily increasing: at the beginning of 1942 there were 249 U-boats in service; by 1943 this would increase to 393 and by 1944 (production having been slowed by Allied bombing) to 436. In addition, changes in naval Enigma again left Allied codebreakers groping in the dark for some months.

The Allies learned from the costly experiences of the war's earlier phase and slowly but steadily put new resources into place. The introduction of aircraft with a longer patrol range of 800 miles, as well as the use of aircraft carriers, closed the air gap. More sensitive radar was developed, and the introduction and improvement of 'Huff-Duff' (high-frequency direction-finding equipment) meant that the Allies could pinpoint the positions of U-boats with greater accuracy. Initially based ashore, Huff-Duff was later carried aboard ships. For attacking submarines the 'hedgehog' was developed – a 24-barrelled rocket launcher whose bombs detonated on impact with a U-boat's hull, and was thus deadlier than depth charges. Most importantly, the team in Hut 8 broke Shark, enabling the naval planners to reroute convoys away from U-boat packs, and confirming that the Germans had been reading the Admiralty's own Number 3 code; after March 1943 they were no longer able to do so. As a result of this knowledge and the subsequent measures taken by the Allies, almost 100 U-boats were sunk during the first months of 1943.

Dönitz, whose son was lost aboard a U-boat during this period, was astonished by the success of Allied convoys in avoiding his submarines. He realized that, somehow, the enemy must be gaining access to his vessels' communications, but the notion that Enigma codes had been broken was not taken seriously. It was therefore assumed that the problem was caused by some superior form of radar. There seemed to be little that could be done about this, and no attempt was made to change the Triton code.

***

As the North Atlantic became more dangerous for submarines, they sought softer targets and found them in the seas off the Americas; and the fact that they were hunting elsewhere did much to save British shipping during the spring and summer of 1942. Though the United States was now at war, the American coast was not subject to blackout and neither was its shipping. Oil tankers and other merchant vessels did not travel in convoy. The constant traffic from the oil refineries of Texas and Trinidad provided a target too tempting to ignore and the U-boats took full advantage. There were so many of them in the western Atlantic that their wolf packs often comprised 20 boats – twice the number that had been common further north. The early part of 1942 became a second 'happy time' as three million tons of shipping went to the bottom in the first half of the year, a rate of sinking four times higher than in the Atlantic. Germany's official history of the naval war, published many years later, commented that:

> **Convoys in the Caribbean and on the Brazilian and African coasts were not only less strongly escorted, but the escort vessels**

themselves were regarded by U-boat crews as being 'harmless' in comparison with those in the North Atlantic. A single U-boat had more chance of firing torpedoes at a convoy sighted in these areas than had a whole group of boats against a US–UK convoy.

Though these easy victories gave the submarine crews a certain amount of euphoria, they were clearly not enough. The vastness of America's resources meant that it could continually replace losses, and even the destruction of its merchant shipping was not proving fatal. US shipyards embarked on an accelerated programme of construction in which 'Liberty ships' were assembled by skilled teams from prefabricated sections. The fastest recorded time in which such a vessel was built was 80 hours 30 minutes. The average was longer, but the ships were so simple in design that they could be completed in less than two weeks and were soon being built at the rate of 140 a month. Germany's senior naval officer, Grand Admiral Reader, had told Hitler: 'The sinkings of the U-boat war are a race with merchant ship construction.' He had estimated that, in order to cripple the Allies, German submarines would need to sink 800,000 tons a month. Only once – in November 1942, when the figure was 802,000 – was this ever achieved. In 1943 the Allies lost 3.22 million tons through enemy action, but built 43.59 million tons. This was a contest that Germany could not possibly win.

In the meantime, other Allied advantages steadily grew. America's entry into the war after the attack on Pearl Harbor in December 1941 had meant that half of the US Navy was now assigned to the Atlantic, and the number of available escorts therefore vastly increased (it was estimated that to ensure success there must be two escort vessels for every U-boat). RAF Coastal Command received more aircraft and some of these, such as the Sunderland flying boat, were specifically designed for U-boat hunting. Aircraft also targeted the Bay of Biscay, through which submarines had to travel when leaving or returning to their home ports, and this small area quickly became a killing ground that was feared by U-boat crews. In 1943 the Allies occupied the Azores, gaining a strategic base in mid-Atlantic.

These factors made the U-boat campaign increasingly expensive and the month of May 1943 brought the highest price yet. By 23 May, 47 U-boats had been lost – a rate of more than two a day. Dönitz conceded defeat. He knew that such a casualty rate could not be sustained and withdrew his fleet from the offensive. It was no longer worth spending lives in large-scale attacks when the odds were so steeply against success. For the remainder of the war, the U-boats concentrated on tying down Allied resources to keep ships and aircraft away from the coasts of Europe.

***

By 1944 the stream of Allied shipping across the ocean had become a torrent. The vessels now carried human cargoes, as well as freight, for the Allies were building up armies in England for the invasion of Europe. Their control over the Atlantic was by that time so overwhelming that not a single troop-carrying vessel was sunk. U-boats were deployed in a defensive role during Operation Overlord (13 of them were sunk in the Channel during the invasion) but as the Allies overran France the Atlantic ports from which the submarines had sailed were either captured or cut off, and the fleet was obliged to retreat to the Baltic, to help Germany's increasingly desperate rearguard action against the Russians, or to Norway.

They were never, however, defeated entirely. In 1944 the introduction of a snorkel device made it a great deal more difficult to detect U-boats, for they could travel submerged for much longer; combined with a practice of keeping total radio silence during missions, this added considerably to their effectiveness. In the last year of the war two entirely new models appeared. The Type XXI and the Type XXIII were the most advanced submarines yet produced. Equipped with snorkels and with a speed of 17 knots (10 knots faster than the Type VII) they could have made a considerable difference to the German war effort if they had been introduced sooner and in greater numbers. They were preparing for a new offensive, as if unaware that the Third Reich was collapsing around them. They were, of course, too late. The U-boat war ended with the surrender of Germany on 8 May 1945.

And the role of the codebreakers in the Battle of the Atlantic? Their work had been vital in keeping supplies of raw materials flowing to Britain, thus preventing capitulation and complete German victory before the US became a belligerent. It had seriously hampered the efforts of the enemy submarine fleet and had saved, according to Hinsley's estimate, about 350 vessels – one and a half million tons of shipping – from destruction.

5
NORTH AFRICA AND ITALY

The enemy never quite knew where the Allied landings in North
Africa, Sicily and Italy would take place. It is true that our plans
for these operations had been based on the information from
ULTRA as to where there would be least opposition, but if for a
moment one reverses the roles of ULTRA there would have been
little chance of our amphibious invasions in the Mediterranean
or in Normandy achieving the successes they did. It is, I think,
true to say that on these counts ULTRA was the vital factor.[i]

The middle phase of the war against the Axis powers was fought in the
Mediterranean – in North Africa, Malta, Sicily, Italy, Greece and the Balkans.
In this theatre of conflict, as in the others, the information provided by
Bletchley was crucial in bringing victory. The Allies faced two highly gifted
opponents, Rommel in North Africa and Kesselring in Italy, either of whom
could have defeated them, and the edge given by access to the German
commanders' thoughts enabled the Anglo-American commanders to exploit
their own strengths and their enemies' weaknesses.

The Mediterranean might seem an unlikely or even unnecessary place in
which to conduct a war between Germany and the Allies, but certain factors
gave this region strategic importance. First, Germany's co-belligerent, Italy,
was a dominant power in the region. The Italians boastfully called the
Mediterranean '*Mare Nostra*' – 'our sea' – and had colonized several parts of
it: Libya, Tripoli and the Dodecanese. Other Italian territories – Somaliland
and recently conquered Ethiopia – posed a threat to East Africa and the
Persian Gulf. Britain too had possessions, or mandated territories, in the
area: Gibraltar, Malta, Cyprus, Palestine and Egypt.

Second, the Mediterranean was the key to the Suez Canal, and the canal
was the key to India and the Far East. Even more importantly, the oil fields
of Iraq were vital to Britain's war effort. Mussolini wanted a share in the

[i] FW Winterbotham (*The Ultra Secret*, Futura, 1975)

glory that he expected the war would bring, and it could be assumed that he would attempt to seize British territory if opportunity offered. In any case he decided to conquer his neighbours and attacked Albania, forcing its king into exile. He found himself opposed by tough Greek armies and became bogged down in the mountainous terrain through the winter of 1940–41. Italian efforts were proving inadequate, and Mussolini (who had acted without Hitler's support) was saved from disaster and humiliation only by the arrival of German armies to assist him. They went on to invade Greece itself. Britain assisted by defeating the Italian navy at Taranto in November and by sending its own troops to the aid of the Greeks. The Balkans became the scene of some of the war's most bitter fighting.

The defeat of France had led to the creation of the collaborationist Vichy Government, and French colonies in North Africa (Algeria and Morocco) became enemy territory. When Vichy refused to hand over to Britain its Mediterranean fleet, which was in port at Mers-el-Kebir, the ships were shelled and sunk by the Royal Navy on Churchill's orders, to prevent their use by the Axis.

With Western Europe in a state of impasse, the Mediterranean was thus growing into a major theatre of conflict and a natural arena for the contest between the Axis and the British Commonwealth – for troops from India, Australia, New Zealand and South Africa fought alongside the British. The region's importance could be gauged by the fact that in July 1940, with invasion of southern England a stark possibility, the government despatched to North Africa the only significant number of tanks it possessed that had not been abandoned at Dunkirk.

There they were put to good use. The loss of face caused by the British Army's retreat from France was avenged to some extent by success against the Italians. At the end of 1940 the British, commanded by General Richard O'Connor, broke through the Italian lines at Sidi Barrani, surrounded a large enemy force and took 38,000 prisoners. During the next few months the Italians were driven out of Egypt and Cyrenaica. These victories on land were matched by a decisive success at sea, when Admiral Andrew Cunningham's Mediterranean fleet delivered a crippling blow at Cape Matapan, off the southern tip of Greece, in March 1941. Cunningham had his headquarters in Alexandria and he and his officers had been under close observation by the Japanese consul there, who was a member of the same club. Aware, from the reading of Axis code messages, that his movements would be reported to the Italians, Cunningham deliberately allowed himself to be seen relaxing there on the Friday before the battle and was heard loudly making arrangements to play tennis the following day. After dark, however, he and his fleet sailed quietly out of harbour and caught the Italians entirely by surprise. This was to be the last occasion on which the Italian surface fleet was brought to battle.

ULTRA AND THE SPECIAL LIAISON UNITS

Cunningham had known exactly where to find his opponents – as well as their number and firepower, and even the fuel situation of their ships – because of the work of the Station X codebreakers, who had been listening to the signals traffic of the enemy fleet. Bletchley housed an Italian section, whose codebreakers had found this enemy's ciphers easier to read than those of the Germans. It was to score numerous successes during the Mediterranean war, but perhaps Matapan was its greatest triumph.

Getting such information to commanders in distant fields of conflict was problematic. To protect the secrecy of its source, the smallest possible number of people must see the messages or know of their existence. They were therefore too sensitive to send abroad through even the normal secure channels, and at the receiving end could not be trusted to the eyes of secretaries or adjutants. The solution was that Bletchley sent its own representatives to the theatres of operations. These security-vetted specialists, rather than ordinary army signallers, received the messages sent from Station X and ensured that they reached their destination. This meant the establishment of small units that accompanied the armies in the field. There must in each case be several men for they, like their counterparts at Bletchley, would need to work round the clock in shifts, and might, of course, expect to suffer casualties. Though they shared the discomforts of their comrades, sleeping in slit trenches or jolting in convoys along dusty roads, they were self-sufficient. Operating their radios from tents or the backs of vehicles, they would receive the information in code and write it out for delivery to the recipient. No one else, no matter how exalted in rank, would be permitted so much as a glance at it. These groups of operatives – the link between the huts of Bletchley Park and the battlefields on which the results of their work were put to use – were the Special Liaison Units, or SLUs. They were set up and controlled by Group Captain Winterbotham. They derived their information from another close-knit communications group, the Special Communications Unit (SCU). The latter, according to RT Jenks, had a comprehensive array of functions:

> Duties of SCUs ranged from interception of enemy traffic, direction finding, mobile D/F and location of enemy agents in the UK and abroad, relaying of traffic across the world, operation of deception traffic, supervision of turned agents, co-operation with clandestine units overseas, to handling of the traffic for SLUs.
>
> SCU 1 was formed about August 1941 above the Passport Office in Petty France (a street in London). It later moved to the Bletchley complex. It is thought to have been formed initially from a mixture of RSS and 'Y' service personnel. It was the 'mother hen' of the organization, supplying staff for other SCUs.

The origins and organization of the SLUs have been described by army signaller RT Jenks, who served in one:

> The Special Liaison Units were masterminded by Group Captain Fred Winterbotham. The German Enigma and other traffic intercepted by SCU 3 was decrypted at Bletchley Park. The vital traffic intended for German commanders in the field was given the code name ULTRA, and was sent immediately, after receiving by one-time pads or Typex machines, from Windy Ridge by SCU operators to the appropriate SCU/SLU in the field. The SCU operator received the traffic and handed it to the SLU (RF cipher sergeants and officers) who decoded it and passed it to the Allied General Staff Officer. An apocryphal story, which could well have been true, tells of a message which due to poor radio conditions and/or poor German operating had to be repeated innumerable times. The SCU intercept operator, however, took a solid copy first time and the traffic was passed as above, with the result that the Allied General knew the orders before his German counterpart.
>
> Within an SLU there could be several groups, each serving a particular command in that area, Army, Navy, Air Force, British and US. A group usually consisted of 3–6 SCU operators, drivers and up to six RAF cipher sergeants with an RAF officer. The CO varied as to who the group served, British or US, Army or Air Force. Groups might be combined for a time and then split

up as required. Each group was usually given a code name, e.g. CROWN, HANS. Not all SLUs had radio links, but were supplied with their information by teleprinter or dispatch rider.

Initially 'one time' pads were used for encryption but the Typex machine became available later in 1942.

The units served all over the world and at every stage of the conflict:

Most of the radio links worked direct to Windy Ridge [Whaddon] but some worked through relay stations in India, Egypt and Morocco. Some SLUs are reported as having travelled with Churchill to conferences, e.g. USA, Casablanca, Teheran, Yalta.

There was an SLU of a sort with Lord Gort in France (1939/40) and also at Meaux (Paris) with Air Vice Marshal Barratt. They evacuated via Brest at the time of Dunkirk (May 1940).

There was an SLU at Fighter Command (Stanmore) working by teleprinter to Bletchley at the time of Operation SEA LION (the proposed invasion of Britain) and the Battle of Britain (Operation ADLER, August 13 – September 15 1940). An SLU in Cairo served General Alexander and later General Montgomery (8th Army) and Air Marshal Cunningham (Desert Air Force), with an extension to Alexandria for Admirals Ramsay and Cunningham. An SLU in Malta served all three services.

Personnel for SLU 9 went by sea to Canada and USA, then by train and flew to Australia. HQ for SLU 9 was in the A.M.P. Building in Brisbane and it appears that they became members of the Royal Australian Air Force. There were groups in Laye (New Guinea) for Australian 1st Army and RAAF, Manila for General MacArthur, Morotai in the Moluccas and Laubaun Island (Borneo) for 1st Tactical Air Force, RAAF. A group was due to move from Borneo to Manila when the atom bomb was dropped on Japan and the move was aborted. Information from London and US went to Brisbane by cable and radio.

In 1943 an SLU, and presumably associated SCU, was provided for C in C India at Delhi, and another for General Slim, C in C 14th Army at Comilla in Assam. About September 1944 an SLU was provided for Admiral Mountbatten (SEAC) at Kandy in Ceylon. These SLUs also provided service to US Army and Air

Force in China with Chang Kai Shek. Information to them came from London, Brisbane and Washington.

The men (for this aspect of the communications war was an entirely male preserve) recruited for work in SLUs were already serving in the Forces as signals specialists. They were otherwise a disparate bunch. Most had undertaken, or would be sent to complete, the necessary crash courses to bring their knowledge and abilities to a suitable level. They were summoned, as needed, from all manner of different places and postings. They were interviewed and then trained in London, living in hostels and receiving instruction in converted private houses or, more intriguingly, in commandeered national museums (rooms in two of the great treasure houses of South Kensington, the Victoria and Albert and its neighbour the Natural History Museum, were used for this purpose). Most were puzzled to receive a summons to London that gave no indication as to why they were wanted. All of them recall the sense of excitement at the job they were to do, and the continuous emphasis on the penalties for divulging anything of what they knew. Squadron Leader Oliver Reece described his experience:

> After two weeks at the officers' training school at Wolverhampton, designed to convert Erks like me to officers and gentlemen, I was summoned to an interview at Air Ministry to determine if I were fit for an intelligence commission, for which I originally applied, in the belief that my knowledge of Spanish and French might be useful. They sent me to Highgate for a crash intelligence course for two weeks, mostly devoted to aircraft recognition and security.
>
> From there I was sent for an interview at Victoria Street at which I met Wing Commander (Tubby) Long. He asked me if I was willing to go overseas and I told him I would have to go wherever they sent me. He emphasised that he could not tell me where and he came on strongly about security and secrecy. So that was my entry to SLU.
>
> Next came a crash course in coding with one-time pad, taken at a boarded-up house near Sloane Square, inside which was a multilingual hive of agents in training. My instructor was Squadron Leader Macdonald, a university French professor.

Sergeant Frank Brailsford's training had been a combination of square-bashing and cipher work:

I joined the RAF and served in the RAF Regiment until the spring of 1943. An IQ test was then carried out to select personnel who were capable of doing a different type of duty, and I was selected to become a clerk c.c. [Clerk and Cipher]. After passing the drill course at Cardington I took a code and cipher course at Oxford. I found the work most absorbing and at the end of the course we had a final lecture from a senior RAF officer about the absolute necessity for complete secrecy in dealing with cipher work of any kind. To emphasise this point he concluded by quoting a biblical verse from the first epistle to Timothy, chapter 6, verse 20, which reads: 'O Timothy, keep that which is committed to thy trust, avoiding profane and vain babblings and oppositions of science falsely so called.'

From Oxford I was posted to a cipher office at RAF Annan where I spent the autumn and winter of 1943–4. In the spring of 1944 I was posted to SLU 8 and commenced by attending the cipher school in Hamilton Terrace, north London, to learn the mysteries of the Typex cipher machine and to be told of the Ultra secret intelligence.

Josh Reynolds had also done all the right courses:

For me, one of the most fascinating jobs of World War II started after I had passed through the normal RAF Code and Cipher School known as No. 5 Radio School, Oxford, and was waiting at Winslow for posting overseas.

Flight Lieutenant Gibson, whom I later learned was one of the four original RAF officers recruited by Group Captain Winterbotham for the Ultra Intelligence team in Hut 3 at Bletchley, came down to select cipher sergeants for the Special Liaison Units in North Africa. I was, I think, picked because I knew German, and together with several others was then sent off on leave only to find we were being very thoroughly checked on by our local police for every aspect of security. It was an odd experience since we didn't know at that time what we were going to do. Anyway, I seemed to pass the test because I then reported to London and about eight of us did the special course in 'one-time-pad' and also on the new Type X cipher machine, and it was here that Group Captain Winterbotham indoctrinated us in the mysteries of 'Ultra', and suddenly the war had come alive. We were to be right at the centre of the whole business.

Every morning a black Foreign Office van [with an] armed guard brought to our empty house in Sloane Square locked and sealed boxes and cases with the machine and books and Ultra material and each night it was taken away again. It was my first lesson in security. There was a Squadron Leader Long who taught us all that we should have to do in the field, and reiterated the warning that if ever the enemy were given any cause to suspect we were reading their most secret signals, Ultra would cease, and with it a large part of our chances of winning the war. There was a nice touch too when we were warned that if there was any leakage of the secret to anyone who was not entitled to know it, the guilty man would be shot. We very soon realized why such care had been taken in our selection and security checks. There was a strangely close-knit companionship between all the men I was to meet in the various Special Liaison Units in which I served, for we could never mix with other units of either service. It was at first a rather difficult situation but I think it made us all the more self-reliant.

One other thing we all had to learn was a thorough maintenance course on the Type X cipher machine. I suppose the RAF who designed this cipher machine had learned what to avoid after we had succeeded in breaking the supposedly unbreakable German Enigma [code]. We had to be able to keep our Type X in top working order under all conditions.

It gave our morale a tremendous boost to feel we were considered so important despite the fact that we were only sergeants, and the signing of the Official Secrets Act was to us a significant moment.

Sergeant Jack Mellor found difficulty in attending the interview:

I remember when I first reported to Hamilton Terrace for the special cipher course, prior to being posted to SLU 8 at Bushey Park, I was met by an army officer, I think it was Lieutenant Colonel Gore-Browne, who – patting an enormous Smith & Wesson revolver on his hip – said he would shoot me with his own hand if ever I revealed the secrets I was about to learn.

My reporting to Hamilton Terrace did, in itself, have a funny side. Due to an error in the transmission of the signal to my Coastal Command station at Beaulieu in the New Forest, where I was working as a cipher clerk, my instructions read to report to '8 Hamilton Terrace.' I duly arrived at No. 8 only to find that it was a completely empty and deserted house. This was a bit of a puzzler, I remember thinking 'By God this IS a secret outfit!' Using a bit of initiative which I didn't know I had I tried No 18, much to the surprise of the civilian residents, and then No 88. So commenced my career with SLU 8.

THE BATTLE OF CRETE

Commonwealth forces attacked the eastern Italian colonies and, despite sporadic but spirited resistance, had taken control of Ethiopia and Somalia by the end of 1940. These victories were helpful in protecting the Suez Canal, but were otherwise of no great significance, because while the Allies had captured vast areas of enemy territory in East Africa, they had lost a more important conflict farther north. The Allies had been driven out of Greece by Axis armies (despite a warning from Ultra that German forces were building up in Romania to strike) and after fighting a rearguard action were forced to withdraw to Crete in what seemed a weary repetition of Dunkirk. According to Anthony Beevor's book, *Crete: The Battle and the Resistance*, a signal from Bletchley on 22 April 1941 to the British Legation in Athens requested urgently the destruction of Ultra signals:

> Take greatest care to burn all deciphered material this series.
> Vital security our source.

On Crete a force of British and Commonwealth troops, commanded by the New Zealander General Bernard Freyberg, dug in. Though it was expected that the island would in turn be invaded, his men had adequate time to prepare. The defence of Crete was the first occasion on which Ultra intelligence made a significant difference to a major land battle. Thanks largely to the laxity of the Luftwaffe in observing security procedures when signalling with Enigma, eavesdroppers in Bletchley's Hut 3 had gained an immense amount of detail about the enemy's organization, supplies and, most crucially, mode of transport, and this was relayed to Crete from Allied

Headquarters in Cairo. The Germans had the option of a seaborne invasion or an airborne assault. For the defenders it was vital to know whether to spread their resources around the coasts to repel landings, or to concentrate them on plains inland to prevent paratroops from seizing the heart of the island. Ultra made available to Freyberg information so comprehensive that the enemy attack could have been decisively crushed had it been taken at face value.

This type of signal would be handed to commanders by their SLU officers throughout the rest of the war. Summarizing the results of many hours' interception, decrypting and translation by a team of experts, these slips of paper must have seemed, to those with the responsibility for making weighty tactical decisions, like a gift from heaven. It is worth examining one of these messages in detail, as quoted by Beevor, because (despite some inaccuracies in the figures) it demonstrates the depth of knowledge, and thus the scale of the advantage, that was given to the Allies by Ultra:

OL 2/302 1745 hours 13.5.41
The following summarises intentions against Crete from operation orders issued.
   Para 1. The island of Crete will be captured by the 11ᵗʰ Air Corps and the 7ᵗʰ Air Division and the operation will be under the control of the 11ᵗʰ Air Corps.
   Para 2. All preparations, including the assembly of transport aircraft, fighter aircraft, and dive bombing aircraft, as well as of troops to be carried both by air and sea transport, will be completed on 17ᵗʰ may.
   Para 3. Transport of seaborne troops will be in co-operation with admiral southeast, who will ensure the protection of German and Italian transport vessels (about twelve ships) by Italian light naval forces. These troops will come under the orders of the 11ᵗʰ Air Corps immediately on their landing in Crete.
   Para 4. A sharp attack by bomber and heavy fighter units to deal with the allied air forces on the ground as well as with their anti-aircraft defences and military camps, will precede the operation.
   Para 5. The following operations will be carried out as from day one. The 7ᵗʰ Air Division will make a parachute landing and seize Maleme, Candia and Retimo. Secondly, dive bombers and

fighters (about 100 of each type) will move by air to Maleme and Candia. Thirdly, air landing of 11th Air Corps, including corps headquarters and elements of the Army placed under its command probably including the 22nd Division. Fourthly, arrival of the seaborne contingent consisting of anti-aircraft batteries as well as more troops and supplies.

Para 6. In addition the 12th Army will allot three mountain regiments as instructed. Further elements consisting of motor-cyclists, armoured units, anti-tank units, anti-aircraft units will also be allotted.

Para 7. Depending on the intelligence which is now awaited, also as the result of air reconnaissance, the aerodrome at Kastelli south east of Candia and the district west and south west of Canea will be specially dealt with, in which case separate instructions will be included in detailed operation orders.

Para 8. Transport aircraft, of which a sufficient number – about 600 – will be allotted for this operation, will be assembled on aerodromes in the Athens area. The first sortie will probably carry parachute troops only. Further sorties will be concerned with the transport of the air landing contingent, equipment and supplies, and will probably include aircraft towing gliders.

Para 9. With a view to providing fighter protection for the operations, the possibility of establishing a fighter base at Skarpanto will be examined.

Para 10. The Quartermaster General's branch will ensure that adequate fuel supplies for the whole operation are available in the Athens area in good time, and an Italian tanker will be arriving at Piraeas before May 17th. This tanker will probably also be available to transport fuel supplies to Crete. In assembling supplies and equipment for the invading force it will be borne in mind that it will consist of some 30 to 35,000 men, of which some 12,000 will be the parachute landing contingent, and 10,000 will be transported by sea. The strength of the long range bomber and heavy fighter force which will prepare the invasion by attacking before day one will be of approximately 150 long range bombers and 100 heavy fighters.

Para 11. Orders have been issued that Suda Bay is not to be mined, nor will Cretan aerodromes be destroyed, so as not to interfere with the operations intended.

Para 12. Plottings prepared from air photographs of Crete on one over ten thousand scale will be issued to units participating in this operation.

Unfortunately, the army was not yet accustomed to working with Ultra. Freyberg could not be told the source of the information (presented as the result of espionage) so could not be expected to accept its accuracy entirely. He did not study some of the signals and did not entirely understand others. He had made up his mind that an attack by sea was the most likely situation, and he shaped whatever Ultra intelligence he was shown to fit his expectations. His troops were placed in coastal defence positions.

On 16 May, an Ultra signal gave him even more information about the enemy's intentions. Another message announced:

OL 10/341 0155 hours 16.5.41
From further information postponement day one for operation against Colorado (Crete) confirmed. 19th May seems earliest date.

It was on 20 May that German parachutes began to open in the skies above Crete. Allied defence was spirited, but much manpower and energy had been wasted on the coasts when the enemy's clearly stated objectives were inland airfields. The defenders had no chance of seizing the initiative, though the attackers suffered heavy casualties. Given the enemy's superiority in numbers and equipment, the outcome could not be in doubt and in a matter of days they had overrun the island. Allied survivors retreated to the south coast where, thanks to the Royal Navy, they were evacuated from Greek territory for a second time. Winterbotham later suggested that, despite the defeat, disaster had been averted:

In Crete ULTRA denied surprise to [General] Student's parachute invasion and, although the island was lost, our knowledge undoubtedly saved most of our forces from capture.

Also significant was the fact that the island would have proved very difficult to hold, requiring a garrison of several divisions that could not have been spared from fighting elsewhere. In the event it was the Germans who had to provide a garrison, depriving *them* of much-needed manpower.

BACK AND FORTH

In North Africa, Hitler had decided to intervene and rescue the Italians from further debacle. He sent Erwin Rommel, a gifted commander whose tanks had helped to win the Battle of France, with a German 'Afrika Korps' to reverse the tide of Allied successes, and Rommel did so almost at once. He found Commonwealth troops entirely unprepared. Their commanders assumed that, with the vanquishing of the Italians, enemy forces in Africa had been defeated and, with worries elsewhere (it was necessary to suppress a revolt in Iraq), many experienced soldiers had been moved out of the area. Rommel's Afrika Korps swept westward, wiping out earlier Allied gains (with the exception of Tobruk, which was besieged) and heading for Egypt.

The Allied Eighth Army began at once to counterattack. 'Operation Crusader' was a trek westward to raise the siege of Tobruk, and after heavy fighting it succeeded. The war then ranged back and forth across the desert, with both sides advancing or retreating according to their fortunes. In the first half of 1942, Rommel scored a series of successes that included the capture of Tobruk. The defence of this city during the previous year had been presented to the world as an epic of heroism; its loss was thus a propaganda triumph for the Axis. The fall of Tobruk, which was no longer of great strategic importance, was one of the most important landmarks in the desert war. The Allies were pushed eastward to the Egyptian border, and preparations were made to evacuate Cairo. Rommel was promoted to Field Marshal.

He and his men may have savoured this triumph, but this time it was the Afrika Korps whose fortunes were about to turn. A few months later, in July, his forces were stopped at El Alamein, an insignificant railway junction in the desert, by a combination of well-prepared Allied defences and the sheer exhaustion of his soldiers. He paused, for the moment, to gather strength for the next stage of his march to Cairo. FW Winterbotham commented that:

> During the long fighting withdrawal of our Middle East forces
> from El Agheila back to Egypt, pressed all the way by the
> relentless Rommel, it is doubtful whether, without ULTRA,
> Wavell or Auchinleck (successively Commander-in-Chief Middle
> East) could have so cleverly boxed him to a standstill.

Thanks to Ultra information relayed by the SLU attached to Auchinleck's headquarters, the Allies had known a great deal about Rommel's intentions. Bletchley had read the communications between the 'Desert Fox' and Hitler but, tragically for the Eighth Army, it was not only the British who had access to the details of the enemy's plans. A well-placed source in the Allied camp was unwittingly providing German Intelligence with a continuing stream of information. Britain was anxious to bring the United States into the war, and the American military attaché in Cairo was given access to battlefronts and to highly classified material in order to influence him favourably. He was naturally reporting his impressions to Washington. He did this in considerable detail, using the State Department's Black Code. Historian Barrie Pitt described the circumstances:

> The Axis powers had broken the American State Department cipher by which its military representatives reported from the field. Since early 1941 one such representative – Colonel Bonner Fellers – had been in Cairo, and his genuine sympathy with the British cause had so impressed Middle East HQ that he had been allowed to witness the whole of the Crusader operation from whatever vantage point he requested, and after Pearl Harbor was admitted to the innermost circles at GHQ.
>
> As such, he attended General Auchinleck's morning conferences with his army chief, navy and air force staff officers which, as the day of battle came nearer, went into more and more detail of the deployments of the Eighth Army. And every evening, Colonel Fellers sent the details to Washington, and busy interceptors in Bari recorded them, busier interpreters translated them, and their superiors forwarded to Rommel whatever they considered relevant.

Hitler remarked:

> It is to be hoped that the American Minister in Cairo continues to inform us so well over the English military planning through his badly enciphered cables.

For several months the Führer's hope was fulfilled, and the damage was considerable. The enemy was given vital information about the reinforcement of the besieged island of Malta. They also discovered the exact details of commando raids to be carried out against airbases in Italy, with the result that the men involved were wiped out as soon as they reached their targets. David Kahn, the author of a book on German Intelligence, wrote that:

> Fellers' messages provided Rommel with one of the broadest and clearest pictures of enemy forces available to any Axis commander throughout the war.

Fortunately for the Allies, the Black code was replaced by the Americans just as Rommel was about to attack Alexandria, and the new code was not broken. At the moment that Montgomery was preparing for his stand at El Alamein, the Axis suddenly lost its source of information and consequently the battle that ensued. The Allies, too, had detailed knowledge of their opponents' intentions and continued to receive reports up to and throughout the battle. Winterbotham commented:

> Before Alamein, Rommel might have caught Montgomery by surprise. At best it would have totally disrupted the preparations for Alamein. With our exact knowledge from ULTRA of just what Rommel was going to do, his attack was met and beaten off. Alamein became the turning point from bare survival to aggressive victories.

There had been significant changes in British command. First Wavell and then Auchinleck had been replaced as Commander-in-Chief Middle East. The job was given to General Harold Alexander, and command of the Eighth Army was vested in Bernard Montgomery, a charismatic and determined leader who had a personal fixation with defeating Rommel. He did this by waiting for months, during which he organized the operation in intense detail, made contingency plans for every possible situation and ignored demands by Churchill for a swift victory, while building up men and resources until he had absolute superiority in both. When finally he was ready, in October, Montgomery launched a massive offensive from El Alamein that sent the Afrika Korps reeling westward again. This was to be their final retreat.

VITAL SUPPLIES

A self-evidently crucial factor for both sides was supplies. The movement of both these mechanized armies depended on a steady supply of fuel, and they required immense amounts of ammunition. More mundane items, such as uniforms, wore out rapidly in desert conditions and had to be frequently replaced.

Ultra informed Montgomery of an acute supply shortage for the Afrika Korps which, despite having captured vast quantities of Allied equipment at Tobruk, was desperately short of fuel and ammunition. Supplies were brought to the Afrika Korps largely by sea and, unable to reach the Mediterranean via Gibraltar, the convoys sailed from southern Italian ports. Because Enigma told the Allies precisely when those convoys would be sailing, it was possible to arrange their sinking by the Royal Navy. Since the precise nature of these attacks might have suggested to the enemy that their ciphers had been broken, a ruse was customarily played out: a spotter aircraft, or a squadron of planes on patrol, or a stray Allied vessel, would be sent to the convoy's route. Once the ships knew that they had been seen, there would seem to be nothing unusual about the fact that an attack swiftly followed.

The role of Ultra in preventing supplies from reaching Rommel's armies was thus highly effective and absolutely vital. Not only materiel but also men were prevented from reaching the enemy through the work of the codebreakers. A member of a North African SLU, Squadron Leader AL Thompson, remembered a successful interception:

> There was one incident in North Africa at this time that got rather near the bone. We had an Ultra signal in the middle of the night that fifty JU52 aircraft laden with German paratroopers were flying into Tunis. I had to rush down a rough hillside covered with stones and rocks, and the haunt of puff-adders, with only a small torch to guide me. Half-way down a bird shot up from under my feet and gave me a bad fright. Eventually it was arranged that two squads of Spitfires on patrol accidentally ran into the German formation and shot down 39 of them. For some time after this I was a bit worried that the Germans might consider this a bit too much of a coincidence, but fortunately nothing happened at all, so obviously they didn't suspect anything unusual.

Group Captain Winterbotham knew where the credit belonged for winning the supply war:

It was ULTRA which denied all seaborne supplies to Rommel's retreating army and forced him to withdraw right into Tunisia.

At this time Ultra was giving us a very full picture of not only the enemy's intentions but of his build-up of troops and even the ports and times of departure of his supply ships. As the war progressed and more and more sophisticated weapons were employed the value of Ultra became more and more a question of denying the enemy his supplies of arms and fuel, and for this purpose our information was proved to be completely accurate and of course invaluable. There were one or two occasions when we sank their transports where the German Abwehr were asked to investigate. We saw the signals both for the requests and for the replies, and it was a great relief when the replies were always completely negative. Another factor which always assisted us was the strange German way of thinking which seemed to make them run on rails so that when they did anything, one could be pretty certain that they would do it again.

From the other perspective Rommel himself, looking back on the campaign, acknowledged the fact that lack of equipment had cost his soldiers victory at a time when, before the arrival of major Allied forces, it might well have been within their grasp. He had:

> ... discussed the possibility of surprising the British at Agedabia and knocking out the limited force they had there. This was something that could naturally only remain a theoretical discussion, since not only had we no petrol, we didn't even have the anti-tank units necessary for such a plan. The central point for supply was no longer Tripoli as at the end of 1941, but had to be Tunisia, making it yet more impossible to assemble the stores and equipment needed for such an operation.

Once driven into Tunisia, Rommel's troops faced a large and fresh Anglo-American force supported, as always, by a seemingly uncanny knowledge of his own plans. Winterbotham wrote that:

> In North-west Africa we and our new allies, the Americans, were ensured by ULTRA of both surprise and almost total lack of resistance for the seaborne operation, and the final battles in

Tunisia were fought with full knowledge from ULTRA of Rommel's and von Arnim's counter-attacks and the details of the positions held by the enemy.

An important element had been added to the Allied effort with the arrival in the eastern Mediterranean of SLUs that served both British and American commanders. Oliver Reece remembered that, before they deployed on the African mainland with the invaders, these codebreakers were obliged to operate from cramped quarters in a nearby British territory:

> Gibraltar was bursting with personnel and SLU was packed into a small office in the army barracks. To ensure radio silence, and to prevent the enemy detecting the presence of our crack operators, whose Morse touch would be recognizable to their German counterparts, all communication from UK was by commercial cable on one-time pad, messages reaching the SLU office in batches by 'hand of officer on a motor-cycle'.

SAFEGUARDING ULTRA

Operation Torch, the Allied occupation of Morocco, took place on 8 November 1942. SLUs were attached to General Patton, General Spaatz (US Army Air Force), Air Marshal Sir William Webb (Royal Air Force) and General Anderson (British Army). At least one of the groups went ashore as soon as the landings had taken place. Squadron Leader SF Burley was with one of these and explained how the unit operated:

> We arrived at Algiers in the early days of November 1942. Our first set-up was in a small hotel off the square close to the Place du Gouvernement. It wasn't funny working in a bathroom and a bedroom but now we were receiving 'real' signals and we were to put into action our one-time-pad training. Signal reception was under the control of the Special Communications Unit (SCU) and it would seem at times wasn't very good and there were many garbled groups to be sorted out, but overall we were able to deliver the material. Our radio operator was then working a suitcase receiver.

As the campaign in North Africa gathered momentum, an increasing number of senior generals arrived in the theatre. All had access to Ultra, and therefore required the service of an SLU. Units were set up in Gibraltar, Oran and Casablanca, and there were ultimately to be another six in the Mediterranean. The commander of the invasion force, General Eisenhower, established his headquarters in Algiers, at the Hotel St George. With him were a galaxy of talented subordinates: General Alexander, Admiral Cunningham, Air Chief Marshal Tedder and General Bedell Smith.

Squadron Leader 'Tommy' Thompson's SLU worked with Eisenhower, and explained that the low profile adopted by SLU was a matter of policy:

> I often met General Eisenhower in the St George Hotel and if
> it was first thing in the morning he invariably said 'How are
> you?' which I soon learned was the American way of saying good
> morning. He was of course extremely glad to get anything in
> the way of information from the material we could give him.
> The material itself went under the code name of Ultra and the
> number of people at the headquarters who were allowed either to
> see it or even to know of its existence was very limited. Its security
> was considered above that of Top Secret.
>
> It had been explained to me that one of the reasons why the
> SLUs were kept on a form of low rank was to make them
> inconspicuous wherever they went. For instance, the cipher
> personnel with the SLUs were sergeants – true, they had been
> hand-picked and were a wonderful lot of men. I myself started off
> as a Flight Lieutenant but became a Squadron Leader later on. The
> Group Captain explained to me that he himself retained the rank
> of Group Captain so that he could slip in and out of any
> headquarters without any undue fuss or anybody asking what he
> was doing, so that it was really a matter of personality with our low
> ranks that enabled us to get on with the commanding generals.

When not quartered in hotels or villas, the units travelled with fighting units, eating and sleeping in their own tents. AL Thompson remembered that they shared every form of discomfort with the troops:

> Life up in the mountains was fairly hard. At about 10,000 feet,
> the nights were cold with rather leaky bell tents and hurricane

lamps by which we had to work all night to keep the flow of
Ultra going and there were morning mists up to your knees.
One of our customers whom I had to go and see each day was
Air Marshal Cunningham commanding the Tactical Air Force.
It was a rough path through the scrub and I found myself
being followed by a dozen wild dogs. I knew they all had
rabies so I had to shoot one before they left me alone.

Their true function had to be concealed not only from their own comrades
but from occasional visiting neutral observers, no matter how seemingly
benevolent they were:

We had a visit from a Turkish military mission. Quite
naturally I didn't want these people wandering about
my tent and complained, but the British escort said
don't worry, they always sleep very sweetly after lunch,
so I presumed they put something in their drinks.

They discouraged the curiosity of those around them by giving the
impression that they were merely a signals unit. Unlike an ordinary unit,
however, they could invoke some highly impressive influence if necessary.
As SF Burley remembered:

It wasn't funny being asked what your function was and having
to find a suitably evasive answer. The question of obtaining
transport sometimes raised difficulties and it was necessary to
resort to telling the [Motor Transport] people that if they wanted
confirmation that they were to let us have what we required then
they should ask the Commander-in-Chief. That always did the
trick. Most times we received every support. They were so
appreciative of getting Ultra from the SLU that it was important
we were able to function properly. We also had the added help of
knowing that should it become necessary, owing to the lack of
co-operation, we had only to send a signal back to Group Captain
Winterbotham and he would put the pressure on. His 'special'
pressure was of the highest order!

The SLUs also differed from virtually every other military formation in that they had no clearly defined hierarchy or obvious commanding officer. Thompson explained:

> I was not under the command of anyone at all in the theatre of war, but only under the command of Group Captain Winterbotham in London, so that although I was attached to various commands I didn't come under their jurisdiction and was completely independent except for being fed. I always made it a rule to avoid making my unit look anything out of the ordinary, particularly in tented areas so that one became part of the landscape and no-one ever bothered us. We carried no papers as proof of what we were and there were times when one had to push one's way through interference.

SF Burley outlined the significance of the material with which even a humble mobile SLU was dealing:

> It was now clear to us that we were receiving from the UK the decoded original signals of the German High Command, even from Hitler himself. This was the information we passed on to General Anderson and his intelligence staff who were in fact in the position then of knowing exactly what the German High Command were proposing to do in the future, or an appreciation of the battle state, movements of troops, aircraft, naval ships etc. etc. Such was the vital importance of this information that the material received from BP had been given the code name Ultra, the most secret of any intelligence information used during the Second World War. The army commanders and those of his intelligence staff who were to handle it were very limited and it was made very clear to them that any question of its misuse would [mean that] the whole operation would be compromised and the Germans would immediately realise that their codes had been broken, and [therefore] the security of Ultra was only passed on to those restricted few who were briefed a) on its contents and b) as to the use thereof under no circumstances whatsoever was it to be repeated, certainly not to be relayed by signal. Ultra was only transmitted on special high frequencies by the SCU to the SLU unit attached to the Commander. It came no other way and was only handled by them.

He described the tight security surrounding every scrap of paper that contained Ultra information:

> Once again our unit was in a somewhat 'no-man's land,' isolated in our bedrooms etc. Security as ever was No 1 priority. As our signals were not received through the usual links we were something apart. A very secret unit doing a job that was distinct from any other in the HQ. It should be pointed out however that it was always necessary for the SLU to make itself as unobtrusive as possible. Its function was to deliver to the commanding generals and their intelligence staff the material we were receiving direct from England on our own wireless link. This was the primary object of its operational performance. The signals were delivered by the hand of officers and it was their duty to see that they were then handed back. No recipient was allowed to 'slip them into their pockets,' so to speak.

The temptation to do precisely that was sometimes too much for senior officers to resist, and the job done by SLU members required considerable diplomacy. John Lamont found that problems could also arise with the adjutants and assistants of commanders, who had to be tactfully prevented from seeing the messages:

> We were on attachment to the army HQ and had responsibility for security of the unit and particularly for the security of the Ultra intelligence material fed to General Anderson. In this respect we were under the clear orders of Chiefs of Staff in London. This sometimes put us in some difficulties with a variety of majors and colonels who, of course, were not in our picture. Often they tried to pull rank on me, at that time a Flight Lieutenant.
>
> The most notable event was a brush with General Anderson himself. Our modus operandi was that we handed a message to Colonel Dawnay (Anderson's Number Two) and collected them for burning shortly afterwards. On one occasion I found that a very high priority message had not been returned, and saw Dawnay about this. He said that although he had asked Anderson for the message, he had decided to keep it. He also

said the General was going forward in the next few hours. This was obviously up to me as Dawnay refused to try again. Perspiring slightly I went to see Anderson and asked for the message to be returned to me for destruction. He categorically refused to hand it back. I was obliged to remind him of the vital need for security of the source, both in necessity to avoid compromising the information by precipitate action, and the physical existence of the message itself. He claimed it was perfectly safe with him. I was obliged to tell him that I was under strictest orders to burn the message and report direct to Chief of Staff if prevented from doing so. Anderson was a dour, taciturn Scot and with a very bad grace indeed pulled it out of his pocket and handed it to me.

Fortunately not everyone regarded Ultra signals as their personal property and most recognized that, if security were breached, the source of this war-winning intelligence might dry up:

As a contrast a similar matter occurred with General Alexander, who was just taking over the new 18 Group and was due in North Africa. We had high priority information addressed to him and handed it over to him. He wanted to take the message forward with him to Anderson's command post. I reminded him of the security vital to protect the source and that I had responsibility for destroying the physical message. His reaction was immediate and he was delighted that I had reminded him.

Like Alexander, the senior American General, Dwight Eisenhower, was polite and appreciative of the rules governing the use of Ultra. Squadron Leader SF Burley commented:

The requests to receive Ultra were so vital that we were providing all Commanders-in-Chief of both the army and the air force with an SLU attached to their headquarters. During the night, after a very busy day, we received a signal 'Ultra Eyes Only' for General Eisenhower from the Prime Minister. It was only to be delivered to the addressee himself. I took it along to his sleeping quarters, and having been stopped by the guard, was passed over to his G2 Intelligence Officer and was duly ushered into General Eisenhower's bedroom. A somewhat sleepy 5 Star Commanding General woke up to see one RAF officer with a slip of paper for him. He put on his glasses and read it, re-read it and thanked me and handed it back to me. This only goes to prove how much the material was appreciated. There was no question of a senior officer saying something to the effect – 'I'll take that and pass it on'. For one thing, we wouldn't let it out of our hand, and in this instance 'eyes only' meant what it said. We endeavoured as far as possible to be unobtrusive, but such was the importance of our work that entry to see Commanding Generals was never queried.

It seemed to be an almost universal experience that a commander would be delighted to receive a visit from an SLU officer, while his assistant – a man of high rank himself – was irritated at being bypassed and kept from knowing the contents of the messages that were delivered. Squadron Leader OB Reece recalled that:

All of the recipients were very appreciative of our service, indeed quite avid to receive Ultra. Our service to the Navy was limited and I suspect complementary to their own channel. However, such personal messages as came in for Admiral Cunningham were received by him with great courtesy. Also Air Marshal Tedder always received any 'personal only' messages with appreciation. However, Tedder's outer office assistant, you might say his 'doorkeeper', a certain Wing Commander, was anything but courteous. On one occasion, having unsuccessfully tried to get a 'personal only' message off me, when I came out of Tedder's office he said 'What shall I do with that tripe when it comes out of his waste-paper basket?' to which I replied, 'I do not think you will find the message in the Air Marshal's waste-paper basket, sir, but I do assure you that if I ever have a personal only message for you, I will make certain that nobody but you receive it.' In general I found a better welcome from the 'top brass' than from their underlings. It seemed as if bypassing them with personal messages resulted in disturbing the cathedral calm to which they liked to accustom themselves.

No doubt in the many cases that occurred similar to the above, higher ranks for SLU personnel would have much facilitated the presentation of Ultra. However, we did not sign on for an easy job and speaking personally I was never much impressed by rank, my own or anyone else's.

Reece found that the perspective – the historical overview – he gained on the war was more than adequate compensation for the monotony that often characterized his job:

Despite the long hours of prosaic drudgery entailed in providing a day and night Ultra service, I found the job fascinating. Unlike the average wartime job which confined the view to a minute fraction of the whole, Ultra provided a spectator like myself with a panoramic view of the entire war operation. Also, unlike the 'need to know' limits imposed by conventional intelligence, in Ultra one was able to see the start and finish of an operation, thus appreciating the value of one's contribution. For example, in the evening a signal about a tanker leaving Bari with fuel for Rommel is rushed to the customers and the following morning comes the news that the tanker is sunk, an immediate confirmation that one's vigilance and despatch have helped to put a nail in the coffin of the enemy's plans for Egypt.

Pursued after Alamein by Montgomery's much larger armoured force, the Afrika Korps had once again retreated westward. With America in the war, Allied troops (four divisions of the US First Army) had been landed at Tunis and blocked his way. He was not yet defeated – indeed he was able to beat the Americans in battle at the Kasserine Pass – but with hostile armies on two sides and Montgomery pressing hard from the east, with supplies disrupted and uncertain, and with control of the air in Allied hands, the Afrika Korps was doomed. By the summer of 1943 it had surrendered. The Eighth Army had pursued it 1,500 miles in just three months. The Allies took more than 150,000 prisoners.

As with much else in the war, the codebreakers were the first to know of important developments. A young woman at Bletchley Park remembered when confirmation arrived of the Axis withdrawal from North Africa:

In early 1943, I was on duty on the night shift alone. We were going through a sticky period; the Italian codes were making no sense. I decided to have one more go ... suddenly a message began to appear. I shouted for Leonard Hooper in the next room and he rushed in and I told him the message was making sense. He literally seized my paper, shouted 'You've done it! You've broken it!' and tore out of the room and down the passage to Josh Cooper. There was great excitement that night, for the message was that the Italian air force was preparing to leave North Africa. The news was radioed to the RAF in Egypt and subsequently night fighters shot down almost all the Italian transport planes. For this breakthrough, I was summoned to Josh Cooper's room and congratulated.

On 20 May 1943, the Allied victory parade took place in Tunis.

SICILY AND ITALY

Once North Africa had been won by the Allies, the war was to be taken to Axis territory. The Italian satellite islands of Lampedusa and Pantelleria were seized without difficulty. The next island objective of Allied planners was Sicily. Code-named 'Operation Husky', this task would involve American, British and Commonwealth troops in a combination of airborne and seaborne forces. The invasion would be launched from Alexandria in the first days of July 1943. Once Sicily was cleared, the Allies would cross the Straits of Messina and invade the Italian mainland. For the first time, one of the enemy powers would be fighting on the soil of its own homeland.

Winterbotham, who was visiting the Mediterranean theatre at the time, stressed the role of Ultra in the execution of this plan:

I found that at all the main SLU stations a great deal of high-level traffic was being sent over the SLU channels by the chiefs of staff in London to Eisenhower and Alexander, and also between the various commanders-in-chief in the Mediterranean area. This was primarily because so much of the planning for Sicily and Italy was based on Ultra information and any discussion or change of plan based on intelligence had rightly to be sent over our own channel; added to which the top brass as well as Winston Churchill found our channel quicker than the normal signals organisation, and its maximum secrecy was useful when personalities had to be discussed. The SLUs were, in consequence, working flat out.

He also observed that the SLUs were now an accepted, essential and greatly appreciated part of the entourage of the senior commanders, who had become not only accustomed to a regular supply of information but also almost entirely dependent on it:

> All the SLUs were now old hands at the game. They had worked out methods of keeping on the air even in times of rapid movement, since they told me that the commanders didn't like being without their Ultra even for ten minutes.

The staff had to work round the clock to process a workload that could reach as much as 200 enemy signals a day. Some of these signals had given away the location of the headquarters of General Kesselring (Commander-in-Chief Mediterranean) in Sicily, which was in a hotel at Taormina. As a result, the RAF shortly afterwards destroyed the building in an air raid. Though their intended victim was elsewhere at the time, a number of his subordinates were killed.

Ultra made an immense, immeasurable contribution to Operation Husky because it described in exact detail the enemy positions and revealed that neither the Germans nor the Italians knew when, where or even if the attack would come. It showed that Hitler shared this uncertainty, and therefore that it was unlikely that reinforcements would be sent to Sicily in time to have any effect. As a result of this intelligence, Allied paratroops were able to capture strategic points that prevented German panzer units, held in reserve in the centre of the island to be rushed to any invasion beach, from doing so.

When it arrived off the coast on 10 July, the invasion fleet (which had been spotted only the previous day by German observers) had achieved surprise, and thus tactical advantage. Though Kesselring was an able commander and signalled for reinforcements as soon as he knew that the Allies were about to land, it was too late. John Lamont was with an SLU that went ashore after the initial assault:

We had very strict orders not to be taken prisoner! This was possibly the first time an SLU had to go in on a landing from the sea in a landing craft. It was almost certainly the first time an SLU unit had been attached to General Patton, who was well known as a very adventurous type. He was considered to have a certain contempt for the word security in terms understood in SLU. However, it was very good to have a session with our chiefs, and we acquired the necessary equipment to destroy our documents and w/t equipment at short notice.

On the morning of the 15th July, we located it and reported to General Patton at Gela. Despite prior warnings that the General was a real rough type, I was surprised at the very cordial reception we had. He said: 'Mighty pleased to have you British boys come along with me.' He introduced me to Colonel Koch [his Assistant Chief of Staff] and to [General] Bradley and several of his Corps Commanders. Koch arranged a camp site for us alongside his tent and we discussed the security arrangements to be made in the present and anticipated moves of the command post for future operations. We moved our unit up and located tents and vehicles on the area.

Several units of panzer troops and parachutists were ordered to Sicily, but it took valuable days, and even weeks, for them to arrive. General Patton knew, through the efforts of Lamont and his colleagues, that the enemy did not yet have the necessary strength to oppose him and he drove his armoured units across the island to Palermo, reaching the Straits on 8 August. Less than ten days later the conquest of Sicily was complete. Winterbotham wrote that:

> In Sicily Patton, who was made aware by ULTRA of the precise position of the German panzer units and the direction in which they were moving after the Allied landings, slipped round their flank and got to Messina almost before the Germans could get across to Italy.

The capture of Italian territory precipitated a collapse of extraordinary speed. Italian soldiers had been expelled from the African colonies and defeated in the desert. They were fighting and dying in terrible conditions on the Eastern Front. At home, civilians were enduring rationing and air raids. War-weariness and disillusionment with Fascism were widespread. Many Italians saw the arrival of Allied troops as a signal that the war was lost. To avoid the devastation of their country and its priceless artistic heritage, an immediate end to the conflict was necessary.

On 25 July, while the Allies were still fighting in Sicily, Mussolini was dismissed by Italy's king, Victor Emmanuel, from his position as prime minister. He was also removed from office by the Fascist Grand Council, placed under arrest and sent to the far north of the country. His successor was a senior military man, Marshal Pietro Badoglio. Trusted by both Allies and Italians because of a long history of aversion to Fascism, Badoglio sought to sign an armistice as soon as possible. The necessary approaches were quickly made – through the medium of a captured Special Operations Executive radio operator. Italy was not only to leave the Axis camp but to join the war against its former comrades. It took some weeks to negotiate conditions, but peace was finally signed on 8 September, the day on which the Allies crossed to mainland Italy. John McCaffery, a member of SOE, recalled the circumstances. A colleague of his, a fluent Italian speaker, was parachuted into Lake Como by British aircraft on their way to bomb Milan. No one had appreciated, however, the interest taken by local people in these operations, and thus the agent's chances of making an inconspicuous arrival were extremely slim. As McCaffery wrote:

> It looked a fine plan on paper. But first of all there was bright moonlight, and seemingly, many people living on the shores of the lake had the habit of turning out to see the Milan bombings as if it was a fireworks display. Dick and his parachute therefore floated down to the water before a large fascinated audience.

Quickly arrested, he spent three weeks in captivity before being summoned to an unusual task:

> When the King and Badoglio decided to sue for peace, they thought that initial radio contact would be faster and more secure than attempting to approach through emissaries. Incredibly, using state radio technical experts, they failed to make the contact they desired; and then someone remembered the British parachutist and his W/T set dropped into Lake Como. Dick was fetched poste haste and asked whether he would

oblige them. He replied that most certainly he could, and to the astonishment of the experts, who had viewed his small set with incredulity, within half an hour he had done so.

It was thus over Dick's little W/T set that the first Italian peace overtures were made, and his ducking [in the lake] had been justified on a bigger and more historic scale than we had ever imagined.

Hitler at once sent more German divisions to the north of Italy, to hold any Allied advance up the peninsula, but also to be prepared for an attack on the Balkans, which the Führer considered likely. He created a new army, comprising both reinforcements and formations already in the region, commanded by Rommel. During this period of frantic reorganization, the signals sent by Enigma told Allied commanders everything they needed to know about the strength and dispositions of the German units.

The Germans were expected to evacuate the south of the country and withdraw toward Rome. Movement was slow and German divisions were still in the south when the Allied landings took place, which meant that resistance was fiercer than had been hoped. The landings were carried out first in Calabria, then farther north at Salerno, south of Naples. Opposition there was insufficient to stop the invaders getting inland. The geography of the country had made it comparatively easy for the defenders to create the 'Gustav Line', a protective wall across the narrow peninsula from the Tyrrhenian Sea to the Adriatic. Italy's long coast, of course, made it possible for the invaders to bypass this. While troops already ashore drove north toward the Gustav Line and the capital, another force came ashore in January 1944 at Anzio – halfway up the boot of Italy and a short distance from Rome. Within this region would be fought the two most significant battles of the campaign, at Anzio and Monte Cassino.

Alexander may initially have been pleased at progress, but he was to have little cause for long-term satisfaction. Ultra had suggested to the Allies that they need not expect fierce opposition, and they had got ashore without difficulty. The failure of General Mark Clark, the American commander, to follow through by moving swiftly inland was to squander this advantage. The Germans counterattacked with vigour and almost succeeded in wiping out the beachhead. The Allies were to spend four months clinging to their toehold on the beaches, protected largely by the firepower of the ships offshore. The Italian campaign was to be slow going.

The troops farther south had troubles of their own. Monte Cassino was an ancient monastery set on a mountaintop that commanded the road to Rome. Such a setting for defence could not be ignored and the Germans had fortified it. On 12 May, in the middle of the night, the assault on it began. It was suicidal. Though Allied airpower quickly reduced the venerable buildings to rubble, the defenders had dug into the surrounding rock and were making the most of the mountain's protection. Any waves of attackers fighting their way up the steep slopes had little hope of avoiding the raking artillery and machine-gun fire that poured down from above. Days and nights passed, and still the ruins held out.

In London, Churchill was becoming anxious. The Germans' successful containment of the Anzio beachhead had been of immense value to their morale. Now Cassino was proving another debacle. Churchill needed the campaign speeded up – and Rome taken at once – because Operation Overlord, the long-awaited stab at northern Europe that would open the final chapter in Germany's defeat, was scheduled to begin in early June. To capture Rome would, in a symbolic sense at least, suggest that the Italian campaign was won.

Winterbotham remembered the anxious days during which he, and Churchill, followed the progress of the armies:

On May the 13th I had a telephone call from the Prime Minister. He asked that I meet him at his flat that evening at 9 p.m. and would I bring round all signals dealing with the Cassino front. It was a cold evening for May and the Prime Minister was sitting in his boiler suit deep in his green leather chair in front of a good fire. He looked tired. I had given him the various small details of the fighting which had come in during the afternoon. When he said 'Is that all?' I had to say that I was afraid it was so. We went across to the map room where the few alterations I had brought over were flagged up, but Churchill was obviously puzzled and disappointed. In his usual courteous manner he thanked me for coming over and then, with a broad smile, he said, 'See that I get anything more first thing in the morning. I think you will find there will be something of interest.' It was now late but I phoned the watch at Bletchley and warned them to keep their eyes skinned. It came through about 3 a.m. and Mrs Owen's knock on my office door with a welcome cup of coffee. The French Moroccan troops had scaled the mountains south of Cassino. Kesselring had reported to Hitler that 'the whole Cassino line was now in danger'. That day signals reported to Berlin that now both the British and the Americans were gaining some ground. On the fifteenth Kesselring sent a signal to Hitler reporting a breakthrough by another strong French force over the massive Monti Aurunci which dominated the Liri valley and the supply routes to the Cassino line. On the sixteenth came reports from Kesselring of the successes of the British and Polish forces around Cassino, and then on the seventeenth came the one we had been waiting for: Kesselring ordered the evacuation of the entire Cassino front, since, as he said, the French had penetrated twenty-five miles behind the German lines. Bletchley was in good form and Churchill, Alexander and the US chiefs of staff in Washington had it within a few minutes of its despatch by Kesselring.

Cassino was captured, though at a terrible cost in lives and destruction.

Having broken out from Anzio, General Clark disregarded instructions to cut off the retreat of Kesselring's troops by moving east. Instead he headed north for Rome, 30 miles away, in a vainglorious desire to be first to enter the city. Kesselring had decided not to defend it, thus saving considerable bloodshed as well as the ruination of what is perhaps the world's most culturally important city, and the Allies knew this through reading the signals that passed between him and his chief. They marched into the Eternal City on 4 June 1944, 48 hours before D-Day. Winterbotham was scathing about the chances that had been squandered:

> It was Mark Clark who, in that dreary slogging match up through Italy, three times did not use the opportunities ULTRA had provided, and which Alexander had planned for him: first at Anzio, then after the fall of Cassino and later north of Rome, to cut off and surround Kesselring's armies. It was Alexander who, knowing the precise distribution of German troops at Cassino, planned the surprise attack over the mountains and it was France's General Juin who so brilliantly carried it out.

To reach Rome the Allies had passed through two further German defensive barriers – the Adolf Hitler Line and the Caesar Line – which Kesselring had chosen not to contest. The Germans withdrew northward to a further position, the Gothic Line, which ran from Pisa across to Rimini over the Apennines. Here they intended to make a stand, and defences were rapidly constructed. Though many British military clerks and other administrative staff were to remain in the capital serving the Allied Control Commission, the fighting troops continued their trek northward, and with them went the SLU. Miss L Addey explained that travel in the slow-moving convoys was a dispiriting experience, and efficient organization was vital:

> A rapid advance by road was very complicated because of the vast amount of traffic that a mechanised army needed to maintain itself, and this put a great deal of strain on the existing roads. When a unit like ours moved with all its vehicles, between 90 and 150, very careful timing of convoys was required to avoid a snarl-up of traffic. In fact, the problem was almost like railway signalling in the rush hour.
>
> There had to be traffic control points every 10 miles or so to ensure that convoys were on time, and to make alterations if they were not. There had to be signposting of roads, police, guides and so forth. Provision also had to be made for recovery posts and vehicles so that damaged trucks and tanks could be got off the road. In addition, there was usually a mobile recovery patrol and this was as busy as the AA on a Bank Holiday Sunday. Recovery was a REME [Royal Electrical & Mechanical Engineers] responsibility and the Brigade REME vehicles travelled with our convoy to deal with breakdowns.

Kesselring's retreat was ragged, and had the Allies chased their enemy more decisively they could have got between the German armies. Clark, once again, was too hesitant to seize the opportunity. The Germans fell back on the Gothic Line and waited.

Ultra remained as important, and as forthcoming, as ever. The traffic between Kesselring in the Apeninnes and Hitler in Berlin had included an order from the Führer that the Futa Pass, one of the few paths through the mountain range, was to be defended (in the phrase that Hitler had used since Stalingrad) to 'the last man and the last bullet'. Armed with the information that defences would be concentrated there, Clark's Fifth Army was able to launch its attack through a nearby pass instead. Though fighting was heavy, the American armies had enough momentum to push their way through into Lombardy. The last and most formidable barrier had been crossed. Though Kesselring appealed for reinforcements, he received in return the demand to release men from his own armies for service in France, where the advance of Anglo-American forces made the need for men far more urgent. Continuing his retreat north Kesselring, as he had done in Rome, spared Florence the agony of defence and therefore destruction.

The Italians had switched, in a moment as it seemed, from enemy to ally and for members of the Anglo-American forces this could create difficult situations. AL Thompson, attached to General Alexander's headquarters, was concerned at the presence there of a distinguished guest who roamed at will among the secrets. This was Victor Emmanuel, still for the moment King of Italy (he would abdicate shortly afterwards). Howard recalled:

> It was [at General Alexander's villa on Lake Bolsena] that the late King spent some time staying with Alexander under a nom de guerre as General X. They had erected a nissen hut war room in which maps based on our material were displayed. It was guarded day and night by a duty Intelligence Officer who was in the Ultra picture. I may have been too security-minded, but seeing the King wandering about everywhere and bearing in mind that no-one not directly involved could see our material I wondered whether he was allowed to do so. I sent a personal signal to London asking whether General X was allowed to see our material. It took quite a long time before I got a reply and the answer was no. It was only at the end of the war that they told me I had got all the security services running around in circles as no-one had told them who this general really was.

Winston Churchill paid a visit to the Italian front to see the conditions there for himself, and for a few weeks Thompson found himself acting as SLU officer to the prime minister. Churchill, like most of the military commanders, treated Ultra staff with particular kindness, perhaps because he knew that they would receive no adequate recognition for the contribution they had made:

> After a somewhat idyllic stay at Bolsena we went forward again and made camp in a great feudal estate a few miles south of

Siena. It was here that Winston Churchill stayed with us for about three weeks. He was actually living in a villa close to the camp and I began to give him the full service. He was very pernickety about the way our signals were presented to him and they had to be typed in capital letters in three-lined spacing. I think my face must have fitted as he was very friendly to me from the start and grew increasingly so as the days went by. It may have been of course that I gave him everything he wanted and there was never a slip-up. I remember one occasion when he put his arm around my shoulders and dragged me to a large wall-map saying: 'Come along my friend and tell me how the war's going.' Another night I had to find him to deliver a message and discovered him in a small marquee having dinner with Alex and a very distinguished company indeed. I gave my name to the Warrant Officer at the entrance and Winston turned round in his chair and said: 'Come in and sit by me my friend, get a chair for the Squadron Leader, and what are you going to have to drink?' So there I was plonked down beside him on his left hand side at the top of the table as one of the party. I already knew quite a few of these people through previous contacts and Winston turned to me and said: 'I don't think you know the Chief of the Imperial General Staff, Alan Brook,' and I replied, 'No, sir, I haven't had that honour,' whereupon Sir Alan rose to his feet and solemnly shook my hand across the table. It was a marvellous gesture by Winston. I think I stayed for some considerable time before I made my excuses because I was listening to a most fascinating high-powered policy debate.

Though clearly Kesselring's absolute defeat was now only a matter of time, his armies remained dangerous until the end of hostilities. He negotiated their surrender on 2 May 1945, only a week before the war in Europe ended, and his forces at that time numbered almost a million men. This was the largest army in history to capitulate.

The Italian Campaign could not have been won without the information provided by the SLUs. It had proved so fundamentally vital to Allied chiefs that Winterbotham was later to write:

Not only the commanders in the field, but also Churchill, Roosevelt, and the Allied chiefs of staff had all the cards in the pack spread out on the table face upwards.

By that time, however, most of the codebreakers had long since departed. The war in Italy had clearly been winding down for some months and attention had shifted to other theatres. Principally this meant the Far East, where resources were being assembled for the final showdown with Japan. SLU members were posted back to Britain for retraining, or were sent direct to join units in India and Australia. Flight Lieutenant (Josh) Reynolds wrote:

> November 1944 and the situation in Italy was gradually closing on the enemy and on the other side of the world attention was concentrating on Japan. Work for the large SLUs in Italy had decreased considerably so we were not surprised when a call came asking for volunteers to strengthen the SLUs in India and South East Asia Command and also Australia and the South Pacific area now that the Americans and Australians had gone over to the offensive.

Captain JN Howard's last memory of Italy was of a trophy he carried with him on the journey home – a highly appropriate souvenir:

> I have a hazy recollection of flying back to London with the innards of an Enigma machine which was found at German army headquarters when they bunked out of Italy. I remember something about fears that had been expressed that the day settings had been mucked up by a crowd of sergeants who had found it. It seems they had been using it to gamble on like a fruit machine but happily no damage had been done and the back-room boys at home must have found it very useful.

6

THE RESISTANCE

In no previous war, and in no other theatre during this war, have resistance forces been so closely harnessed to the main military effort.[i]

At 4:00 a.m. on May 10, 1940, Queen Wilhelmina of the Netherlands awakened her only daughter, Princess Juliana, with the words: 'They have come.' She did not need to elaborate on who 'they' were; she had been expecting the Nazis for a long time. In this she was almost alone in Holland. Even after Austria, Czechoslovakia, Poland, Denmark, Norway – the entire Dutch nation refused to believe that we would be next. When nevertheless the war engulfed us, we didn't have the slightest idea what to do about it.[ii]

The suddenness and the unprovoked nature of the German Blitzkrieg in 1940 gave its victims no opportunity to reflect or react, which was of course deliberate. There had been little that trained and organized troops, let alone civilians, could do to halt the juggernaut. With western Europe under German control from June 1940, the armies of France, Belgium, the Netherlands, Denmark and Norway had either been defeated or simply disarmed. Their heads of state were under house arrest (as in Belgium), had escaped to England (as was the case with the rulers of Norway and Holland), or had come to terms with the occupiers (as in France). Their populations, subjected to strict and increasingly draconian regulations, were cowed. An uneasy 'peace' settled over Europe and in many respects life could continue as before (the time of hardship – hunger, air raids, conscription for forced labour and German reprisals – were to come later). Erik Hazelhoff, soon to depart for England to join the exiled Dutch forces, outlined the options facing those who remained:

[i] Dwight Eisenhower
[ii] Erik Hazelhoff

Except for the Jews, the choice of existence for every Hollander
lay between extremes. He could either live in safety and comfort
by complying with the authorities, or in mortal danger by defying
them. In the latter case you enjoyed life quite normally, in your
home, with your friends, in your job, on the beach, at the movies
and ballgames and parties, until something went wrong and you
were beaten, kicked, and sometimes shot to death. And once in
trouble, you were on your own.

Naturally, there were many in these lands who wished to continue the
fight. Largely young men, they could attempt to reach Britain and enlist in
the armed forces there, or they could remain at home, organize themselves
into clandestine units and carry out as many acts of subterfuge, espionage
or harassment as were offered by circumstances.

This resistance did not begin at full strength. It built up slowly (the best
known of the underground armies, the French Maquis, did not come into
being until 1943) as the harshness of German policies took an increasing
toll on the conquered peoples. Its numbers swelled in response to the
setbacks suffered by German armies in the field, whether at Stalingrad or
in Normandy, just as defiance of the regime in Germany itself increased
after these events.

Communications were a vital part of any resistance organization. London
was the source of most necessities, whether weapons, money, medical
supplies or military advisers, and therefore any cell that wished to be effective
needed to be able to contact the Allies by wireless. Because German experts
could easily listen in (they would be hunting for the transmitter), messages
had to be encoded and the resistance could not function without men and
women who possessed first-rate communications skills. Britain's codebreakers
would play a major role in the success of the resistance movements.

Those movements had two enemies: the occupying power and their own
compatriots who collaborated with that power – and who often proved
more ruthless and dangerous. Resistance actions varied in character from
the deliberate misdirecting of German soldiers to the destruction of railway
bridges, and members ranged from conservative, monarchist patriots to
outright Communists. In a country with a small population such as
Norway, the resistance units acted from much the same shared motives. In
France or Italy, the underground forces were a wildly disparate collection
of social and political groups who often had nothing in common except a

desire to defeat the Axis and who did not trust each other enough to coordinate their efforts. A British officer, Major DE Longe, recalled that:

> Anyone in France seemed able to form a centre of resistance provided he was willing and able to get followers, and there were scattered groups all over the country of various political creeds and formed for numerous reasons. The largest group was the FFI [French Forces of the Interior] which was well organized and in constant contact with HQ in London.

Men in specific occupations frequently found that their circumstances made them well suited to carrying out undercover work. Priests and pastors in country districts, for instance, often became adept at working as couriers because they were able to visit houses all over their parish without arousing suspicion. Men who maintained communications also had obvious advantages, as another British officer, Captain CA Watney, explained:

> Railwaymen, PTT [post and telecommunications] and Roads and Bridges workers were quite numerous in the ranks of the 'Armée Secrète.' They were in many sectors the real backbone.

Men and women going about their business in occupied countries could be invaluable sources of information regarding the enemy's numbers, equipment, methods and movements, and many were willing to perform such low-level espionage. Means were devised by which the results of their observations could be relayed to London. Groups of *résistants*, though they might sometimes be unreliable and difficult to control, could carry out general acts of nuisance or specific acts of sabotage that would 'hit the enemy where it hurt', such as disabling transport or factories that made war materials.

In Quercy, a district in central France, the infrastructure for an active unit was put in place within a few months of the Germans' arrival. Captain Watney described the arrangements:

> On November 20, 1940, Etienne Verlhac went to the central telegraph office in Cahors to meet Raymond Picard, who was in charge of all transmissions there. Verlhac had already had a visitor from London, and it was decided to set up a communications network. At this time the

first job was to find reliable men who were well placed to distribute news and orders and to obtain vital information. By the end of 1940 they had 12 men doing just this.

At the centre of this work in Cahors was Raymond and in Paris his pal Henri Chapuis. By the combined efforts of this group calls and correspondence to and from the Resistance was kept from the authorities and, on the other hand, important information was passed on about the enemy's intentions. Officials of the prefectures, of the larger 'mairies' and of the army were under surveillance. All official telegraphic messages were intercepted and passed on, and those to the 'combat troops' kept safe and delivered. Picard himself developed the French radio in the service of the Resistance. His old boss and friend François Deveze took on the national aspect of this service.

The orders were to 'monitor all emissions from Vichy, and all orders given to the administrative authorities. To make for presentation to the officers of the Resistance sets which would more readily receive transmissions from London. To reduce, and if possible suppress the noisy interference with the radio broadcasts of "France Libre".'

Picard was ideally situated for this job and his official vehicles enabled him to travel freely throughout the region. He could and did make regular contact with his colleagues in neighbouring districts. He was therefore charged with this responsibility.

In one of the cellars at the house of Mme Almus at Belaye were stored the radios and transmitters and other technical equipment for the combat units. Jean Lagarde and his wife were given the job of delivering these because they had a van with a false floor, specially designed, of course.

The success of the resistance movements often depended on geography: ideally, they needed remote terrain in which they could hide. Norway, Greece, Italy and much of France enjoyed these advantages. Denmark, Belgium, Luxembourg and the Netherlands did not. Erik Hazelhoff joined the Dutch Resistance and explained the difficulties caused by this lack of cover:

The German occupation killed more people in Holland than in any other country in Western Europe. One reason stood out: there was nowhere to go. Squeezed between Germany and the

North Sea, our country lay farthest from the neutral sanctuaries of World War II – Sweden, Switzerland, and Spain. Within this political isolation no area was less suited for a resistance movement. Small, flat, highly cultivated, intensely populated, it offered no natural hiding places. No room here for the familiar features of the 'underground' – the safe redoubt in swamp or mountain, the hidden cave, the band of heavily armed desperadoes, the campfire meetings. The coast stretched straight and bare as a speedway – no hidden coves for sneak approaches by Allied submarines, as in Norway. The land, densely populated, lay open and observed – no improvised air-strips marked with flashlights for fast pick-ups by RAF planes, as in France. The only two-way contact with the free world existed via wireless set, a deadly short cut to the firing squad. Holland's secret struggle took place in cafes full of people, quiet board rooms, cellars, busy shipyards, dark city streets, and always under the only cover available: everyday life.

In spite of all the difficulties they faced, networks of agents were established throughout occupied Europe. They were coordinated and supplied with both equipment and trained leaders from Britain. Though they would often choose their own missions and targets, they might also carry out missions directed from England by nationals who had been given the requisite preparation abroad, as happened in 1942 when two Czech agents attempted to assassinate Reinhard Heydrich in Prague. Their main function during the war's early stages was to keep the Allies informed regarding enemy troop movements, to pinpoint targets for the Royal Air Force and to operate escape routes for shot-down aircrew.

SECRET ARMY: THE SOE

To carry on this clandestine war, Britain organized a secret army of its own: SOE, or Special Operations Executive. This recruited and trained men and women to infiltrate occupied territories and work with the local resistance units – a job that required not only physical courage but a fairly high level of skill in sabotage, unarmed combat and, crucially, communications, in which the use of codes would prove essential.

The operatives needed fluency in languages, and sufficient mental and physical toughness to face possible torture and imprisonment. The function of the SOE, as well as the type (and motivation) of those who volunteered, was explained by Captain Watney, who belonged to it:

> Churchill knew that [it] would be difficult to start, and there could be no question of creating a centralised organisation in France which could eventually be at the mercy of a coup d'état by the German forces which could enable them to crush the resistance at one blow.
>
> It was, therefore, in June 1941 that the British premier decided to put on the ground a service whose role would be to enrol secret agents charged with infiltrating wherever possible the occupied countries, to aid and co-ordinate the resistance movement, to arm and help them. He gave the order 'to set Europe on fire', to mount operations with specially trained troops to develop a reign of terror such as would make life untenable for the occupying forces, to light and fan the flame of revolt. This was the basis of S.O.E.

Watney recalled that the range of qualities, including circumstances of birth as well as personal abilities, made recruits very difficult to find:

> In the beginning recruitment of agents posed many problems. First of all they had to have a perfect knowledge of the French language and a wide knowledge of France itself. Again, only volunteers were acceptable, but it was not feasible to advertise for candidates! It was not possible to accept volunteers from those who had escaped from the French forces to England. This was because they had a duty to join the Free French forces, and it would be wrong to tempt them to do otherwise. There was also the fear that there might be some Nazi sympathisers among them who might betray their comrades. It was therefore not until early 1944 that the SOE finally accepted agents who had already proved themselves as sort of 'associate agents'. These were for the most part men and women of British nationality who had been brought up in, or had spent many years in France, or were people of mixed French and English parentage and who possessed dual nationality. This choice

was the more happy since the first were Francophiles of long standing, the latter had two countries to defend and therefore they had the conviction and will to work for a final victory.

Even when suitable individuals were available, they might not survive the lengthy conditioning process:

There were no rules, no tradition on which to base a system of secret agents, so it was worked out piece by piece. Colonel [Maurice] Buckmaster (placed in command of SOE) and his aides put in train a programme to prepare us for the difficult role we had assumed. The 'schools' were situated in diverse regions of England and Scotland. Generally they had as base one of the magnificent mansions in isolated countryside. The 'candidates', chosen by personal contact and having volunteered, were received and interrogated by an officer who, if he appeared to meet the standards required, then sent him on to a house near Guildford to pass a series of physical and psychological tests. Later, assuming he stood the strain, he was sent to join his comrades on the banks of a Scottish loch. There, in the solitudes of a vast domain surrounded by woods and mountains, he would follow the first stage of training.

Followed by their 'teachers', and under their direction, the 'candidates' would learn the use of arms, sabotage, unarmed combat, judo, use of explosives, the means of forming and directing a 'commando' to accomplish a mission, and to organise a military operation. They learnt to poach, to scale a wall, to camouflage and to move quickly and silently by night or day, to surmount obstacles, to resist cold, hunger, fatigue.

At the end of the first stage, those selected were sent to the parachute school. They were sent to other schools where they learned other specialities, such as secret radio operation, sending of 'parcels,' sabotage, how to blow a safe or a lock, send a message without being seen, and to enter by fraud a military building without detection.

The use of the French language was compulsory at all times, and they had to live and behave, dress, eat, and write as if they were French. Even their teeth fillings were checked, and if necessary changed to French fillings. They were taught to stand interrogation, even against threats and brutality. Only after passing this rigorous training were they despatched on secret missions on French soil.

Though these criteria seem formidably narrow, a number of members of SOE seem to have arrived there through the traditional British route of the 'old boy network'. They were, in other words, recruited informally in the context of a social situation because they appeared to have the general qualities that fitted the organization's needs. Such methods often proved surprisingly successful. Major DE Longe remembered how he and a friend (John Houseman):

> ... became bored with the Phoney War and while on leave in January 1941 we lunched in London with Lt. Gen. Sir George Cory KBE, CB, DSO, who had helped me to enlist. He was at that time Inspector General of Allied Contingents. He listened sympathetically to our tale of boredom and offered to give our names to a certain Brigadier who wanted young bloods. Thus we came in contact with Brigadier Colin Gubbins ... and soon we became two of the 'earlier birds' in the Special Operations Executive.

He described their subsequent experiences, which suggest that, given the speed with which a complex system of schools was being set up and recruits passed through it, there might be no more than a few weeks' accumulation of knowledge separating teacher and pupil:

> We were given a very intensive commando training at Lochailort and Arisaig in Inverness-shire and were then posted as Chief Instructors in guerilla warfare and sabotage at schools established in large country houses in England to train potential members of the underground in various occupied countries ...
> John Houseman went to train Poles who were to prove such gallant men behind the lines in their own country and I went to train Norwegians and Danes.
> After some weeks John and I applied for and were granted leave to qualify as parachutists in order to have a better chance of accompanying our trainees on operations. We did our jumps

at Ringway Aerodrome, Manchester in April 1941. As I lay on the ground after my qualifying jump I was offered one of two postings. To Canada to instruct at the school to be opened there, or to West Africa to train natives to operate against Vichy French territory. I chose the latter and sailed in May 1941 ...

CODES AND THE SOE

Communications were a major and vital part of the world that the SOE recruits would inhabit, and skill in using codes was as important as the ability to operate wireless equipment. The nature of codes and ciphers had to be thoroughly understood, for any mistake in interpreting a secret message could have disastrous consequences. A syllabus for trainees in September 1943 explained the different aspects of this subject, providing a useful insight into the education of agents for communication in the field:

ESSENTIAL REQUIREMENTS
a) The Need for Security.
Discovery of coded documents or secret ink preparations place possessor in a very suspicious position.
Essential to destroy all paper used in enciphering or deciphering messages, and all materials used in to reduce this risk to a minimum.
b) The Need for Secrecy.
No one except the actual correspondents should know the system, keywords or ink used.
An organizer could make different arrangements with each member of his organization. He would know all the systems, but each member should know no other than his own.
c) The Need for Care.
One error may result in the message being indecipherable.
General carelessness may arouse suspicion in the mind of the censor.
d) The Need for Concealment.
As stated above, the fact that a secret message is passing must be concealed from the enemy. This will usually be done by the code system itself. But special papers may help a person carrying a message to conceal it. Practise writing on thin paper.

<u>CODES AND CIPHERS</u>
SAMPLE CODE WORDS.

a) General. A simple word code is the arrangement by conventions of certain words or phrases to mean other words or phrases. Only a limited variety of messages can be sent by such a code as this.

b) When used. Telegraph. Telephone. Personal advertisements.

c) Examples In a telegram: NO NEWS RECEIVED FOR AGES ARE YOU WELL might be agreed to mean: CARRY ON WITH THE SCHEME AS ARRANGED

On the telephone: Heavily veiled and guarded language would usually be sufficient, such as 'usual time and place;' but code names can also be used, e.g. the word 'cat' can be a word of warning that a third person has just entered the room.

In a personal advertisement: 'Gold ring lost in Café de la Paix, night of 24 Sept; if found, please return to 6 Rue de la Croix,' might be a general warning to all members not to visit the organizer until further notice.

INNOCENT LETTER CODES.

3) General. A code which is concealed within a communication which looks completely innocent.

4) When used. To send a message through the post within the country and from the field to headquarters.

PLAYFAIR CIPHER.

a) General. A substitution cipher in itself easily susceptible of solution.

b) When used. To conceal a message in clear which is itself to be concealed in an innocent letter. The combination intensely difficult to break.

DOUBLE TRANSPOSITION CIPHER.

a) General. A 'straight' cipher, i.e. a cipher that looks like a cipher. Very secure if proper precautions taken.

b) When used. Transmissions by w/t.

c) Message carried by courier.

d) Used in conjunction with invisible ink, e.g. through post.

e) As a military cipher in the event of an armed rising.

Leo Marks, a scholarly young man who already possessed an ability to work out codes with or without the assistance of 'cribs', undertook this specialist education, and shortly afterward was lecturing on the subject to audiences of young women at Grendon Underwood, one of the SOE outstations. He gave them examples to decipher, including a poem:

I asked them to help break the code as if they were the Gestapo, I showed them what enemy cryptographers would look for if they had intercepted the message. I began to anagram and asked them to join in. They were shy at first – but soon suggestions were being called out from all round the room and those from 'the gigglers' were among the brightest.

It was oversimplified, of course, but it gave them the 'feel' of codebreaking, and the principles they were shown were absolutely valid. I let them finish the message themselves. The clear-text read: 'From the coders of Grendon to the agents of SOE. THERE SHALL BE NO SUCH THING AS AN INDECIPHERABLE MESSAGE.'

I knew I would be overloading them if I continued but I couldn't resist it. I wanted them to see how the enemy would now mathematically reconstruct the five words on which the message had been encoded. It took them twenty minutes to recover those words but no one could identify the rest of the poem ...

Two days later they sent me a message on the teleprinter: 'WE HAVE BROKEN OUR FIRST INDECIPHERABLE. THE CODERS OF GRENDON.'

Early in 1942, some months after candidates began to receive training at SOE schools, the number of recruits to the French section was expanded by including women. The work was self-evidently dangerous and it was not to be assumed that educated, bilingual young ladies would be able to work with the peasants who made up much of the rural French Resistance. However, women were as liable as men to have the necessary background, abilities and motivation, and their employment also carried decided advantages, as a later article in the *Sunday Times* by Jerrard Tickell in June 1949 explained:

The question was considered from every angle, and it was agreed that they would have certain practical advantages over men agents. All men were automatically suspect when travelling, whereas women could move about France rather more freely. This rendered them especially suitable for the job of courier or radio operator. The feminine 'cover story' was easier to devise. From women could be expected a great deal of subtlety.

Out of a final total of 13,000 SOE volunteers, about 3,000 would be female. Once they had been through the necessary schooling, they proved as adept as their male colleagues. In view of the fact that the most famous members of SOE were to be women, this proved to be a momentous decision.

Leo Marks described the workings of the communications department:

> SOE's code department and teleprinter rooms occupied the whole of a mews building at the back of Michael House [the headquarters of Marks & Spencer on Baker Street]. The Baker Street code room was essentially a main-line code room. Its function was to communicate with embassies and base stations around the world using code books and one-time pads which provided the highest possible level of security and were cryptographically unbreakable.

Putting their theoretical knowledge to use under 'real' conditions demanded versatility:

> The agents in the field had to use their codes in conditions of difficulty and danger which were unique in the history of coding. Their traffic was handled in that main-line code room by anyone available to do it. The volume of main-line traffic allowed no specialisation. Each girl had to be a multi-purpose coder, able in theory to switch from main-line traffic to agents' at a moment's notice, though the system called for very different aptitudes, attitudes and disciplines.

SOE used an intriguing system to help agents retain vital information:

> The agents were using poems for their codes. Or famous quotations. Or anything they could easily remember. This concept of clandestine coding had been adopted by SOE because of a theory, traditional in Intelligence, that if an agent were

caught and searched it was better security if his code were in his head. The slightest mistake in the coding, a second's lapse of concentration, would render the entire message indecipherable. Frequently as much as 20 percent of SOE's traffic could not be decoded due to agent's errors. Whenever SOE received an indecipherable the agent responsible was instructed to re-encode it and have it ready for his next transmission ...

To encode a message an agent had to choose five words at random from his poem and give each letter of these words a number. He then used these numbers to jumble and juxtapose his clear text. To let his Home Station know which five words he had chosen, he inserted an indicator-group at the beginning of his message. But if one message was broken – just one – the enemy cryptographers could mathematically reconstruct those five words and would at once try to identify their source.

One agent had been allowed to use the National Anthem, the only verses which he claimed to remember; suppose the enemy broke one of his messages and the five words he'd encoded it on were 'our,' 'gracious,' 'him,' victorious,' 'send,' then God save the agent. They could sing the rest of the code themselves and read all his future traffic without breaking another message.

The reasoning behind the practice was brilliantly simple:

If all your poem-codes were original compositions written by members of SOE, no reference books would be of the slightest help in tracing them. It would make it slightly more difficult for SOE's messages to be read like daily newspapers if we started a Baker Street poets' corner. Striding up and down the corridors like the Poet Laureate of Signals, I did what I could to make my poems easy to memorize, less easy to anticipate, but I was obliged to turn to the country sections for help with their respective languages.

SOE's security checks were ... to tell us whether an agent was coding under duress. To convey this to us without the enemy being aware of it, he was required to insert various dummy letters in the body of each message – and their absence or alteration in any way was supposed to alert us immediately to

his capture. As an additional 'precaution' he was instructed to
make deliberate spelling mistakes at prearranged spots. The
whole concept had all the validity of a child's excuses for staying
up late, with none of the imagination. It took no account of
the possibility of an agent's code being broken or tortured
out of him, when the Gestapo would be in a position to work
out the security checks for themselves. Nor did it make any
allowances for morse mutilation, which frequently garbled
so much of the text that it was impossible to tell whether the
security checks – for what little they were worth – were present.

All the resources of the Gestapo would not force an agent to
reveal a code that he could not possibly remember. Destroying his
worked-out keys as soon as he had used them must become as
reflex to an agent as pulling the ripcord of his parachute.

But there was one thing for which he could still be tortured. His
security check. And this to me was the most haunting and
daunting issue of all. If we couldn't solve this problem, we had
solved nothing.

Marks explained further how the system allowed captured agents to
protect security:

Imagine I'm an agent, and I've been caught with my ... code on me.
I've destroyed all the previous keys I've used but the Gestapo know
that if they can torture my security check out of me they can use the
rest of these keys to transmit messages to London and pretend
they're from me.

Opposite each pair [i.e. set of numbers or letters, not necessarily
two of something] of keys there are five letters printed. These are
indicator-groups to tell London which pair of keys I've used to
encode my message. The next pair I'm due to use are the ones at
the top – starting 14.2.13.4. The indicator group is CEDQT. After
this I'm due to use the next pair of keys – starting 9.10.1.7. The
indicator-group is PKBDO. But I never use these indicator-groups
exactly as they are printed. I have prearranged with London
always to add 3 to the first letter and 2 to the fourth. Take the
indicator CEDQT, C plus 3 is F, and Q plus 2 is S. So, instead of
sending CEDQT I send FEDST. Instead of sending PKBDO I send

SKFBO. At least, that's what I'm telling you because you're the Gestapo. All my previous indicator-groups have been destroyed; how can you know if I'm telling you the truth? Rough me up and I'll change it once again. When do you stop?

When sent into occupied Europe, agents had a highly structured set of procedures to observe. A glimpse of a typical set of orders gives an idea of the way in which British-trained agents worked in conjunction with the resistance:

For Lieutenant Marcel Clech, wireless operator to INVENTOR 11.5.43
Operation: GROOM
Christian name in the field: BASTIEN
Name on papers: Yves LE BRAS
<u>MISSION</u>
You are going into the field to work as W/T operator for two organizers, PAUL and ELIE. You will be under the command of Elie, whom you have met here and who will be travelling with you. Besides his job as organizer, he is to act as your liaison officer with Paul, who has an organization already established in the district bounded by Troyes, Nancy and Besançon.
<u>APPROACH</u>
You will go into the field by Lysander with Elie and his courier, Simone, to a reception committee at a point
14 km. E.S.E. of Tours
11km. W.S.W. of Amboise
As soon as possible after your arrival you will make your way to Paris to a safe address which you already know and stay there until you receive further instructions from Elie. This address is:
Monsieur Cornie,
22 bis rue de Chartres,
Neully s/Seine.
If, by any mischance, you should lose contact with Elie, the following address is given you to enable you to get in touch with Paul:
Mme. Buisson,
203 ave. du Roule,
Neully. Password: Amour, amour.
There you should ask to be put in touch with Monsieur Frager or

leave a letter for him. Frager is the name by which Paul is known at this address. It is stressed that you should contact him ONLY if you lose contact with Elie.

METHOD

1. You have been given a cover story and papers in the name of Yves Le Bras, which you will use for your normal life in the field. To cover your personality as an agent you will use the name BASTIEN.

2. You will receive and send messages for Elie's circuit. You will send only those messages which are passed to you by Elie or which are approved by him. Although you are under his command and will take your instructions from him, you are the ultimate judge as regards the technicalities of W/T and W/T security. We should like to point out here that you must be extremely careful with the filing of your messages.

The circuit password of Elie and Paul is:

'Je viens de la part de Celestin.'

'Ah, oui, le marchand de vin.'

('I come on behalf of Celestin.' 'Ah, yes, the wine-merchant.')

COMMUNICATIONS

1. You will sever your contact with the people who receive you as soon as possible and, after that, will refrain from contacting members of any circuit apart from your own.

2. As regards your wireless communication with us, we would stress that you should only be on the air when necessary and that your transmissions should be as short as possible. You will encode the messages yourself.

3. You will send us as soon as possible the address of a postbox through which we can contact you personally should the wireless communications break down.

4. You will also send us the address of a 'cachette.' Should you be in difficulties you will go to your cachette and advise us of the circumstances by coded letter or card to this address:

Snr. Leonel Martins,

20 Travesa Enviado Inglaterra,

Lisbonne.

We will then contact you at the cachette with a view to getting you out.

5. For communicating with us by other means than W/T, you will use your personal code.

CONCLUSION

You have had your personal training, our W/T training and a W/T refresher course during your visit to this country. You have had our general briefing and with regard to the briefing herewith you have had an opportunity of raising any questions on matters that have not been clear. You have also had a trial viva voce of the methods outlined. You understand that you are to receive your instructions from Elie and that you are to carry them out to the best of your ability. If, through any unforeseen circumstances, Elie should disappear, you will advise us and receive further instructions direct from us.

CAMP X

SOE training schools were established all over Britain, almost always in the incongruously gracious surroundings of country houses, to teach the particular arts necessary for agents. Some specialized in unarmed combat, some in explosives, others in disguise. These facilities were not only to be found in the British Isles. The most important training facility was in Canada, on a lakeshore near Toronto, where 'Camp X' was a university of espionage. At this secluded former farm, all the necessary skills could be learned by students during a 10-week course.

Rural Canada might seem an unlikely setting for the establishment of the Allies' most important training facility for secret agents, but the location offered several solid advantages. Its comparative safety was significant, for Britain itself still faced the theoretical danger of German invasion. There was a military airfield a short distance away. Unlike any British city at the time, Toronto, 30 miles west, contained sizeable communities of Italians, Hungarians and other ethnic minorities, from whom spies could be recruited for service in occupied Europe (French Canadian agents were to prove similarly effective in working with the French Resistance). Proximity to a large city also meant access to useful skills and equipment: in Toronto a sophisticated industry developed forging documents for the agents.

Perhaps the most significant advantage, however, was the fact that the camp was situated only 30 miles across Lake Ontario from the United

States. It opened on 6 December 1941 – the day before the attack on Pearl Harbor and America's entry into the war – and was thus well situated to train US agents as well as those from Britain. Britain's, and Canada's, new ally was quickly going to need these skills, and could gain them unobtrusively in this quiet corner of Ontario. Alfred Taylor, a businessman who acted as SOE's go-between and bought the site for $12,000, remarked that:

> **Toronto is within two hours of New York by air with thrice-daily service, so that communications with HQ and with America are extremely convenient.**

Another of Camp X's founding fathers, Inspector George McClellan of the Royal Canadian Mounted Police, remarked that the remote farm, with its neglected appearance and deserted orchards, looked like 'a good place to make hooch'.

There was a library of military history that also contained spy novels, and a collection of captured enemy weapons, uniforms and insignia. There was an underground shooting range and a 90-foot 'jump tower' (parachuting was an integral part of training of the recruits). A Canadian Pacific main line provided them with opportunities to learn railway sabotage techniques, and 30-foot lakeshore cliffs – similar to those along the Normandy coast – enabled students to practise landings and climbing. Most significantly there was a telecommunications centre, code-named HYDRA, which received top-secret data from across the world. Radio hams were discreetly recruited from all over Canada to staff the centre and they worked round the clock, in shifts.

Trainee agents came from a wide spectrum of Canadian society as well as from several foreign countries, but had in common a spirit of adventure and a hatred of Hitler. Eric Curwain, chief of the British Security Service's Canadian Division, described some examples:

> **One was a Yugoslav named Paul, one of the last blacksmiths working in Toronto. He was preparing to drop into Yugoslavia and the final meal [we shared] in his home in Toronto was truly his last meal, for Paul was killed in Yugoslavia. His views on the war were simple – the Nazi doctrine was evil. He shared the same view as an unfrocked Italian priest who left the Church and his teaching profession to train with us to fight the Fascists. In Italy**

he was killed, fighting against Mussolini's troops. The arrival at the camp of an ebullient medical man from Brazil was another indication of the extent to which the war was becoming a global affair. The Brazilian was a champion high diver and judo expert in his own country, and, first and foremost a Don Juan. After seeing him throw a six-foot man across the training mat, one wondered how the ladies fared.

Another of the students was Ian Fleming, who doubtless gathered useful information for his future writings.

The participants went through a gruelling course in guerrilla warfare, escape and evasion, and weapons handling. Their experiences included standing behind bullet-proof glass while being sprayed with gunfire, assembling and firing weapons in pitch darkness – and learning to drink huge amounts without becoming indiscreet. They also practised the use of explosives, the setting of ambushes, and the infiltration of a local munitions factory to steal documents and weapons.

A DANGEROUS GAME

Despite the meticulous nature of the preparations and organization, service in occupied Europe was extremely dangerous. A man or woman dropped by parachute in the darkness, especially in the forested or mountainous regions favoured by the resistance, might come to grief before their mission had even begun. Their radio set might be lost or damaged in the jump, rendering them unable to make contact. The historian MRD Foot cited one such instance:

> One agent, Brian Stonehouse, a young Vogue fashion artist, was dropped in France at the end of June 1942. The container his set was carried in hung up in a tree, and it took a week before he could get it into his hands. Then he had a lot of technical trouble before he could make contact with England; then his set broke down altogether and he caught dysentery. It was not till late August that he got into proper working touch with home station.

In England, operators were manning other radio sets and waiting for the pre-arranged call signs that confirmed the safe arrival of an agent, and for the subsequent regular reports that they were required to make. Doreen Spencer, at Bletchley, always remembered the signals she exchanged with anonymous operators, hidden in distant woods or barns or caves on the other side of the English Channel:

> We were never told with whom we were in contact. We would sit through a whole watch listening for a call sign through all the mush and interference, and trying to locate it. We would send our call sign, then listen and search. Sometimes one would be rewarded with an answering signal and we'd take the message and acknowledge, but sometimes nothing at all.
>
> I have often wondered if the operators at 'the other end' were in enemy territory and possibly resistance workers, or our own people who had been working undercover in enemy territory.

There were built-in safeguards to indicate if something was wrong. The most common difficulty would be that an agent had been captured (direction finding equipment would be used to pinpoint the source of signals and locate his radio, which would have been seized and used by the enemy). Because each operator, when transmitting Morse code, had a distinctive 'fist', the Gestapo would not attempt to send a message themselves but would force the agent to do so. He would try to warn listeners that he was acting under duress by deliberately making some previously agreed mistake.

It seemed a foolproof system, but it was dependent on the alertness of those at the receiving end and in March 1942 it failed. A message received from an agent who had just landed in Holland contained the arranged signal. He was in the hands of the Gestapo, and agreed to transmit for them the news of his safe arrival. His warning was unheeded because it was deemed to be a genuine mistake. He was subsequently sent further messages, announcing the arrival of other agents. Most of these men therefore parachuted straight into a trap.

This kept on happening. One after another, over a period of two years, more than 40 agents were trained, equipped, and sent to join what they believed to be a growing underground organization. Their radio messages indicated that they had rendezvoused with other agents and that the resistance was intact. German Intelligence, for whom catching these men in a web of deceit was a deeply satisfying exercise, called it the '*Englandspiel*', or

'England game'. The Germans, of course, were able to build up a detailed picture of the organization sending their captives across the North Sea.

As well as parachuting agents into the Netherlands, a number of men were delivered by sea. Royal Navy MGBs (Motor Gun Boats) made frequent crossings from the East Anglian coast to drop agents on Dutch beaches. Charles Elwell was a naval officer whose job was to row ashore two Dutchmen. All three were seized on the beach by German troops. Taken for questioning, Elwell was surprised to find that his interrogators:

> ... not only knew the actual numbers of his gunboat, but also the names of many of the officers stationed at Great Yarmouth, where the 16th Motor Gunboat Flotilla was based.

Eventually, two captured agents managed to escape, and succeeded in reaching the British Embassy in Switzerland, where they broke the news that the resistance movement had been infiltrated and compromised. The ambassador reported at once to London:

> Lieutenant Johan Bernhard Ubbink, cover-name Edema and code letters CEN, parachuted into Holland during the night of 1 December 1942, and Sergeant Pieter Dourlein, cover-name Diepenbrock, code letters ACO, dropped during the night of 10 March 1943, have both arrived here. Both report that they were met by a reception committee who knew their cover-names yet turned out to consist of Dutch Nazis and German SD [Security Service], who immediately arrested them. During their interrogations it became clear that the Germans were completely aware of the whole organization with its codes and passwords. For a long time the Germans have been transmitting to England pretending to be agents. They guess that at least 130 men have been arrested in this way so that the whole organization is in German hands. During the night of 30 August 1943 they escaped from prison. On 25 November I can send them to Spain using our normal route, but arrangements have to be made to ensure that they spend as little time as possible in Spain, in view of the importance, in my opinion, of their information.

The two were passed on to London, where they repeated their story, but even this was not the end of the *Englandspiel*. Through its control of the resistance radio network, the Gestapo convinced the Dutch government-in-exile that the men were turncoats who were working for the Germans, and they were arrested. The overall situation was only resolved once the Allied armies reached the Netherlands, but the death toll had been appalling: of 144 agents infiltrated into the country between 1940 and 1944, only 28 survived.

The 'game' could also be played the other way round. If a resistance organization was found to have been compromised, Bletchley or London could maintain a pretence of cooperating with it. This deception might even include making supply drops and providing funds. Such measures, which lured the Gestapo into a feeling of complacency and thus led them to make mistakes, also enabled the Allies to populate the countryside with the radio circuits of imaginary cells. These could tie down German eavesdroppers and distract their attention from areas where operations were actually going on.

Though the *Englandspiel* had some ramifications elsewhere in north-west Europe, the dropping of agents was a good deal more successful in France. Those sent to the Maquis were more commonly infantry officers than radio operators, their job being to plan and direct raids rather than maintain a communications network. Illustrative of how such men could galvanize a unit is this observation by an Englishman, CW Kempson, on the arrival of two compatriots in a nearby district:

> [In January 1944] two English officers were landed near Carennac.
> From now on the Resistance groups would have a regular means
> of direct communication with London, which would help them
> to get arms and munitions and to get organized. Messages relayed
> by the SOE and broadcast by the BBC informed the groups and
> gave them a quicker and safer link than they had had before.

The arrival of Allied personnel by air in occupied countries was a complicated affair, even if the districts in which they landed were not swarming with enemy soldiery. Captain Watney explained how a rendezvous was arranged:

> When organising a 'drop' the local group chose the reception
> site, which was then agreed and co-ordinated by the local British
> officer(s) following his own personal method. He would give it

a coded letter and number, a code name (for all the groups in Quercy this would be the name of a tree), there would be a name code when calling the pilot, a code of light signals to the Morse signals to guide the plane, and finally the 'personal message' to announce the drop. There also had to be alternative plans in case of changes in the weather, unexpected presence of the enemy, etc.

Those aboard an aircraft had to keep to a strict set of rules when flying over enemy territory, looking out for the bonfires, or lights, that would announce the presence of a 'reception committee' below. Communication had to be circumspect because of eavesdroppers. These War Office instructions were given to the pilots of Lysanders – the highly versatile light aircraft that could land in a meadow and were used for delivering, or 'oicking up', human cargo:

> Don't forget that the Germans' wireless intelligence is probably listening with some interest to your remarks. So your RT procedure should be arranged afresh before each operation and no reference should be made to place names or landing and taking off, or to the quality of the ground, unless this information is coded. For the same reason call signs are usually changed in flight so that, although you may start off at Tangmere as Jackass 34 and 35, at the target you may be Flanagan and Allan. There is no need to talk to each other en route, except where the leader of the operation is deciding to scrub and go home.
>   Once you have seen the light, identify the letter positively. If the letter is not correct, or if there is any irregularity in the flare path, or if the field is not the one you expected, you are in NO circumstances to land. Experience has shown that a German ambush on the field will not open fire until the aeroplane attempts to take off, having landed. Their object is to get you alive to get the gen, so don't be tricked into a sense of security if you are not shot at from the field before landing. I repeat, the entire lighting procedure must be correct before you can even think of landing.

CODING DELIVERIES

Bigger cargoes, such as the weapons that *maquisards* so often needed – and people – were dropped by parachute. Captain Watney, as a member of an expedition that sought to infiltrate both British and American personnel into a mountainous region of France, remembered how it was organized:

> The mission was to be dropped by parachute in the next moon period (May 1944) at a 'pin-point' at Vassieux – a small village in the Vercors Plateau. Our task was to contact the leader of resistance in the Vercors and to act as a link between the French Forces of the Interior in the Vercors area and the Allied High Command in England. To help organize and arm the Resistance elements, to carry out acts of sabotage, and report all military intelligence. To prevent destruction of important targets, such as certain bridges which would be required by the Allied armies should they operate in our area ... Our cover stories, were we to be caught, were checked and rechecked until they were known by heart. We were issued with civilian clothes, identity cards and ration books, etc.

The date had to be carefully chosen:

> There were only certain days on either side of the full moon when these operations could take place and the tension grew considerably as the date for the 'Moon Period' drew nearer. As our pin-point was some 300 miles east of the Channel coast the weather had to be exactly right for a lone plane to find the exact little field in a valley in the highest Alps. Sometimes the RAF would raid a nearby target to divert the Enemy's attention from that lone plane going on its secret mission.

For those on the ground, an air drop was naturally an event of huge importance, requiring detailed planning and the tightest security. Captain Watney witnessed the delivery of canisters by the US Army Air Force:

> On 15 June they were told to prepare for two huge 'drops', one of troops, one of supplies or, they were warned, they could be both at the same time and at the same place. The English officers

said they preferred two dropping-grounds, Bouleau for the men and Prunier for the materials. Coded messages were agreed. For 'Bouleau' was to read 'the boss does not laugh,' and for 'Prunier' the message was 'the elephant in the zoo.' The timing of the drops was to be indicated by one or two words, of which each letter represented 30 minutes from 5 a.m.

The markings and the smoke signals were ready for the respective orders. A chain of despatch men linked each post with Michel and his radio and with Raymond. Everything seemed to be covered when among the flood of messages received by Michel came on July 13 'The following takes top priority for Maxime STOP. Be ready tomorrow Friday for a parachute drop during the morning STOP. You need to light strong smoke signals – repeat very strong at 6.30 a.m. GMT STOP. Expect 432 repeat 432 containers STOP. Acknowledge immediately.' Then, that evening, the BBC confirmed 'The elephant in the zoo is named Charles'. So the drop was to start at 8.30 a.m. local time.

They arrived on 14 July – Bastille Day – and, in a gesture greatly appreciated by the watching Frenchmen, flew the tricolor as they passed overhead:

> It was a moving moment. Not a cloud spoilt the purity of the blue, and soon in the middle of all the arms held out these angels of liberation passed and repassed, not only the big carriers but also the escorts, passing and repassing. All of us suffered mixed emotions. The certainty of strength and beauty, and above all the feeling of chasing away the forces of evil. A tremendous hope fell from the sky and doubtless many who had not cried for ages could not suppress a tear.
>
> The great birds were about 1,000 feet above, 432 containers said the message, but there were more than 1,500 pairs of parachutes, for some of the containers weighed more than four hundredweight each. Picard wrote: Wave succeeded wave. The containers dropped, trailing behind them, like a greeting – a salute – our national colour. Delicacy and courtesy, the subtle tact of real friendship which knows which gesture to make, made plain the meaning which moved us, stirred the heart, and filled us anew with hope and ardour.

Despite much success in its European operations, the dangerous nature of SOE's work meant that tragedies were not unknown. The organization's operatives were as liable to betrayal as any other member of the resistance, and those who operated radios were vulnerable to discovery by direction-finding equipment.

This fate befell the agent Noor Inayat Khan, code-named Madeleine, the first female radio operator to work in occupied territory. She was sent to Paris in June 1943 disguised as a governess named Jeanne Marie Regnier. Aristocratic and introspective (she was the daughter of an Indian prince, and a writer of children's stories), she was a most unlikely participant in the ruthless world of espionage. Nevertheless, she was a graduate of the rigorous SOE schools and a trained wireless operator. She coolly set up her equipment in a Paris apartment (it is said that a German kindly helped her put up her aerial). The Paris 'circuit' of *résistants* was large, loose and notoriously prone to infiltration. Only two weeks after her arrival, many of her colleagues were arrested and she was forced to go into hiding. Aware that there was no other wireless operator in the city, she continued at grave risk to keep open this channel of communication. As Jerrard Tickell reported in a postwar article in the *Sunday Express* (5 June 1949):

> Knowing that she was in mortal danger, London offered to send an aeroplane to bring her home. She refused. She was the last link between London headquarters and her hunted comrades, and it was not in her character to desert her friends.
>
> The Gestapo, aware that hers was the only remaining set transmitting in the area, put every available man on the chase, and the capture of the mysterious 'Madeleine' became a matter of the highest priority to Berlin.

Her career as an agent lasted for three months. She was betrayed, arrested and – despite a daring and almost successful escape attempt from prison – deported to Dachau, where she was killed. She had steadfastly refused, under interrogation, to reveal information to her captors, and she was posthumously awarded the George Cross. Though her bravery cannot be doubted, and though her insistence on remaining in Paris to keep open the radio link with London was of value to the war effort, it is clear that she did not possess all the qualities necessary for a successful SOE agent: she made mistakes that did great damage. Professor MRD Foot, the historian, discussed this:

With Noor Inayat Khan were captured not only the transmitter she had in her flat, but also – from the drawer of her bedside table – a school exercise book in which she had recorded in full, in cipher and in clear, every message she had ever received or sent since reaching France. How on earth did she come to make so elementary a mistake? It must have been through a misunderstanding of her orders, for she had of course been trained, as all wireless operators were, to make sure that she did nothing of the kind. Her operation instruction did contain a curious phrase: 'We should like to point out here that you must be exceptionally careful with the filing of your messages.' She was certainly too shy, reserved and conformist a person to think of questioning an order; and, being 'not over-burdened with brains' (a phrase used in her final report from training school), might have managed to misunderstand it as an order to file and keep the messages she sent; worse, as an order that overrode her explicit training instructions to the contrary.

[Her] set, her codes, her security checks [were] in enemy hands.; and all her back-messages in clear, from which the Germans could study her style of writing. Her style of W/T transmitting they had carefully studied already. So they launched a wireless operation they called DIANA, playing her set back to London by the hand of one of the operators who had often listened to her touch.

BROADCAST MESSAGES

The question of contacting the multitude of disparate and far-flung resistance units was solved by a practice ingenious in its simplicity. The BBC's foreign department, situated at Bush House in central London, was already in use as a means of spreading Allied propaganda to the occupied countries. Exiled heads of state regularly spoke to their peoples from its studios. SOE began to make use of its nightly broadcasts to send coded messages to listeners in the European underground. Twice each evening, at about 7.30 and 9.00 pm, the radio played the adapted Beethoven 'V-for-Victory' theme and then a voice announced '*Voici quelques messages personnels*' ('Here are some personal messages'). They were read twice, in French (or other appropriate language), the second time more slowly so that they could be written down. Some may have been genuine greetings or announcements, but the wild phraseology of others made it clear that they were code words. The recipients would have been told by other means, such as Morse signals, what phrases must be listened for and what they meant.

In his official history of SOE, Professor MRD Foot explained how these messages were interpreted by their audience:

It was Georges Begue who proposed in the summer of 1941 what became the most conspicuous thing SOE ever did: the nightly broadcasting on the BBC's foreign programme, through some of the most powerful transmitters in the world, of scores of sentences which sounded either like family greetings or like Carrollian nonsense. 'Romeo embrasse Juliette', 'la chienne de Barbara aura trios chiots', just might mean what they purported to mean to somebody; but 'Esculape n'aime pas le mouton' or 'La voix du doryphore est lointaine' were clearly enough codes. Only the staff and agents concerned knew that such messages announced respectively the safe arrival of a courier in Switzerland from Toulouse, the impending arrival in Barcelona of three passengers on VIC's best line (escaping prisoners of war), a drop that night on a GLOVER ground near Chaumont, or a call for immediate telephone sabotage in RF's region R3, which ran from near Le Puy to Perpignan and the Spanish border. The Germans wasted a lot of time and emotional energy in trying to unravel this sort of indecipherable coding. This in itself was some gain to the allied effort. A greater gain was that agents in close touch with London could use BBC messages to demonstrate their own bona fides to people in the field who were doubtful about them, by getting London to transmit a message of the doubter's choice. And of course it was an enormous convenience to reception committees to get definite information that the RAF were going to attempt to drop on a particular field; in fine moonlit weather scores of messages announcing drops that night would go out each evening in the summer of 1944.

As a method of passing messages the BBC could not have been more public; but with one fearful exception its security was sound. The rate of traffic passing was kept fairly constant; dummy messages were passed if not enough real ones were available. However, there was one disaster:

the Germans claim that some code 'action' messages calling sabotage groups out to work were known to them, and thus enabled them to discover on the evening of 5th June 1944 that a main Allied landing was to take place overnight.

Having secured full control of wireless on the home front, SOE's high command was disinclined to part with it to agents in the field. The whole business of encoding and enciphering wireless traffic with the field was naturally both complicated and highly secret. In the early years every operator took with him to France a personal code which he had memorised; this might be as simple as a Playfair code based on a single word, or consist of a string of numbers to guide him in transposition. A rather more elaborate system, called the 'worked-out key', followed; this was based on a phrase, usually a line from a poem, chosen by the agent because it could easily be remembered. This was less easy to break than the previous ciphers, and no evidence suggests that the Germans did in fact decipher SOE's messages of this kind before they had discovered from prisoners what the phrase for a particular message or set of messages was. However the Paris SD was able to manipulate worked-out key ciphers with complete dexterity, while working some captured sets back to London.

Another author, David Kahn, added that:

No cryptanalyst could break these messages, for nothing in the open text implied its hidden meaning. But, like all secrets, they were vulnerable to betrayal. During 1943 German counterespionage, through questioning of a suspicious person who proved to be an underground courier, had broken up a resistance net named BUTLER.

The airwaves were busiest in western France at the beginning of June 1944. The resistance had known for months that the summer would bring an invasion. Many units had a specific task to perform – blocking roads, destroying bridges, disabling railway tracks, or reporting the movements of enemy units. Captain Watney, as a British officer serving with a formation of maquisards, remembered the night before D-Day on which,

German army signallers. Such was the confidence of Hitler's generals in the invincibility of the Enigma ciphers that they never seriously considered the possibility of interception. Nevertheless, German commanders were frequently baffled by their opponents' uncanny ability to find and exploit weaknesses. Some suspected a highly sophisticated form of radar, rather than eavesdropping, was the cause.

As portable as a typewriter, Enigma machines went wherever German forces were serving, and were used to send signals from the fighting fronts. When the war was going badly, decoded messages informed Allied listeners of increasing acrimony between rival generals or services, and provided a useful indication of Hitler's state of mind.

General Heinz Guderian in France, 1940. This photograph illustrates the interior of a communications vehicle of the type that accompanied Hitler's armies during a Blitzkrieg campaign. The machine is operated by members of a Panzer unit, and would have conveyed orders in code direct to the General from the Führer's headquarters.

Two members of the French Resistance operating a radio in the field. The wireless was a vital part of the equipment of Resistance units and of Allied agents. It provided the most efficient – and often the only – means of sending information from occupied Europe and of receiving news of supply-drops or other operations. Sets were supplied from London.

A Maquisard sending a radio message. The demands of the undercover war in occupied Europe brought about an intensive development of gadgetry, ranging from portable transmitters to innocent-looking, but explosive, lumps of coal. Ian Fleming, later to write the James Bond novels, gained much of his inspiration from wartime service in Naval Intelligence.

A clandestine radio, hidden in a city attic or remote farm, formed the centre of a circle of agents. The Germans, however, used efficient direction-finding equipment to locate these transmitters, and wireless operators ran the greatest risk of capture. As the Gestapo closed in on her group, the SOE agent Violet Szabo courageously maintained a radio link from her Paris apartment until she too was arrested.

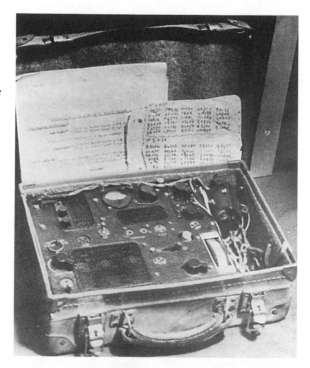

Information was passed to Europe through the BBC, which every evening broadcast apparently nonsensical messages to underground members. A sentence such as 'The children have gone to the seaside' could mean a Resistance official had safely escaped to England. Coded wireless signals would have explained the meanings and given the dates on which messages might be expected.

Royal Navy coders, aboard HMS Shropshire, at work decoding messages from other ships in the region. Codebooks were weighted with lead. If a ship was sinking the first duty of coders was to throw them overboard.

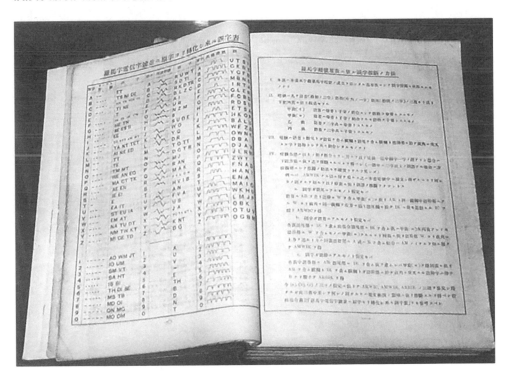

A Japanese code book. In 1941 the Allied countries did not have sufficient graduates with a knowledge of this language. Recruiters therefore targeted those with a background in Greek and Latin, on the basis that these were difficult to grasp. Mathematicians and crossword-solvers were also sought. Their mental processes were considered suitable for tackling an oriental language.

A Royal Air Force wireless operator attached to the Chindits in Burma. This undercover force – whose scruffiness became a symbol of their ability to live and fight in difficult terrain – depended on radio to ensure supplies and to track enemy movements. On Saturdays, an operator could sometimes raise morale by picking up a British football match on his set!

A supply-drop from one of the ubiquitous C47s that provided transport for men and equipment in all theatres of war. The silk or nylon parachutes were in great demand among those on the ground, for they were swiftly converted into tents, sleeping bags or clothing. The material would be shared with locals who helped unpack the goods.

In the jungle, supplies could often be delivered only from the air, and a constant and important task of SOE and OSS operatives was to arrange these drops. Weaponry and ammunition, food and medicine all arrived in this way. Another vital cargo was replacement wireless sets and radio parts, since these were continually lost or damaged in the rough conditions.

Navajo Indian signallers, or 'wind talkers', were an important aspect of frontline communications in the Pacific, and the men were kept out of danger whenever possible. Nevertheless they ran the same risks as others in combat zones – and might also be shot at by fellow Marines who mistook them in the heat of battle for Japanese.

Navajo Indians were used in the Pacific Theatre by the US Marine Corps to send signals. Japanese eavesdroppers, many of them educated in the States, had an impressive command of American English, but were stumped by hearing chatter in Navajo. A number of native American signallers were attached to each unit. They communicated between themselves, translating as they went along.

after years of clandestine activity, these underground soldiers could at last come out of hiding, openly wear quasi-military insignia, and take on the enemy face to face:

> There were many strange messages on the air on the night of June 5/6 1944; among them 'it's a simple comedy', 'they chatter ceaselessly' and 'contradictory'. Each strange phrase meant something special to the eager listeners who were waiting for the call into open battle with the Nazis. Now their period of waiting was nearly over.
>
> On receipt of their particular message each unit or group set its team at their planned preliminary tasks. Deafening explosions were soon echoing round the hills and valleys, brilliant flashes lit the sky, bridges crashed into ravines, and there was a sudden movement of vehicles in the night. Now they would show what they could do! Everyone sported the 'A.S. (Armée Sècrete) Veny' flash on their left arm together with the cross of Lorraine.

Men like these had not been the only ones listening to the radio. German Intelligence closely monitored all of these announcements, and the enemy, too, knew that an invasion was imminent, though they did not know where it would come. They were aware, however, of the signal that would announce its start. The effect that this news produced was described in one of the most memorable passages in Cornelius Ryan's epic history of Operation Overlord, *The Longest Day:*

> At Fifteenth Army headquarters near the Belgian border, one man was glad to see the morning of June 4 arrive, Lieutenant-Colonel Hellmuth Meyer ...
>
> Besides being the Fifteenth Army's Intelligence Officer, he also headed the only counter-intelligence team on the invasion front. The heart of his set-up was a thirty-man radio-interception crew who worked in shifts around the clock in a concrete bunker crammed full of the most delicate radio equipment. Their job was to listen, nothing more. But each man was an expert who spoke three languages fluently and there was hardly a word, hardly a single stutter of Morse code whispering through the ether from

Allied sources that they did not hear.

Meyer's men were so experienced and their equipment was so sensitive that they were even able to pick up calls from radio transmitters in military police jeeps in England more than a hundred miles away. This had been a great help to Meyer. American and British MPs, chatting with one another by radio as they directed troop convoys, had helped him no end in compiling a list of the various divisions stationed in England. But for some time Meyer's operators had not been able to pick up any more of these calls. This was also significant to Meyer; it meant that a strict radio silence had been imposed. It was just one more clue to add to the many he already had that the invasion was close at hand.

In January Admiral Wilhelm Canaris, then chief of German intelligence, had given Meyer the details of a fantastic two-part signal which he said the Allies would use to alert the underground prior to the invasion.

Canaris had warned that the Allies would broadcast hundreds of messages to the underground in the months preceding the attack. Only a few of these would actually relate to D-Day; the remainder would be fake, deliberately designed to mislead and confuse. Canaris had been explicit: Meyer was to monitor all these messages in order not to miss the all-important one.

At first Meyer had been sceptical. It had seemed madness to him to depend entirely on only one message. Besides, he knew from past experience that Berlin's sources of information were inaccurate ninety per cent of the time. He had a whole file of false reports to prove his point; the Allies seemed to have fed every German agent from Stockholm to Ankara with the 'exact' place and date of the invasion – and no two of the reports agreed.

But this time Meyer knew Berlin was right. On the night of June 1st Meyer's men, after months of monitoring, had intercepted the first part of the Allied message – exactly as described by Canaris. It was not unlike the hundreds of other coded sentences that Meyer's men had picked up during the previous months.

Daily, after the regular BBC news broadcasts, coded instructions in French, Dutch, Danish and Norwegian were read out to the underground. Most of the messages were meaningless to Meyer, and it was exasperating not to be able to decode such cryptic fragments as 'The Trojan War will not be held,' 'Molasses tomorrow will spurt forth cognac,' 'John has a long moustache,' or 'Sabine has just had mumps and jaundice.'

But the message that followed the 9 pm BBC news on the night of June 1 was one that Meyer understood only too well. 'Kindly listen now to a few personal messages,' said the voice in French. Instantly Sergeant Walter Reichling switched on a tape recorder. There was a pause, and then: 'Les sanglots longs des violins de l'automne' (The long sobs of the violins of autumn). Reichling suddenly clapped his hands over his earphones. Then he tore them off and rushed out of the bunker for Meyer's quarters. The sergeant burst into Meyer's office and excitedly said, 'Sir, the first part of the message – it's here.'

Together they returned to the bunker where Meyer listened to the recording. There it was – the message that Canaris had warned them to expect. It was the first line of 'Chanson d'Automne' (Song of Autumn) by the nineteenth century French poet Paul Verlaine. According to Canaris' information, this line from Verlaine was to be transmitted on the 'first or fifteenth of a month ... and will represent the first half of a message announcing the Anglo-American invasion.'

The last half of the message would be the second line of the Verlaine poem, 'Blessent mon Coeur d'une langueur monotone' (Wound my heart with a monotonous languor). When this was broadcast it would mean, according to Canaris, that 'the invasion will begin within forty-eight hours, the count starting at 0000 hours (12 midnight) of the day following the transmission.

From 6 June 1944 onwards, the Maquis came out of the shadows and merged into the French Forces of the Interior. It was thenceforward a semi-official army. The same had happened in Italy the previous year, and was true in most other liberated countries. For them, the secret war ended when the first Allied troops arrived, though in many cases factions continued to struggle for political causes.

BALKAN OPERATIONS

SOE agents operated wherever there was a need to work with local partisans against the occupying power, and another theatre in which they were heavily involved was the Balkans. This region, overrun by German armies in 1941, was ideally suited to guerrilla warfare. All the necessary conditions were to be found in abundance in Yugoslavia: rugged mountain ranges, remote valleys, deep forests and meandering coastline. Bands of partisans, recruited from a fiercely proud population that was skilled in hunting and thus in bearing arms, could live off the land, carrying out raids and ambushes from hideouts far in the hinterland. German units were highly adept at tracking them through the mountains. Both sides were determined, and quarter was seldom given by either. The Balkans probably saw the most vicious irregular warfare of the entire conflict. SOE provided much of the armament and equipment for the partisans, sending operatives to lead bands of men, coordinate their efforts and liaise with the Allies. British agent RC Grindlay served as a radio operator with a unit in Montenegro. Like many of his colleagues throughout the conflict, he arrived at night and by parachute:

> At about 0130 hours we arrived over the target area. The despatcher, an RAF corporal, motioned me to get ready and I moved over to the centre of the plane and sat with my feet in the hole facing the rear. A tube extended a short way beneath the plane so that I could not feel the slipstream.
>
> We checked that my static chute was hooked up and I noticed the aircraft being levelled off and the engines being throttled back. Slowing down, we were now flying at about 110 mph. I watched the two lights on my left up on the roof and waited for the red light to go on. A few seconds later it came on followed shortly afterwards by the green light. When this showed, the despatcher hit me on the shoulder and shouted 'Go!'
>
> The drop was so accurate that I almost landed in one of the [signal] fires. I can remember privately thanking the RAF crew.
>
> Once I got to my feet and removed the chute there were plenty of hands to grab hold of it to stop me being carried over the rough ground. The ground was heavily strewn with boulders and I thought that this was hardly the ideal spot to have chosen for a night drop.

Obviously in the dark it was a bit difficult to see the faces of all the people, especially now that the fires had been extinguished. However, I was introduced straight away to Major Owen and Corporal Campbell – the latter I knew from our training course.

He quickly learned about the size and nature of the group, and came to appreciate the danger of failing to keep on the move:

Campbell told me they had had a hectic time in recent weeks as the enemy had been very active – both the Germans and the Ustashi. The latter being a fascist lot, who were around in great numbers. These traitors, as the partisans called them, were perhaps even more hated than the Germans. My second attempt to get in had been aborted as they were on the run at the time and obviously could not accept visitors like me. The general situation in this area, some 40 miles south east of Ljubljana, was such that partisan groups were ordered to spend only one night in one place – so we were to be almost continually on the move.

Our mission was attached to a group of about 200 troops and all were well armed, mostly with the British Lee Enfield rifles and mortars. Whilst on the move we were always kept in the middle of the column and had assistance given us for the portage of our equipment. Life was certainly made as easy as possible for us.

He also found a member of American OSS (Office of Strategic Services, America's clandestine espionage and warfare unit, a forerunner of the CIA) operating with the unit, and discovered that sometimes those sent on such missions were not quite as skilful as they should have been:

We had a most unusual character in this group by the name of Bob Peric. He spoke the languages and was a sergeant in the O.S.S. This man had been parachuted in on his own with a radio set which, it appeared, he had no idea how to use. I asked him if he was in regular contact with his base and to my surprise he told me 'I have not been able to get through.' So far as his unit was concerned he was not much use and no doubt they would have given up on him by now. I offered to try and get a signal through for him which he agreed to. We went through his signal plans to see what call signs were to be used etc. It was quite obvious he had been sent into this situation inadequately trained.

However, the radio was set up and I called his home station. Contact was made quite quickly and I offered a message. The operator at the base, wherever it was, readily accepted this but I felt that he was not too sure that this was coming from the right source. I managed to convince him and he took a message which Bob Peric decoded. At least they knew he was in the land of the living. I cannot remember how many messages I sent and received on his behalf but he never seemed at all bothered whether they went or not.

He used his own radio to arrange frequent drops of supplies, requesting whatever specific weaponry was needed and agreeing locations at which the drops would take place, and he was also able to summon the might of Anglo-American air power to the aid of the partisans:

> For my part I was regularly in touch with our HQ in Bari and many drops of guns, ammunition and anti-personnel mines were sent to us. As soon as these drops were made we moved at least 4–5 miles away from the dropping zone ...
>
> Major Owen instructed me to send a number of messages over the weeks for the railway bridge at Maripor to be taken out by bombing. This was very important to the Germans as it was one of the main supply lines to the eastern front and the Russians were steadily rolling them back.

The war in the Balkans did not end decisively. The partisans did not drive the Germans from their country, nor did the Wehrmacht succeed in the impossible task of rooting out the bands of guerrillas. The Allies did not attempt a large-scale invasion of the Balkans, so there was no question here, as there was in northern Europe, of the resistance linking up with advancing Anglo-American forces and then laying down their arms. The conflict against the Germans dragged on until the day that the war in Europe ended, after which there were local scores to be settled. The partisans would then revert to ordinary banditry or to political infighting.

RESISTANCE IN THE TROPICS

Though conditions were extremely difficult in the mountains of Eastern Europe, the most challenging terrain in which SOE had to operate was half a world away, in the jungles of Burma. This land, too, provided an ideal setting for partisan warfare, and was both mountainous and thickly forested. The weather, for months at a time, could be almost unbearable, and was famously summed up by the American General Stillwell as:

Rain, rain, rain, mud, mud, mud, typhus, malaria, dysentery, exhaustion, rotting feet, body sores.

Like the Balkans, Burma was inhabited by hardy and fiercely proud peoples. Although the Japanese had overrun this British colony in December 1941, the native races had not been subject to straightforward conquest. Their new masters had sought to harness their desire for independence by creating a locally recruited 'Burma Defence Army', a small but enthusiastic force charged with controlling the country's internal security and led by 'Thakins' – Japanese-trained native commanders. As in other Axis-occupied countries, the savagery of the conquerors and their collaborators created a resistance movement, and this was based among particular hill tribes: the Kachins, Karens and Chins. The Allies were able to coordinate these peoples into an effective fighting force that could carry out ambushes and acts of sabotage under the leadership of Allied agents and officers.

Hatred of the Japanese meant that Burmese tribesmen, who like the Balkan partisans would normally have regarded all outsiders with suspicion or hostility, welcomed Allied agents into their midst. They were willing to serve under British, American or Commonwealth officers in 'levies' or irregular units. Their ranks were swelled considerably in early 1945 when Aung San, one of the Thakins, went over to the Allies and brought with him the Burma Defence Army. By that stage of the war, the Japanese were retreating from Burma. The defection of their local supporters, as well as a rebellion by the Karens, would seal their fate in the country.

Just as in Europe, Allied agents arrived by parachute, their aircraft guided to the drop zone by fires lit on the ground. Radio operator D Gibbs recalled his introduction to the Karens:

I noticed that I was drifting fairly rapidly away from the fires, and it looked as though I should be about three quarters of a

mile away when I landed. I saw that I was near the ground and that the outlook was not promising; for I saw a very large tree at the landing point. In no time at all I was rushing past the trunk and then the chute caught in the upper branches, and I was left suspended several feet above the ground. It appeared that the harness had caught round the holster of my automatic, and I could not free it though I struggled for several minutes. Then I heard voices not far away, and hoped it was not Japs. Suddenly the harness gave way, the pistol disappeared somewhere, and I fell on my back into the ditch. The voices were those of local villagers, and they now appeared and helped me to my feet. It turned out that I was not the only one to land in a tree, and Major Denning had landed in the local cemetery! But we had had no casualties.

The Advance Party had not been so fortunate. One of our Burmese boys had landed in a tree and had been strangled to death through his kit coming up round his neck. In addition, Major Lewis had broken his ankle, and after marching some distance in considerable pain, had been left in a cave guarded by Lieutenant Rennie.

Planes were now arriving, and soon stores and arms were being parachuted down to us, and there was feverish activity – opening containers and sorting supplies, etc. I went and gave a hand and found my rucksack had arrived safely.

We were lucky to have got in that night, for an incompetent base-wallah had sent a message saying that we were coming at 11 p.m. whereas we were over at 9 p.m. Luckily Pop [Lt. Col. Tulloch, commanding the men on the ground] had heard the planes and got the fires lit just in time at 9.45 p.m.

Reaching his destination, he set up his equipment. Much of the work of a radio operator in this theatre consisted of relaying or receiving coded messages. Local groups were often left to choose their own targets rather than acting on orders from outside, and much of the radio traffic therefore dealt with the arrangement of supply drops:

We arrived at Tirkule at 11 a.m. after a long climb. We were now in Karen country and their villages were nearly all on or near the tops of hills as a protection against attack from other tribes. I had brought a radio and immediately set it up (watched by a crowd of visitors) and tried to contact Pop at HQ, but was unsuccessful. After having food, we climbed to the DZ [Drop Zone] which was a flat clearing on the summit of the hill. The drop was expected at 2 p.m., but did not arrive, and I had to come down after a further attempt at radio contact with Pop. I was again unsuccessful, and felt rather miserable, as this was the first time on this op. that I had been on my own as an operator.

Another SOE radio operator, RA Leney, described the difficulty of keeping the tools of his trade in working order under tropical conditions:

The radio set was not working at all well. Apart from the fact that I did not have much confidence in that model, it was much too fragile for work in rough country and also the pre-monsoon storms were getting more frequent and trying to work a 'sked' in an electric storm was a bit scary, at times lightning seemed to be running up and down the aerial wire and the static noise made it impossible to hear incoming signals. So I asked the Colonel in a message if I could have a type B2 set sent in to us by air drop. Several days later, to my delight a couple of porters turned up from the Colonel with a B2 set and crystals and sked plans for a direct link with 14th Army so we could now call for air strikes with the minimum of delay.

The weather was now getting pretty bad and at times it rained without stopping for a couple of days. The radio set had to be kept on a frame over a fire in the house to keep it dry and in working order. The pages of code books tended to stick together and clothes sprouted mushrooms.

It was not only the radio that might suffer in the climate. The operator was also prone to 'malfunctions':

I developed a swelling on my right forearm. This got very painful and stiff, it got to the stage that I was unable to use my right hand to operate the Morse key for transmissions.

Being right handed it was a slow process to use the key with
my left hand and I made mistakes, all of which I had to explain
in a message.

As well as arranging drops of supplies to keep the tribal levies in guns,
ammunition and medicine, the radio operators had an important role in
evaluating information gleaned by locals and passing on the details of
potential targets to the Allies. They had the only radio, so all communication
with their scattered colleagues had to be by more traditional methods:

Morris' scouts came back from Shwegyin and Nyaunglebin with
some good information which we passed on to the RAF, resulting
in the bombing of food and ammunition dumps and the
destruction of the Japanese Kempetai HQ in Nyaunglebin.
    With all the officers down at the river, each commanding a
sector, I was tied down at Htilerkekhi keeping radio
communication open, sending messages down to Fred Milner by
runner and getting his messages back to be sent off. All had to be
coded or decoded which was time-consuming as well as sending
out the hourly weather reports.

Local villagers provided the labour to carry from drop zones the large
amounts of equipment that littered the ground. With the help of
elephants (when these were available), they also transported the unit's
baggage and weaponry from place to place. When assistance was needed
with these tasks, Allied operatives were surprised by the nature and
calibre of those who came forward. Richard Dunlop, an American OSS
officer, remembered that:

[British Lt Col] Gamble sent a Kachin boy up into the
mountains to ask the Kachins to provide porters, and the
next morning a bevy of Kachin girls and women hiked into
Fort Hertz. They laughed and giggled, and their diminutive
frames seemed incapable of carrying anything at all. But on
December 30, when the party set off, elephants and all, on the
rutted road to Sumprabum, the Kachin women lifted loads of
from thirty-five to fifty pounds onto their heads, or strapped
them to their backs, and set off down the trail at a pace that

left the Americans and the Anglo-Burmese floundering in the rear. Hour after hour the Kachin women kept to the trail.

'My God,' groaned Allen Richter, as he watched the group depart. 'If the women are like this, I can't imagine what the men must be like.'

Dunlop discovered that the Kachins possessed another ability that could be put to use by the Allies. His unit:

> ... flew young Kachins out of the Burma jungles to be trained as radio operators. They showed remarkable talent for electronic gadgetry.

By the latter stages of the war, drops could be very frequent, though they did not always contain the items that had been requested. One difficulty that was never solved by SOE operatives was the constant breaking of radio equipment, either in parachute drops or while being manhandled through the jungle. As a result, there were constant pleas for new sets or spare parts.

Always welcome were the silk or nylon parachutes that brought the containers to earth. They were invaluable as tents, blankets and even garments. After every drop, they were scrupulously divided up among those who had taken part in the recovery. As Gibbs remembered:

> We were rather disappointed. We got several hundred arms, but the only wireless equipment was smashed and it seemed that every spare space had been filled with field-dressings. There were hundreds of them! On the other hand there were no rations other than 'K's and Australian, and nothing in the way of luxuries. There were also some nylon parachutes, one of which was shared by Neville, Captain Troward and myself.
>
> After the drop Nev, Captain Troward and I made a tent from a cotton parachute. We got it up just in time, for it rained heavily again that night. I spent most of the day making myself a sleeping-bag with one light-weight blanket and my share of the nylon.

They were sustained throughout months in the field by a combination of army rations and the tribesmen's simple fare:

Our food consisted of American 'K' Rations which are reasonable in small quantities, but become exceedingly monotonous after a day or two. These were supplemented with rice, chicken and eggs brought up by the villagers, together with fresh water. We were to become very familiar with this diet!

DIFFICULT CONDITIONS

As a force of irregulars moved through the jungle, it was often difficult to find suitable places in which to set up a radio and attempt to transmit. All manner of difficulties – altitude, tree cover, rain clouds – might prevent messages from getting through. It was also much easier to transmit from inside a dry building, which could be difficult to find since the local people lived entirely in bamboo huts. The loss, breakage or wearing out of equipment remained the greatest difficulty suffered by radio operators in this environment, and they had to improvise, or call upon local assistance, in any way that they could:

> There was another drop the next day, including food and a steam generator which I had been frantically signalling for since our batteries were on their last legs, and the hand generators were of little use and were always getting broken.
>
> I had brought only one battery with me and I soon found that Gallear's batteries were flat; and as he proceeded to use mine, that was soon flat too. He had only hand generators, so we had villagers turning them all day and night (the night shift got double pay). [The next day] Gallear and I got our wireless kit packed up and stood by to scram. One of the bods who had been generator-turning was around so we asked if he would go with us. He agreed, so we took him on the permanent staff at 30 rupees a month. It turned out his name was something like 'Silence', so that was what we all called him.

The objective of this unit was to harry the retreating Japanese troops as they passed, with Field Marshal Slim's Fourteenth Army in pursuit. The radio operator was too valuable to be allowed in the forefront of the fighting, however. His orders were to depart for safety, with his vital code books, the moment shooting began. Though it was his responsibility to look after these codes, Gibbs was relieved to find that other members of the unit kept an eye on them too:

> Our purpose coming to Kyebogyi was to ambush Japs nightly passing down the road which was only 2 miles away at the nearest point. It seems incredible, but we stayed there for 7 weeks and almost every night attacked the Japs without them doing anything about it. The reason was that the 14th Army were advancing quite rapidly. When they slowed up later the Japs turned their attention to us.
>
> Finally, on Sunday, June 10th, the expected attack came. The Japs started by firing 75mm shells into the village, and when we heard the rattle of machine-gun fire, we realised that this was the real thing. I was instructed to take a small party with essential wireless equipment to the cache. We hid the wireless kit and codes in the bushes (a foolish move on my part), for [later, when I] sent two levies back for the radio and codes, they soon came back with the news that Japs were all round the position and it was impossible to get the kit.
>
> Soon after lunch time Sam Zai and I arrived at the village to find the codes no longer there. However we made enquiries at the village and were eventually led to the villagers' hide-out in the jungle and contacted Mang U who had left Kyebogyi with me and who had moved the codes to a safer place. Having got the codes and eaten regally off some rations we found in the cache together with some Bren guns, we set off for Dawtama.

The guerrillas did not always have things their own way. In the world of swift movement and running firefights that their lives involved, the precious equipment could be lost. Radio operator GH Tack remembered how, when surprised by a party of Japanese:

> We opened fire and ran, all separating. The radio, complete with codes and all our remaining money and personal kit, were inevitably captured.

No disaster seems to have arisen from the Japanese seizure of these codes, and the troops involved may have had no idea of what they had, but radios, once lost, would naturally cut communications until word could be sent by some other means asking for a replacement to be dropped. Tack recalled sending an important message to headquarters but that:

> The answer was never received as our radio was captured the next night.

When they encountered Japanese, the tribesmen were not accustomed to letting them live. Prisoners were a nuisance. They had to be fed, and might try to escape. It was easier simply to eliminate them. They could sometimes, of course, provide valuable information. Richard Dunlop remembered one occasion on which a downed Japanese pilot, seized by his men and delivered to an OSS radio operator (whose report of the capture caused jubilation at headquarters), was allowed to live:

> Kachin villagers saw the Japanese pilot come floating down to earth. They waited for him to land. He smiled when he saw the villagers, but at the same time he loosened a pistol in its holster at his belt. He unstrapped his parachute, and in his impossible-to-understand language asked for an easy-to-understand thing. He wanted to be led through the jungles to the nearest Japanese position. The Kachins smiled, and several young men pointed the right way to go. They would lead the Japanese up into the mountains. Their faces indicated that it was the right way to go, but they led the pilot farther and farther away from [his airfield at] Myitkyina at every step. It began to rain.
>
> The Japanese scowled, pulled out his pistol, and brandished it at the Kachins. These brown natives were playing some sort of desperate game with him. Two Kachins hit him from behind, and others jerked up his arm so that his shots went wild. The Kachins trussed their captive up with vines and brought him deeper into the mountains to Pat.
>
> Pat's evening radio schedule with Nazira contained surprising news. We have captured a Japanese pilot. Should we try and smuggle him out through the Japanese lines or should we kill him? When the message was deciphered at Nazira's message centre, a whoop of triumph went up. The air force had been searching for months to locate the hidden fighter-plane bases

from which the Japanese Zeros rose in such a deadly swarm.
The Japanese had done a masterful job of secreting the planes.
American bombers had attacked and attacked again the
known bases, but the attacks had not affected the Zeros in
any significant way. Now perhaps this captured Japanese pilot
could be made to tell where his base at least was situated.

'Hold him. We'll get him out,' was the return message
from Opero.

The pilot refused to reveal the location of his airfield, but study of snapshots found in his possession enabled Allied Intelligence to identify topographical background details, and it was bombed shortly afterward. The war in Burma, like the successful campaigns in other theatres, owed a great deal to the information provided by the undercover armies and the communications experts – the radio-cryptographers – who served with them.

7
TOWARDS VICTORY IN EUROPE

**If you had to have a desk job, it was satisfying to have one you
believed was extremely important to the war effort as well as
offering a heavy mental challenge.[i]**

In 1942, the tide turned against Hitler. His forces suffered resounding
defeats in Russia, North Africa and the Atlantic. The years of triumph were
over and there would be no more German victories. Instead, Wehrmacht
troops would find themselves fighting costly rearguard actions in the
east, the west and the south, while behind their backs their homeland was
systematically laid waste by the Allied bombing offensive.

For the rest of the conflict, Anglo-American codebreakers would
decipher messages that reflected a steadily mounting despair on the part of
enemy commanders as manpower and materiel ran out, territory was given
up, and the Führer maintained a stubborn refusal to grasp the realities
of the situation. In fact Hitler knew as well as his generals that, without a
miracle (and he fervently believed that one would occur), the war was lost.
He was aware that he could not hope for a separate peace with the Western
Allies and that there would be no mercy after surrender. His insistence
on fighting to 'the last man and the last bullet', was dictated as much by
desperation as by determination.

Bletchley Park and its maze of outstations had continued to grow, and
the estate resounded with constant hammering and sawing as carpenters
laboured to erect yet more wooden huts. When Japan entered the war, a
section had to be created to deal with Far Eastern intelligence. Alan Stripp was
recruited from Cambridge and described the setting in which he worked:

**The administrative offices were in the mansion itself, which
also housed Nigel de Grey, one of the team which had solved the
Zimmerman telegram of January 1917 [see Chapter 1] , and at one**

[i] Anonymous American officer

stage Colonel John Tiltman worked there too. He had already
done brilliant pioneering work on Japanese and other military
codes and played an important role in expanding and recruiting
for the Japanese section. At first most of the rapidly expanding
staff worked in the huts, with trestle tables and folding wooden
chairs. More and more huts were built until they sprawled over
most of the grounds, whether singly, in pairs or grouped in T
or H patterns. They were urgently needed, because the number
of staff was growing out of all recognition. In 1939 the official
budget had provided for Head, Assistant Head, three chief, 14
Senior and 18 Junior Assistants, together with clerks, typists,
telegraphists and others making some 150 in all, plus a handful
of ancillary staff. By late 1942 the total had risen to about 3,500,
and by early 1945 to over 10,000.

A large percentage of the staff continued to work in the temporary huts that
had proliferated all over the grounds. A few more substantial buildings had
also been erected, though the bustle and clutter inside was much the same.
'E' Block was a square, two-story concrete building. On its top floor a central
passageway ran its whole length between rows of long tables covered with
clattering equipment and piles of paper. Each was staffed by four operatives,
and from the confines of this claustrophobic room they routinely exchanged
signals with the far corners of the earth as well as with the war's decisive
battlefronts. Though repetition might make the work seem dull, most young
women were impressed by their first sight of this bustling environment. One
remembered:

> You saw benches situated at right angles to the central walkway,
> solidly built and quite long, loaded with equipment – typewriters,
> perforating machines, autoheads, Morse keys and other
> paraphernalia. On a board above the bench was a row of pegs
> where tapes hung, wound into a figure of eight, waiting to be
> transmitted or typed. Each bench had the name of the place that
> particular operator was in contact with. Exotic names to me then
> such as Melbourne, New Dehli, Alexandria, Suez, Port Said,
> Malta, Cairo, Calcutta, Colombo, Toronto. There were clocks on
> the wall showing the different time zones in these parts of the
> world.

The mathematicians, the eccentrics, the military men and the armies of clerks had developed since the beginning of the war into a highly efficient corporate machine, accustomed to their particular tasks and performing them with smooth professionalism. Marion Hill, in her history of the Park, commented that:

> In order to process enemy messages each unit of people had a specific, often repetitive task to complete, like a self-contained link in an unknown chain. They only knew they had to do the task, pass the material on to the next and repeat the task – a human conveyor belt.

The technology they used was undoubtedly advanced for its time, but some aspects of their work would raise a smile among users of today's computers. Pat Wright, the operator of a Type-X machine, remembered:

> Anybody who works a computer now that has this light touch would be horrified. The keys had to be pressed right down and came up with a clackety bang. It was very, very noisy. It printed out onto a long strip of sticky tape a bit like you used to get on old-fashioned telegrams. When we finished we took the message and stuck it on the back like an old telegram. Then we would send it through and say, 'Shall we go on with this?' and they would say: 'Yes, keep going,' or 'No, don't bother.'

The one-time pad, which was a standard means of coded communication, was used extensively because of its secure nature. The Type-X machine was the other stalwart of the coders. Patricia Penrose (née Rattray), an operator whose work with the machines was rather more routine and less sensitive than that of most SLU members, explained its workings and described one of the unusual, but commonplace, tasks it carried out:

> At Signals HQ partitions were built to section off the new 'Type X' machines. This way the calm silence of the main office was not broken by the constant 'chug-chug' noise from the machines. These huge mechanical monsters had a key-board similar to a type-writer. Having set the machine to the necessary code key and switched a lever marked 'Encipher,' the operator

then punched out the message in 'clear'. The address being enclosed within the message, as normal cipher procedure. A long, thin, wormlike tape poured from the left side of the machine, recording the clear message for checking. On the other side a similar tape bore the cipher groups. On completion, this tape was stuck across a message form and passed to the morse operators for relay. The procedure for decrypting was the reverse. As well as the extra personnel needed to 'stick up' messages, it was always necessary to have at least one specially trained mechanic on duty, more at peak periods.

The 'X' messages were considered high in security. The code key being changed at exactly the same time each day, wherever the Allies used machines. However, the force needed to push the keys and the consistent deafening noise they made proved a great strain on the operators, who were all girls.

The War Office Cipher Book which was compiled for the 1914–18 war did not always have an adequate word for the changing times of the later war. Whenever a word was not covered by a group of figures it was necessary to spell out each letter to make one word. We were continually receiving signals from padres or commanding officers stating that such-and-such a man requested compassionate leave to get married, as his girlfriend was – spell a word of eight letters – 'PREGNANT.' This would be followed by the girl's name and address, and a request for a medical check of her condition before leave would be considered. The continual stream of men who got leave this way made us wonder whether it was accidental or well planned. In either case we found such domestic signals irksome and a frightful waste of time when there was so much urgent war traffic. For security reasons the man's name and unit had to be enciphered.

Gordon Welchman, who worked in Hut 6, described the type of enemy signal that he and his colleagues came to know well:

The composition of a typical intercepted Enigma message.
1. The call signs of the radio stations involved: first the sending station, then the destination(s).

2. The time of origin of the message.
3. The number of letters in the text.
4. An indication whether the message was complete, or was a specified part of a multi-part message (for example, the second part of a four-part message).
5. A three-letter group, the discriminant, which distinguished among different types of Enigma traffic.
6. A second three-letter group, which I will call the 'indicator setting'. This was related to the procedure for encoding and decoding the text of the message.

Before this information in the preamble, the intercept operator would include two more items:

(a) The radio frequency used for transmission.
(b) The time of interception.

Note that the British intercept operator would have warning that a message was about to be transmitted, because the control station of the radio net would often be able to enter the frequency and time of interception, and perhaps the call signs too, before the German operator had got started on the preamble and the text.

Though much of the work was undeniably monotonous, there was also a palpable sense of excitement generated by the nature and importance of the signals being received. Alan Stripp remembered how impressed he was on first acquaintance with the place and people that would become familiar:

I joined a roomful of twenty or so young men, mostly undergraduates like myself, presided over by two slightly older men. We were all working on the Japanese Army Air Force code system, called 6633. As a newcomer I was set to work on translating signals that had already been stripped of their key and been decoded. I was at once staggered by the volume of useful information most of them carried. They told of movements of squadrons, described Allied air attacks on airfields and aircraft, fit and unfit airmen, fuel and ammunition stocks, requests for spare parts, and occasionally the impending visit of a senior officer on a tour of inspection. Most of the messages came from Burma, but others were from the areas of south-east

Asia or further afield: the East Indies to the south of Burma, and the Philippines. Even those which mentioned only low-ranking personnel were passed on to the indexing staff, and helped to build up a remarkably detailed picture of the enemy's organisation. Even after my brief apprenticeship at Bedford I was dazzled by the picture which this one code painted of the Japanese military machine in action.

He was also impressed by the dedication of his colleagues:

It was a happy characteristic of Bletchley Park that differences of age, rank or background, as well as departures from convention, were largely disregarded. The atmosphere was often likened to that of an Oxford or Cambridge college. Discipline and hierarchy in the normal sense hardly existed, and in return GCHQ was rewarded with men and women who 'hated to take leave on rest days'; a cautionary notice exhorted them to 'take at least one day off every week'. The 'long haired intellectual', far from being a figure of fun, was at the centre of the imaginative and flexible approach needed for successful codebreaking. Denniston, Travis, Tiltman, Cooper and others put their faith in 'the ability of the highly intelligent amateur to grapple successfully with very complex problems'.

However little they may have known about the work of people who sat for years in buildings only a few feet away, some of the codebreakers developed a curious form of intimacy with those whose messages they were reading every day. Group Captain Winterbotham remembered that:

Over the years of reading the signals of Hitler, Rundstedt, Rommel, Kesselring and other German commanders in Europe, most of us who were closely connected with this miracle source, as Winston Churchill called it, obtained a fairly complete insight into the way their minds worked, of the attitudes of the various generals towards Hitler, and of the reasons behind their various appreciations, which they sent to the OKW [Oberkommando der Wehrmacht], as to when and where we were going to operate. These latter gave us the priceless opportunities to misguide them about our operations with our deception plans.

With America's entry into the war in December 1941, unfamiliar uniforms had appeared at Station X. To these new allies the eccentricity of the surroundings may have been something of a culture shock, but they certainly impressed the British staff, one of whom later wrote:

> The Americans, when they do things, do them quickly and with great aplomb. They had no back-up, no training, but then neither did I when I went there. I'm still amazed at how quickly they did cotton on. They learned darn quick and were very good at it. No complaints about them at all.

Not all strangers were so welcome. In the communities around the Park, security remained as tight as ever. Despite the large number of recently arrived people living and working in the area, individuals could still stand out, as Ann Harding recalled:

> Opposite our billet we had a woman living called Mrs Parrot, and one day a good-looking young man arrived to be billeted with her. He went down to Bletchley Park to work, but before long we got worried about him. He was always asking girls to go out with him, and then he questioned them about their work. The girls pretty soon reported him and he very promptly disappeared from Mrs Parrot's and was seen no more. We had many young men coming and going, sometimes for only a short time, but we never wondered why. Only years after did we find out that they were probably being trained before being dropped somewhere in Europe. After all, Bletchley was the Government Code and Cipher School.

MAGIC INTERLUDE

It was not only at Bletchley that codebreakers were at work. The United States had established its own decrypting centre at Arlington Hall, an imposing mansion outside Washington that had formerly been a girls' school. Having mastered the Japanese 'Purple' code ('Magic' was the equivalent term to 'Ultra' for the information gained from this source), American cryptographers uncovered a significant source of intelligence during 1941. This global conflict was not fought in isolation; both sides communicated with their allies, and a great deal of highly useful information passed between them through channels that were assumed to be secure. It was because of this that Allied codebreakers gained, from Japanese signals, much of the most valuable knowledge they possessed about Germany.

Horishi Oshima arrived in Berlin as Japanese Ambassador in February 1941. He knew the country well, having previously served there as Military Attaché. As the representative of Germany's most valued ally, he was naturally given privileged access to the German leaders and discussed with them the developing situations on the different fronts. He sent to his government in Tokyo scrupulously detailed reports on these meetings, as well as his own shrewd analyses of Germany's difficulties.

No attempt was made to change the codes in which his reports were sent and for much of the war they were therefore available to eavesdroppers. One translator of these decrypts was Henry Graff, an American officer who keenly appreciated the importance of what he was reading and who wrote later that, of the thousands of signals that passed through his hands:

> The ones from Oshima were always the most alluring to me.
> I used to look for them to read, even though we translators
> were supposed to work on the messages in the order of receipt
> regardless of whom or where they came from. Oshima's
> messages, transmitted from Berlin, and often reflecting his
> conversations with Hitler and Albert Speer, seemed to come from
> the very heart of the evil enemy we were fighting. As a fledgling
> historian I felt in reading the words of Oshima that I was
> standing at the center of the universe.

In January 1943, Ambassador Oshima convened in Berlin a conference, attended by all the senior Japanese diplomats attached to missions in Europe and the Middle East, for the purpose of organizing systematic information-gathering. They were instructed to assemble all the information about Japan's enemies and about the Soviet Union, which was of course a potential opponent. The Berlin embassy would be a clearing-house for this material. Unknown to Oshima, Allied listeners had followed the progress of the conference and now had a perfect opportunity to evaluate Axis knowledge of their plans or reaction to their operations. It was from this source that they began to see doubt and anxiety developing behind the façade of German invincibility. The following extract from a report by the Ambassador indicates the extent to which the professional German commanders had ceased to believe in Hitler's infallibility and blamed his amateur leadership, after Stalingrad, for what one of them described as 'the greatest disaster suffered by the German Army since Napoleon defeated them at Jena':

> Since Germany has been fighting Russia, Hitler and his generals have been at odds over the conduct of the war, and now the time has come for the Chancellor to stop and think, because he knows how much criticism is being heaped on his head. The German military insists that a general, well versed in military strategy, be put at the head of the general command, that the Chancellor and the General Staff be in agreement on strategy, and that the military be given more freedom. The military say that it is not that they want to quarrel with Hitler, but winning the war is the first consideration. The Chancellor understands this and will, in all probability, willingly give in.

Oshima also reported the pressure under which he was placed by Hitler to help to bring Japan into the war against Russia. An attack on Siberia from the east would undoubtedly tie up resources and relieve pressure on the Germans: Russia, in other words, would have to fight a two-front war just as Germany was doing. Japan had enough to cope with and did not want another powerful enemy, so the Führer's blandishments were unsuccessful. His tone appears to have been wheedling rather than hectoring, as the following report of the conversation showed:

> Now I don't want you to think I am weakening in my conviction that we will win, but the first question we have to face is disposing of the Soviet Union. It is clear that if, in order to destroy the striking power of Russia, you Japanese would, from the East, take a hand and help us out, it would be very advantageous in getting this job off our hands. But after all, the Japanese officials who understand their national resources better than anybody else must make this decision.

Not all the information gained by Allied codebreakers was flowing from Oshima in Berlin to Tokyo. Extremely valuable intelligence was also travelling the other way. This was particularly the case with a report sent to the Ambassador in the spring of 1943 by Matsuoka Yosuke, the Foreign Minister. It was the result of a fact-finding tour through unoccupied Soviet territory by two expert observers. Despite close ties with Germany, Japan did not join the war against Russia (with which it had signed a Neutrality Pact), and its diplomats were free to visit the country and report on conditions. Their analysis gave a comprehensive overview of Russian resources and morale, a clearer picture than was offered by Stalin to his allies. The authors commented on how Soviet pride and confidence had swelled in the wake of their overwhelming victories at Stalingrad and Kursk:

> The war aims have been well driven home and the determination of the people may be called unshakable. All the people cry, 'Let us slay the German invader!' You get the impression that the whole Soviet nation in its fury is welcoming another attempt by Germany to come back.
>
> The successes of the Red Army during the past winter's drive and the annihilation of the 6th German Army in Stalingrad have given an impetus not easily stopped. They say, 'Look, we have plenty of food and raw materials and can give the Germans two blows for one.' The Soviet officials call their present battle against Germany the struggle for the Fatherland. The propaganda of the leaders seems to have succeeded in making the home front well-nigh impregnable, and the bloodthirstiness of the Soviet masses may be adjudged insatiable. Now the Soviets scarcely ever speak of help from England and the United States, or of a second front. They say, 'We ourselves, alone, can whip those Germans any time.' This attitude is general throughout the [country] and is something we cannot afford to lose sight of.

One reason for this soaring morale was that industrial output was steadily regaining its prewar levels. When Germany had invaded, thousands of Russian factories had been dismantled and shipped eastward, beyond the Ural Mountains, where they were reassembled and went back to work. This had kept the armed forces, and society in general, supplied with necessities. The Japanese Ambassador reported that:

Although it is true that both materially and militarily the Soviet Union has suffered considerable losses, by her policy of moving heavy industries to safe places, her essential industries, particularly her military industries, are now estimated to be about 70% of what they were. Apparently the transference of factories and installations to the East is now about complete and the Ural industrial area is remarkably well organized and prepared.

The observers were able to support their general impressions with a great deal of specific detail. As they travelled the country by train, they noted the immense number of wounded soldiers everywhere, but also recorded the vast trainloads of oil and other raw materials, the sizeable quantities of American-built vehicles (tanks and trucks) rumbling past on flat cars, the numerous airfields, the harbours filled with warships and, everywhere, the countless soldiers heading westward toward the front. This was not a nation on the verge of defeat. Its resources appeared limitless and its desire to carry the war to a victorious conclusion had been brought to boiling-point. This was news that must have heartened the Western Allies as much as it dismayed the Nazis.

At Bletchley, the comparative ease with which Axis Enigma traffic could now be read created a new problem, for it became increasingly difficult for the operators to keep up with the flow of signals. As the workforce became larger, the coordination of effort also began to break down. Mrs J Howard explained how she and some of her colleagues took the situation in hand:

Once breaking became a regular occurrence, the decoding section in Hut 6 began to fall rapidly into arrears because of the time taken in changing machine settings as each watch came in and changed the instructions of the previous watch. So 3L was set up to give priorities to the decoding room and elsewhere.

We arranged to have a daily meeting attended by delegates from all three services, our American allies, the cryptographers (who needed particular ciphers for cribs, for example the Pantelleria weather keys), Traffic Analysis experts, experts from the secret weapons section researching on the V1 and V2 cipher, and the railway cipher experts. This was chaired by Squadron Leader Oeser or, if he was overseas on special missions, one of us, to decide which ciphers should have priority on the Bombes.

So, in early 1943, Squadron Leader Oeser set up 3L at the far end of the operational room in Hut 3, behind a map partition. It was a cold winter, so we were warmed by a paraffin stove which was once kicked over. The ensuing flames nearly put an end to us, our venture and the whole hut. We built a door to keep others out and George Crawford wrote above it in Greek: 'Let no one enter here who is not primarily interested in mathematics.'

We had blackboards on the walls, and Christine drew on them the German w/t stars we were most interested in at that time. So that we should not forget that some frequencies might require double banking. We were sent into Hut 6 to familiarise ourselves with the machines working there. We liaised with the traffic analysis log readers; we also made time and study assessments of how to speed up the flow of decodes to the watch, which bore fruit when we moved into Block D and arranged to time-stamp every signal as it passed through. We tried to get better conditions for personnel working in appalling discomfort and became agony aunts for the miserable and uncomfortable.

We three women read and graded every German Enigma signal which came into the Hut. These had been bound into approximatly 50 separate ciphers, covering the German Air Force, the German Army in North Africa, Europe, Balkans, Russian Front, Middle East, Supply Ciphers and specials like weather Keys, secret weapons from Peenemunde, railway and some diplomatic ciphers. Someone had to read all the German material, published daily in the original, in order to evaluate each individual cipher.

We each prepared a weekly news sheet for Mr Churchill on the areas we were covering. We swapped areas frequently so that we should be competent in all of them.

Any extra research, like: 'Who was killing most Germans in Yugoslavia, Tito or Mikhailovich?,' 'Total forces in Norway for a cover plan invasion?', 'The new German Intelligence Services after the bomb plot, how many and who were running them?' came my way. We were hideously overworked and extended.

PREPARING FOR D-DAY

By the middle of the war, the most crucial enterprise was the preparation for the invasion of Europe in 1944. Colossal numbers of men and amounts of equipment were being made ready. The fields of southern England were filling with the huge, tented cities of bivouacking armies; seemingly endless columns of vehicles sat by the roadsides or made slow and patient progress towards the ports of the south coast. The West Country was almost entirely 'occupied' by American troops, whose task it would be to form the right wing of the invasion. In this atmosphere of mounting tension and excitement, the most exhilarating SLU postings could be within the United Kingdom, even if the 'office' in which one might be working could be rather primitive, as described by Sergeant Douglas Jackson, RAF, who trained as a codebreaker:

> On completion of the special course I was posted to the SLU with General Patton's Third Army at Knutsford, Cheshire. At first, I was a member of the part-time watch using one-time pads and working in cramped conditions in the back seat of an RAF staff utility car.

The major Anglo-American communications headquarters was in the western reaches of London at Bushey Park (near Hampton Court) and several SLU graduates were sent there. Sergeant Jack Mellor, who was subsequently posted to an Air Force headquarters in Buckinghamshire, remembered:

> I went to Bushey Park (USTAF [United States Strategic and Tactical Air Forces]) to swell the existing complement of about nine officers and sergeants who were coming under increasing pressure of work with the approach of D-Day. The messages were received from Bletchley Park by W/T, a small unit of army W/T operators being attached to us but not permitted access to the office in which we deciphered the messages on Typex machines. Very rarely did we have any outgoing messages. I remember that many of the W/T messages were 'corrupt' i.e. errors in receipt or transmission of the 5-letter code groups which of course threw the deciphering into gibberish, necessitating repeats of the W/T messages, unless we could by trial and error figure out the mistakes fairly quickly. We late received direct line teleprinter messages which were more effective and rapid but, if the quality

of the operators at Bushey Park varied, errors in transmission still occurred.

Things were really hectic in the weeks leading up to D-Day. We had two teleprinters, W/T and three Typex machines on the go 24 hours a day and the majority of the messages were of the ZZZZZ [the most urgent] or ZZZZ priority. The normal watch complement was three or four sergeants plus an officer i/c (either British or American). One sergeant would look after taking the message sheets off the teleprinters and then, after the deciphering of the messages by other sergeants, stick these up on message pads. The Officer of the Watch then typed these plain language messages onto special paper stamped Ultra; they were then delivered by hand in sealed envelopes to the appropriate addressees (senior officers on the approved Ultra recipient list).

As usual, the low rank and circumspect nature of the unit's members caused curiosity and annoyance among generals' aides, who were not allowed to handle or know the contents of messages delivered to their superiors. The answer to any such difficulty was to refer back to Group Captain Winterbotham, who would smooth matters over with the help of some suitably illustrious commander. Those at the top who received Ultra did not want the SLUs to be hindered in their work:

> After a few words from our Commanding Officer in the right quarters they came to accept the situation and recognise that we were a rather unusual outfit with special direct access to the hierarchy.

While the seaborne assault on Europe had not yet begun, it had been under attack since 1942 by Anglo-American bomber fleets. The largest component in this operation was the US Army Air Force (USAAF), and Sergeant SF Burley of the RAF was posted to a USAAF headquarters in Buckinghamshire as part of their SLU:

> After a brief tour at Bushey I opened up in April 1944 at High Wycombe. Here the unit served the US 5th Air Force under the command of the celebrated Doolittle. It was comprised of RAF, army and US Wacs, and proved to be an excellent combination of

services. The headquarters was located deep underground below the girls' school and was later to become a war room. The actual construction of this underground building was composed of long corridors and air-conditioned blast-proof rooms, each with heavy steel doors, and included sleeping-quarters etc., canteens and mess halls, entrance to which were down a long ramp, and involved passing through several security checkpoints.

As to the physical setting-up of our SLU, the American effort and support were outstanding. There was indeed no question of requisitioning through the 'usual channels'. A US Major saw me, asked me what I required in the way of equipment, maps, type-writers etc., and within a very few hours it was all done. Our Type X machines were set up and Ultra signals were coming through.

There was one amusing incident. My adjutant was an army captain from the Intelligence Corps who was the Earl of Northesk, a most charming individual and an efficient officer, but there had to be some explaining to do about his signing forms 'Northesk'. When the Americans received these they could not understand why there were no Christian names or initials and when I explained that this was the usual form of signature by a titled person and that he was an earl they exclaimed in amazement, 'What, a REAL earl?' This caused quite a flutter and for our part much laughter. This kind of incident made for a happy relationship among all staff.

The invasion had been expected by the Germans since the spring of 1944, but had been scheduled by the Allies for the end of May or beginning of June. As summer arrived, planners settled on 5 June, a date chosen because the tides and the probable weather conditions would favour a landing. There could be flexibility to the extent of a day or two, but after that the sea would become rougher and the vast fleet of ships assembled for 'Operation Overlord' would have a more difficult task crossing the Channel and lying off the French coast. The attack would thus have to be postponed by at least a month. In the event, rough weather did affect the sailings, which were postponed by 24 hours, and thus 6 June became the date that history would remember.

In fact, the invasion might well have been a disaster, for the Allied plans had been in German hands for some months. Fortunately, the situation seems to have been saved by the same attitude that had lost the Allies their advantage at Mechlin in 1939: an assumption that a discovered document was a deliberate deception. Winterbotham explained:

> Whether Hitler had, in fact, been more impressed than he admitted at the time with the supposed Overlord plans (they had been stolen by a German spy in January from the British Ambassador in Ankara and he had told his generals that they were obviously an Allied trick) or whether he and Rommel were being more realistically briefed by German Intelligence one cannot tell.

He went on to observe that, when the German High Command made an assumption about where the cross-Channel invasion would come and the information was relayed to the Allies through Ultra, it enabled them to put in place one of the greatest military hoaxes of all time:

> Perhaps the best example ... was Rundstedt's appreciation in 1943 that the allied invasion of France would come across the Pas de Calais. This document alone led to a complete chain of events, dictating much of our planning for Overlord and setting up of Patton's phantom army in Kent to fit in with Rundstedt's views, a deception which kept a complete German army around Calais and four panzer divisions away from our landing beaches.

And he made a shrewd observation about the Führer's leadership:

> ULTRA told us, too, that as soon as things started to go wrong with enemy operations Hitler invariably took remote control, which was a bonus, since most of his signals went on the air.
> Although neither Hitler nor his top generals ever gave any indication on ULTRA that they had caught on to the fact that their ciphers were unsafe, they must have wondered why their carefully laid plans never came off.

Hitler had ordered the building of coastal defences – the 'Atlantic Wall,' which ran from North Cape in Norway to the Pyrenees on France's border with Spain. The attack could have come anywhere between those places, but the Führer was convinced – and he in turn convinced his staff – that it would be launched at the Pas de Calais. The Allies had instead chosen the Bay of the Seine in Normandy but, as has been seen, highly proficient exercises in deception created the notion that an entire Army Group was being held in reserve after the thrust at Normandy had been made. The Allied invaders got ashore, experiencing ferocious resistance on only one beach: Omaha. They did not make the progress inland that had been hoped, for the countryside favoured the defenders. Nevertheless, by August they had broken out of Normandy and were heading eastward toward Paris, and Germany.

Within days of the first landings, Hitler launched a secret weapon at London. The V-1, contemptuously nicknamed the 'Doodlebug', was a pilotless plane, designed to explode on impact, which had been launched at southern England from sites in north-west France. To this was added the V-2, a rocket packed with explosives that travelled too fast for interception and whose approach could not be heard. The development of these weapons had been followed by Allied Intelligence, and the fact that the launch sites for the V-2 were almost ready for use meant that the invasion could not wait. As Winterbotham pointed out:

> At the end of May an ULTRA signal reported that fifty sites were ready for launching. This finally determined Churchill to press for the start of Overlord in June at all costs. Time was obviously going to be very precious.

Bletchley was, of course, closely involved in the invasion. To protect security in the months before the great expedition began, Bletchley staff were under virtual house arrest, in that they were forbidden to travel further than 20 miles from the Park. It was obvious to the British public, and even to the enemy, that the assault would begin at any moment. Nevertheless, one young clerk still found it a shock when the news was broken:

> One morning in June 1944, JH (John Herival) beckoned me to a corner and whispered, 'We're invading Europe today!'
> My heart stopped.

The contribution of Station X was neatly summed up by Mrs J Howard:
Our main value in preparations for D-Day was:

1) Our knowledge that the enemy had swallowed the cover plans, believed that the invasion would take place in the Pas de Calais, was still worried about a possible invasion of Yugoslavia and/or Norway.
2) That the traffic Analysis section had prepared cover for frequencies likely to produce new and so far unused and unbroken ciphers, in that area occupied by the German 7th Army which we were going to call Duck.
3) That our knowledge of the German Order of Battle, logistics, secret weapons, railway movements, future intentions, remained as always the best we could achieve, and that we expected far more intelligence once bombing had disrupted landlines to OKW [Oberkommando der Wehrmacht, the German High Command].

The V-2s brought a brief reign of terror to Kent and London, but were too late to save the situation for Germany. In England, the SLUs and their host units were making ready to leave for Europe, while learning to live with the flying bombs. Jack Poole remembered that they quickly became sanguine about this new danger:

The dawn of D-Day brought our staff into full play. The watch system was temporarily abandoned and it was a question of all hands to the wheel. The teleprinter almost became red hot as it churned out thousands of five-letter groups of varying priority and in the radio room the signals boys worked as they never had before. Officers and sergeants decoded the deluge of signals, stuck up the 'clear' strips from the Typex machines (like telegrams), logged them, typed them, checked them and then after embossing them with the distinctive Ultra stamp, passed them to the personnel co-ordinating delivery. Priorities were carefully observed and I have no doubt everything was done to keep General Spaatz right on top of the situation as far as Ultra was concerned.

It was decreed that all staff should take cover when a local warning [of approaching bombs] was given. Slit trenches were slashed in the lawns of the SHAEF [Supreme Headquarters Allied Expeditionary Force] quadrangle and surface shelters were also available. The order to take shelter did not apply to the SLU, however. We remained in our office to protect the security of Ultra in the event of a hit.

Frank Brailsford, working underground in the headquarters of the US Tactical Air Force, had a similar experience:

> When the Allied forces had become firmly established on the Continent, I was posted to Bomber command HQ near High Wycombe. This was housed completely underground and all cipher work was done under artificial light. Towards the end of August [1944] I went to Bushey Park and was there when the V1 flying bombs were coming over. The nearest escape we had was when one dropped in Teddington causing a lot of damage and loss of life. When the V bomb attacks were at their height the tannoy announcements in a nasal American twang saying 'Flying barm – take carver' became so frequent one night that we just ignored them and stayed in our Nissen hut hoping that the worst would never happen.

Regardless of danger, the teams were having to deal with a greatly increased flow of traffic as a result of the invasion. Flight Sergeant Jack Poole recalled that:

> We handled a continuous stream of signals which must have been of the utmost value to the US Strategic Air forces at this crucial point in the 'Overlord' campaign. To me the messages were merely isolated pieces of a jig-saw puzzle I could not complete, but I realised that as the Allied invasion forces were pressing on from Normandy the full comprehensive service General Spaatz was getting from Ultra was absolutely vital to him. Our coded signals were still received by teleprinter and radio, varying in priority, and the enthusiastic staff I am certain got a real kick out of knowing that they were feeding our popular customer with material that was playing a major role in the success of the Allies' effort.

Now these operatives, like their counterparts in the Mediterranean, would get used to sharing the discomforts, and the dangers, of life in the field.

Peter Narey, who had just been recruited to an SLU but saw his chances of taking part in the campaign slipping away, made an urgent – and successful – attempt to join the troops going overseas:

> The headquarters soon was split in two parts with one going to France and the other remaining in Bushey Park. I was in the latter contingent. I had brashly invaded the sanctum of the British War Office and asked Colonel Gore Browne for duty on the Continent. Such orders were soon forthcoming and I joined SLU8 at St. Germain. There were only two Americans attached to this unit and by virtue of rank I found myself second in command of the contingent. We had a very congenial and talented group of men. The work was continuous and it was efficiently carried out.

Sgt Douglas Jackson went across with General Patton's headquarters and his group soon established a good working relationship with the General:

> General Patton set up his first headquarters in Normandy at a place called Nehou, near St Mere Eglise, and once our SLU station was established the work began to increase rapidly. We continued to use one-time pads for decoding the messages received by our special communications radio unit. The material was written by hand as we unscrambled the signals and was passed to Colonel Oscar W. Koch, Assistant Chief of Staff, G2 Section of the headquarters. He in turn prepared a daily Ultra briefing for General Patton and other officers in the picture. All top priority messages were passed to the General immediately and direct by hand of officers.
>
> We were quickly integrated into Patton's G2 Section. Our SLU was not a large one. There were two American officers, two British officers and two sergeants.

AFTER THE INVASION

Throughout the weeks and months that followed D-Day, the Allied armies made slow but steady progress through France, first moving off the beachheads they had established on the Normandy coast, then breaking out of the Falaise region and heading north-east for Paris. Another amphibious landing, Operation Anvil, had brought Allied armies into the south of France and these were moving up the Rhone valley to join the main attack. Paris was liberated at the end of August and the armies next moved into Belgium and Luxembourg. They liberated the southern part of the Netherlands, but in September a parachute assault on the Rhine bridge at Arnhem – a bold attempt to seize a major crossing before it could be destroyed – proved a costly failure. The Germans stubbornly held out in the Rhine estuary on the island of Walcheren, resisting for longer than many of their compatriots, who were overrun on the mainland.

After the Normandy landings, traffic became somewhat less hectic and the SLUs coordinated their efforts as they accompanied the armies or moved into regional headquarters. Jack Mellor, as an RAF sergeant attached to the US Tactical Air Force, found his commanding officer, General Carl Spaatz, highly appreciative of the work done by his SLU. He later wrote:

As far as I can recollect we spent the September of 1944 to early 1945 in St Germain. We received our messages for deciphering by W/T and also collected, twice a day, messages received by high speed Morse from another section of SLU 8 attached to SHAEF at Versailles. The volume of traffic slackened off to some extent, compared with the pre D-Day and immediate post D-Day volume, progressively with the collapse of Germany.

Regarding the reception of the material and the appreciation by General Spaatz, I was told by one of my colleagues later that it had been the General's wish to award the US Bronze Medal of Merit to the NCOs of SLU 8 and the Silver medal to the officers at the conclusion of hostilities. However, this was apparently politely and unilaterally declined on everyone's behalf by someone in the RAF or Ultra hierarchy. Nevertheless I gather that all members did receive a special certificate of commendation from the General for their work.

I greatly enjoyed my work with Ultra and when after the war I was asked 'what did you do?' I had to be very circumspect and untruthful in my replies but am very glad now to have the opportunity to tell my story.

Jack Poole left this account of life in the headquarters of General Spaatz in the autumn of 1944:

As the Allied campaign progressed on the continent we got news of a proposed advanced USSTAF HQ there, a move we all keenly anticipated. The convoy of trucks and caravans which were to form the new advanced headquarters was assembled for inspection. We were allocated one of the huge grey trailer caravans that accommodated the various officers. Ours was fitted out with Typex machines, a typewriter and all the necessary accoutrements for an SLU office. An innovation was a petrol-driven electric generator installed at the end of the caravan in a separate compartment. This was to provide us with our own light and power.

He described life in a caravan:

Our caravan [in Normandy] was sited in an apple orchard and for a time we slept in tents. Contact was made immediately with Britain by radio and, with as little delay as possible, we were receiving Ultra signals. At first we found working in a caravan rather strange after the office at Bushey Park and we had the added responsibility of helping the Typex mechanic look after the generator. Typex machines were activated by electricity and if the voltage dropped below a certain level they would not function. It was essential, therefore, that the generator was kept working efficiently. Occasionally we found the extra task rather irksome, particularly when the petrol engine that drove the generator decided to play up just as we were in the middle of decoding a top priority signal. But SLU staff were nothing if not versatile so tinkering with a carburettor or cleaning sparking plugs were regarded as being all in a day's work.

It was surprising how much room we had in the caravan office. We no longer had a teleprinter and all our Ultra signals came to us through the Royal Signals Communications Unit which had set up its radio station somewhere through the apple trees. No time was lost in getting things organized in the caravan. Our move had not meant a break in the supply

of material to USSTAF for an SLU office was still maintained
at the main HQ at Bushey Park. We picked up the threads
of the Ultra service immediately we arrived at Granville
and quickly got down to the business of dealing with the
signals brought to the caravan door by a radio operator.

Poole's unit remained as busy as ever:

There was no slackening in the number of signals we received
during the round the clock watches in the caravan and
although I cannot remember the substance of them I have no
doubt whatever that Ultra was still making a most significant
contribution to the success of the operations of USSTAF.
There is one signal I do remember and it gave a clear indication
of the accuracy of Ultra information. It came through one
evening and referred to the intention of the Luftwaffe to bomb
railway stations in Paris that night. Several hours after we
had delivered the message the air raid sirens began to wail.

Without the option of negotiation, Hitler's armies fought with the
boldness of desperation. The Führer believed he could stage a final,
successful strike in the West by throwing all his available resources into an
attack through the Ardennes, the scene of his audacious triumph in 1940.
He launched this in December 1944, at a time when bad weather had
grounded Allied aircraft. He caught his enemies completely by surprise in
an action that became known as the Battle of the Bulge. For several days
his troops pushed westward, taking thousands of prisoners and spreading
alarm. Within a week of the start, however, the skies cleared – to fill at once
with massive Allied air fleets – and the German effort disintegrated in a
hail of bombs. The tanks had, in any case, insufficient petrol to reach their
objective: the port of Antwerp.

Poole and his comrades experienced the surprise of the German breakthrough in the Ardennes, though his team were quickly back at work:

The days of the Ardennes offensive were certainly traumatic.
There was the report we received that Otto Skorzeny and a
group of picked men had been sent out to assassinate top-
ranking Allied generals ... At 4 a.m. on a cold, misty morning,

I was sound asleep in the billet when I was awakened by a blinding flash. I realized that it was the electric light above me being switched on and I saw standing in the doorway two strapping G.I. Military Policemen. 'Let's go, buddies!' yelled one of them, 'Get your guns and ammunition, German paratroopers are dropping all around the camp.'

It was immediately obvious that the alarm had caused a real commotion in the camp. My main concern as the senior member of the SLU staff was to contact the duty officer at the caravan. Although our office was not in the immediate vicinity of the camp I figured that a parachute raid might cover a wide area and so threaten our boys on night watch. I was instructed to strengthen the guard as a precaution. During this nerve-wracking vigil in the pre-dawn hours we could hear GIs crashing through the undergrowth in the surrounding forest but no reports came in of encounters with German paratroopers. We were eventually ordered to stand down and it was obvious the whole thing had been a false alarm with good intent. While all the early morning excitement had kept us on our toes, the SLU had carried on calmly and the usual run to Versailles had been made with nothing more than shocking weather conditions to cause any trouble.

If the lighting and power in the caravan had occasionally fluctuated because of the capricious antics of the somewhat recalcitrant generator our efforts to maintain the Ultra link for General Spaatz never wavered. The General's subsequent Unit Commendation for Meritorious Service awarded to the USSTAF SLU vouched for that fact.

The winter of 1944–45 proved to be the most severe for many years but by this time Allied troops and materiel were flowing into Europe in an unstoppable torrent. Many assumed that the war in the West would come to an end in a matter of weeks, and plans were already being made to transfer resources to the East.

Germany, however, was not quite finished. The Allied leaders had already decided, in 1943, that there could be no negotiated end to the war. Germany could not bargain with the victors; surrender must be unconditional, and must be offered to all three of the Allied powers.

Meanwhile, Squadron Leader Oliver Reece was attached to the staff of General Eisenhower who, since the liberation of France, had maintained his headquarters at Versailles. He gave a description of life there in the autumn of 1944:

We must have been the last SLU to set out for France, long after the units attached to the armies and, I believe, after the units at Portsmouth. Our little convoy embarked at Southampton on a landing craft which deposited us at Omaha Beach. [We] established [our operation] in a small cottage, alongside which we set up our telex and W/T reception in a mobile van.

Whilst [at Versailles] we received a long 'personal only' message for Eisenhower from Churchill, which was a bit tricky to put together as it had been encoded into two messages on an alternate line basis so that the first message contained all the odd number lines and the second signal all the even number lines. Thus, after decoding each we had to intertwine them as it were. As I remember now the gist of the message was that Churchill was in favour of pushing into Germany with all speed so as to reach Berlin before the Russians while Eisenhower had apparently in a message under reply espoused stopping at the Rhine.

Eisenhower's office was in a large trailer set up to overlook a small house in which he was apparently billeted and where his mess was. Brigadier Strong, who was Eisenhower's G2 [Intelligence chief] at that time, took me over to the trailer and ushered me in with the message. The General was about to eat but glanced at the signal and thanked me for getting it to him. At Versailles, as in Algiers, I found the panorama of the war as depicted in our Ultra traffic extremely fascinating and, although there never seemed to be the sense of urgency that we had experienced in north Africa and as must have existed in the forward SLUs, our recipients were keen and appreciative. I used to drive over with deliveries and when I mentioned the problem of transportation they gave me a jeep and kept it fuelled. Indeed, in that very cold winter of 1944 the jeep froze up, whereupon they took it back and gave me a second one which I kept until our departure after VE Day.

Not too far down the corridor from our premises was a
Russian Liaison Office. I always thought it a bit peculiar
that they had been assigned quarters so close to our Ultra
set-up. I never had more than a nodding acquaintance with
their personnel but did rather admire a rather comely woman
officer in their crew. She was quite good-looking until she
opened her mouth and displayed her stainless steel teeth,
which somewhat diminished the allure. In the Officers'
Mess their table manners were quite fascinating; it seemed
as if this was their first experience with knife and fork.

In December, Allied troops entered Germany for the first time. In March
1945 they crossed the Rhine and the race was on for Berlin. Eisenhower
had decided to allow the Russians to seize the capital, while the British
liberated Denmark and the Americans stood poised to attack the 'National
Redoubt' that Hitler was expected to defend in the mountains of Bavaria.

In France, Jack Poole arrived at the scene of one of the war's final acts:

SHAEF had moved to Rheims from Versailles and had
established itself in the red-brick 'Ecole Professionelle'
just around the corner from where we were situated.

There were scores of German prisoners of war in Rheims.
A squad of them were employed cleaning the pavements
and gutters in the streets near the USSTAF HQ and it was
something of an ordeal for me at any rate to walk past the
long line of abject sweepers in their war-torn uniforms.
We did not speak to or acknowledge any of these Germans
as they carried out their non-military duties en masse.

It was ironic that while the German prisoners of war
performed their menial tasks virtually on the threshold of
the USSTAF HQ we were handling intelligence material
relating to their countrymen who were still actively engaged
in the struggle, information that was contributing in no
small measure to the ultimate downfall of Germany.

During the final months of the war in Europe Ultra messages
were received, decoded and delivered to General Spaatz and his
staff under what can only be described as the most salubrious
conditions. The optimism we shared as we steered the flow

of material through absolutely water-tight channels to our customer enhanced the relaxation we enjoyed while off duty. We now had the Sergeants' Mess with its pints of beer as a change from the more exotic sparkling champagne so easily available in the cafés, or we could pop down the road to a cinema near the barracks which was run by the US authorities for the troops.

Events were now moving very fast. During our visits to the SLU office at SHAEF we could not help noticing the increased and significant activity that was going on at the headquarters. On May 7th the German surrender was signed.

The ceremony lacked the pomp and pageantry that had surrounded the spectacular historic land-marks at Rheims down the centuries. General Jodl signed an unconditional surrender of all German land, sea and air forces in Europe to the Allied Expeditionary Force and simultaneously to the Soviet High Command in one of the unostentatious classrooms that flanked the expansive quadrangle used by SHAEF as a car park.

Although we of the USSTAF SLU played no part in the actual proceedings we felt we were fortunate to be in Rheims at the time. One of our sergeants spoke to me afterwards of the satisfaction of being in the courtyard of the building where the surrender was taking place in the early hours of the morning. He was on night duty and visiting the SLU office. 'Nothing very special about that I suppose but it was a nice feeling to imagine what was going on behind the closed windows at the precise time.' He did not hear General Eisenhower make his victory address after the signing in the 'surrender' room. He is reported to have said: 'This unconditional surrender has been achieved by team work. To every subordinate in this command of 5,000,000 men who took part I owe a great debt of gratitude which I can never repay. They have earned the deep and lasting gratitude of every citizen of all the United Nations.' Naturally no reference to Ultra or the contribution it had made in securing victory. No compliments to the dedicated men of the Special Liaison Units, but I have no doubt they were all implied.

General Spaatz's Unit Commendation for Meritorious Service reflected to the ultimate the perspicacity and efficiency of Group

Captain Winterbotham and his staff in London for, after all, it
was they who had selected us, trained us, guided and inspired us.

Before the SLUs could be transferred to service in the Far East, the war
against Japan also ended. Frank Brailsford found his unit wandering
Europe without purpose until they were ordered to return home for
demobilization:

> As Ultra messages were no longer required by the Allied
> commanders we were instructed to make our way back to Paris.
> After being billeted in the Montmartre area of Paris for about
> three weeks I was then posted to the 21st Army Group stationed at
> Bad Oyenhausen, and I was there when the first atom bomb fell
> on Japan on the 6th of August. After that the war in the Far East
> soon came to an end, and the long process of demobilisation
> began. I reached Earl's Colne in England some time in September,
> to be released from the RAF by the middle of October 1945.

The war in Europe ended on 8 May 1945, eight days after Hitler shot
himself. When Germany capitulated the codebreakers had the news first, as
Doreen Spencer remembered:

> We were the first to know, we were told before the general public.
> We were given permission to halve the number of our watch so
> that we could go and celebrate.
>   To London and, eventually, to the pictures. At about four
> o'clock in the morning we found ourselves in Leicester Square.
> Here the cinemas were still open. We piled into one, found
> ourselves some seats and settled down to rest.
>   We had been on night duty the previous night and were dead
> tired. It was a strange feeling to know that we were no longer at
> war with Germany but knew there was still a lot to be done
> before we could return to civilian life. There was still the war in
> the far east with Japan where there were still thousands of
> servicemen fighting for their lives.

The codebreakers received a heartfelt message from Sir Stewart G Meade,
their Commanding Officer:

MESSAGE FROM THE DIRECTOR GENERAL
On this ever memorable day, I desire that all who are doing duty
in this Organisation should be made aware of my unbounded
admiration at the way in which they have carried out their
allotted tasks.

Such have been the difficulties, such has been the endeavour,
and such have been the constant triumphs that one senses
that words of gratitude from one individual are perhaps out
of place. The personal knowledge of the contribution made
towards winning the War is surely the real measure of the
thanks which so rightly belong to one and all in a great and
inspired organisation which I have the privilege to direct.
This is your finest hour. (signed) S.G.M. 8th May 1945.

For the codebreakers, the cipher war against their principal foe was over, but
there was still another formidable enemy to confront. Bletchley Park had
been studying and breaking Japanese codes since the war began. Now all its
expertise was to be concentrated on this last remaining foe. However, events
moved faster than anyone had expected, as Doreen Spencer explained:

I was standing on Bletchley Station watching the Flying
Scotsman roar through when my eye caught the front page
picture on a newspaper. It was the late edition. The picture was
of a huge mushroom cloud and the headline said that a nuclear
bomb had been dropped on Hiroshima in Japan.

With the ending of the two wars, things at Bletchley Park
started to wind down, those of us who had served the longest
were released from our duties and relocated in preparation for
demobilisation. I was posted to an aerodrome of Air Transport
Command, RAF Honiley near Knowle in Warwickshire. This was
an operational station and being Transport Command was very
busy at that time. The communications staff didn't know what
to do with us. We were wireless operators of which they knew
nothing. We knew nothing about operations rooms or handling
aircraft and radar.

She was to finish her service career involved in a very different type of work,
after being asked by the Admin Officer:

'Would you be interested in helping out with the pantomime our Entertainments Officer is planning?'

So my last month in the RAF was spent rehearsing and helping to 'get the show on the road', literally. The theme was based on Cinderella. I was fortunate in being chosen to play Principal Boy. It was a really good show. We played to packed houses on the station then went to tour other RAF stations down to London, where there was a huge audience at Aspro Hall and a terrific reception.

For some of the staff at Station X there followed an experience that brought home to them the reality of peace; they were told to dismantle the precious equipment with which they had worked through so many long and difficult years. One of the Bletchley Park codebreakers described the joy:

I remember having to dismantle the Bombes bit by bit, wire by wire, screw by screw. We sat at tables with screwdrivers taking out all the wire contact brushes. It had been a sin to drop a drum but now we were allowed to roll one down the floor of the hut. Whoopee!

In a sense, however, the war did not end for the codebreakers for another thirty years. Not until 1975 were restrictions lifted by the British government on the secrecy to which they had been sworn. Only then did the families of many of them discover the nature, and vital importance, of what they had been doing.

8
WAR IN THE PACIFIC

> Up at Commilla Slim was getting all he needed to know from
> London, Washington and Australia. ULTRA certainly provided
> the information on which the Battle of Imphal and Kohima was
> cunningly fought by General Slim and Admiral Mountbatten, the
> battle which was the turning point of the campaign.
>
>   Perhaps the cryptographers' greatest naval triumph in the
> Pacific was the way in which Admiral Nimitz used it so skilfully
> at the Battle of Midway, the last great sea battle, where the big
> ships never saw each other and where the battle was entirely
> fought by aircraft.[i]

While the expanding might of Hitler's Germany had been causing growing
unease in Europe, a parallel process had been taking place in the Far East.
The Japanese Empire had, in less than a century, developed from a feudal
backwater, which foreigners were not even allowed to visit, into an
industrial and military giant that dealt on equal terms with the leading
nations of the world.

In World War I, Japan had sided with the Allies and its armed forces had
taken part with British troops in capturing the German colony of Tsingtao
on the China coast. Japan was affectionately dubbed 'the Britain of the
East', but it had not joined World War I out of idealism. Its government and
emperor were heavily influenced by militarists who had a single-minded
desire to expand the country's possessions on the Asian mainland.

In 1921, the Japanese signed a naval treaty with America and Britain,
consenting to restrictions that would give them a smaller navy than either.
The story of how this agreement was reached has become one of the epic
tales of codebreaking. Colonel Herbert Yardley had headed America's
cryptographic organization during World War I and afterwards he retained
his interest in this field by working on diplomatic codes. He was particularly

---

[i] FW Winterbotham: *The Ultra Secret*

concerned with those relating to countries with which the US had any sort of rivalry. A history of cryptanalysis described what happened:

Japanese is a unique language. While it may be expressed in ideograms or brush-stroke characters, like Chinese, it may also be written in phonetic symbols like our alphabet, whereby each symbol corresponds to a syllable, not a sound. Thus a relatively short code book can be used to represent everything in the Japanese language except proper names.

Yardley and his associates attacked the Japanese code with spectacular success, the more remarkable since Yardley could not speak the language. On November 28, 1921, while the Washington Naval Conference was in progress, a communication in cipher from the Japanese Government to Prince Tokugawa, its representative at the negotiations, was intercepted and turned over to Yardley. It turned out to be one of the most important secret communications in world history, and Yardley succeeded in unscrambling it.

The decoded cable revealed that if pressed hard enough the Japanese would agree reluctantly to build only three battleships to every five constructed by the United States and England. This information was all the stubborn American and British negotiators needed to put Japan in a subordinate position.

Seven years later, in the spirit of world-wide disarmament and treaties by which countries promised not to make war, the American Government decided to scrap its cryptographic department. Colonel Yardley found himself out of a job. He turned his talents to writing a book, *The American Black Chamber*, in which he told the whole story of America's success with cryptanalysis, including the background of the Washington Naval Conference. This book possibly badly damaged the United States and indirectly could have cost many American lives. Publication so outraged the Japanese that the Government in Tokyo fell, and a wave of anti-American feeling swept the country. The Japanese militarists declared that they wanted no further part in treaties limiting the size of their navy, and they began to lay the keels of the ships that fought against the United States in the Second World War.

In 1931, Japanese troops invaded Manchuria, thus beginning a conflict – the opening salvo of World War II – that would not end until 1945. Korea became a Japanese territory, and was administered with terrible cruelty. Throughout the 1930s, Japan was apparently occupied with consolidating its hold; in reality, its military leaders were preparing for a further series of conquests. Japan was poor in raw materials, particularly oil, so set in train the action needed to seize the resources of neighbouring lands.

This process was prepared by subterfuge and followed by military force. All over East Asia – in Hong Kong, Singapore, Malaya, Java – Japanese began to proliferate as shopkeepers and businessmen. Many owned photographic studios, which gave them a perfect justification for taking pictures of strategic features such as harbours and bridges. They formed a highly developed spy network that prepared the ground for the armies that would conquer these lands within a few years, and they communicated with Tokyo through code that made use of innocuous commercial terminology.

Japan also wished to force a showdown with the United States which, with its large navy and strategic island outposts, dominated the Pacific. During the interwar years the Japanese, like the Germans and Italians, began to use Enigma. The codes were being read by US Intelligence some time before the two countries were at war, though it took many years to break their cipher. The Japanese government had decided to use Enigma as early as 1930 and had acquired an early model of the machine. This was largely used for diplomatic purposes, but was later adopted (in a more developed version) by the armed forces. American Intelligence broke the Japanese cipher in 1940 and began to share its knowledge with the British. The number of ciphers, however, was so large that success could never be universal. Regarding one type of enemy cipher, Alan Stripp commented:

> There can be no simple answer to the question 'Why were the Japanese army codes not broken?' First, several of them were. Second, there were probably as many as twenty.

PEARL HARBOR

Given that US eavesdroppers were able to read Japanese diplomatic ciphers for more than a year before the attack on Pearl Harbor, it may be wondered why America was taken so completely by surprise when, on 7 December 1941, Japanese fighter bombers appeared out of the early morning sky and sank much of the Pacific Fleet. The answer proved to be a matter of tragic human circumstance: an encoded message announcing that the attack was imminent *had* reached US Intelligence, but everyone in authority, who could have taken the important decisions and alerted the navy, was away for the weekend. The facts did not become widely known for some time, even though there was an official enquiry, because they would have made the officials involved seem incompetent. More importantly, they would have shed too much light on the way in which information from Japan was being gathered.

This matter, however, did not go away. In the 1944 presidential campaign one of the most effective means by which the Republican candidate, Thomas E Dewey, could attack his opponent Franklin Roosevelt would have been by bringing up the issue of unpreparedness over Pearl Harbor. But Dewey received a letter from the Chief of Staff, General George C Marshall. Marked 'TOP SECRET FOR MR DEWEY'S EYES ONLY', the letter disclosed the extent to which America's conduct of the war was dictated by the deciphering of enemy messages and stressed the danger that could result from making this knowledge public. Requesting that Dewey abandon the issue as a campaigning tactic (he did, and it may have cost him the presidency), Marshall's letter was a useful summary of the US war effort in the Pacific and the specific events that were affected by knowledge of the Japanese cipher. It also emphasized the fact that the European and Pacific theatres were interrelated: just as the Americans and British shared information through coded messages, so did the Axis powers. The letter said:

> The most vital evidence in the Pearl Harbor matter consists of our intercepts of the Japanese diplomatic communications. Over a period of years our cryptograph people analysed the character of the machine the Japanese are using for encoding their diplomatic messages. Based on this, a corresponding machine was built by us which deciphers their messages.
>
> Therefore, we possessed a wealth of information regarding their moves in the Pacific which in turn was furnished the State Department, but which unfortunately made no reference whatever to intentions toward Hawaii until the last message before December 7th, which did not reach our hands until the following day, December 8th.

Now the point to the present dilemma is that we have gone ahead with this business of deciphering their codes until we possess other codes, German as well as Japanese, but our main basis of information regarding Hitler's intentions in Europe is obtained from Baron Oshima's messages to Berlin reporting his interviews with Hitler and other officials to the Japanese Government. These are still in the codes involved in the Pearl Harbor events.

To explain further the critical nature of this set-up which would be wiped out almost in an instant if the least suspicion were aroused regarding it, the Battle of the Coral Sea was based on deciphered messages and therefore our few ships were in the right place at the right time. Further, we were able to concentrate our limited forces to meet their advances on Midway when otherwise we almost certainly would have been some 3,000 miles out of place.

We had full information of the strength of their forces in that advance and also of the smaller force directed against the Aleutians which finally landed troops on Attu and Kiska.

Operations in the Pacific are largely guided by the information we obtain of Japanese deployments. We know their strength in various garrisons, the rations and other stores available to them, and, what is of vast importance, we check their fleet movements and the movements of their convoys.

The heavy losses reported from time to time which they sustain by reason of our submarine action largely results from the fact that we know the sailing dates of their convoys and can notify our submarines to lie in wait at the proper point.

The current raids by Admiral Halsey's carrier forces on Japanese shipping in Manila Bay and elsewhere were largely based on timing of the known movements of Japanese convoys, two of which were caught, as anticipated, in his destructive attacks.

The Roberts Report on Pearl Harbor had to have withdrawn from it all reference to this highly secret matter, therefore in portions it necessarily appeared incomplete. The same reason which dictated that course is even more important today because our sources have been greatly elaborated.

As a further example of the delicacy of the situation, some of the OSS, without telling us, instituted a secret search of the Japanese Embassy offices in Portugal. As a result the entire military attaché code all over the world was changed, and though this occurred over a year ago, we have not yet been able to break the new code and have thus lost this invaluable source of information, particularly regarding the European situation.

The conduct of General Eisenhower's campaign and of all operations in the Pacific are closely related in conception and timing to the information we secretly obtain through these interrupted codes. They contribute greatly to the victory and tremendously to the saving of American lives, both in the conduct of current operations and in looking toward the early termination of the war.

This overview of American successes was, of course, written at a later stage in the war. In the meantime, the Japanese themselves were having plenty of victories. Having chosen the moment to begin the war on their own terms in December 1941, Japanese armies swept like a prairie fire through the surrounding territories – through China to Hong Kong, into Burma, Thailand and Malaya and down the archipelago to fall upon Singapore, then across the sea to the Philippines, the Dutch East Indies and New Guinea. They were as successful at sea as on land, sinking HMS *Prince of Wales* and *Repulse* off Malaya and the carrier *Hermes* off Ceylon (now Sri Lanka), and obliterating a combined Allied fleet at the Battle of the Java Sea.

Their victories were largely easy. The forces that opposed them were too small and ill-equipped to offer serious or protracted resistance, and local populations, initially at least, often welcomed the ousting of their colonial overlords by fellow Asians. Only in Burma and New Guinea was their expansion to be checked by Allied and local troops.

In the winter of 1941–2 the Japanese seemed unstoppable. Within months they had conquered a huge swathe of territory, wiped out the opposing armies, displaced and interned the colonial rulers, and set up their characteristically cruel form of occupation. Though they called their empire the 'Greater East Asia Co-prosperity Sphere', there was no attempt at sharing prosperity, or anything else. They ruthlessly exploited the natives and resources of conquered lands. Their sights were set on India and Australia.

At the insistence of Churchill, the Allies had given priority to the defeat of Hitler. The Pacific conflict was lost, for the time being. The Allies sought to keep Japan out of India, Burma and Ceylon (now Sri Lanka) but could not yet go on the offensive.

TRAINING FOR THE PACIFIC

Both in Britain and in the United States, training of personnel for the Pacific war was being carried out as a matter of urgency. Cryptographers were needed and one of the training schools for them was opened at Vint Hill Farms in Virginia. This establishment, like Bletchley, was so secret that its inmates were forbidden to talk about it. It was also disguised to look as if it were a real farm. Irene Brion, a young woman who enlisted in the US Army as a cryptographer for assignment to the Pacific theatre, was swiftly processed through it in 1942. She outlined the structure of the course:

> Classes began the following Monday on the principle of self-instruction via a training manual, with each person working at her own speed. We were graded, and anything lower than eighty-five had to be rewritten. The classes lasted for eight hours, except for lunch hour and time off for retreat, and were given six days a week.
>
> We began with cryptography, which involved learning to encipher and decipher messages in code and cipher. Mastering a number of systems was only the beginning; we then had to learn to analyze them, because we were being trained as cryptanalysts. A cryptanalyst had the military occupational specialty (MOS) number 808, which was defined in a current army manual as follows:
>
> 'Decodes and deciphers enemy messages and cryptograms without aid of the device or key used in preparing them. Using deductive reasoning and employing knowledge of the various cryptographic codes, analyses messages and determines key to code. May supervise others in cryptanalysis. Must have cryptographic clearance. Must have training in cryptanalysis and be familiar with all types of cryptographic systems and their variations in military communications. Must possess initiative, patience, and marked deductive ability. Should have some mathematical training and be familiar with at least one foreign language.'
>
> We practiced on messages used by the Union army at Gettysburg, because a similar encoding procedure was used by the Japanese in one of their shipping codes. We worked with only one machine, the M-209, a medium-level cryptographic system.

In addition, we had a daily class in Hepburn Kana, the system devised for converting the Japanese characters into syllables – a necessity for transmitting the language in Morse code. We learned a lot of Japanese military vocabulary and the grammatical structures we'd be likely to encounter in their messages. We 'assumed' (a word used frequently by cryptanalysts, and jokingly among ourselves) that we'd be going to the Pacific, but we dared tell no one.

Finally, the last classes were over. We said our goodbyes to Sergeant Nelson, our 'keeper', and to Tokashi Kajihara, the nisei (Japanese American) who taught us Japanese. The next morning, September 16th, we boarded trucks and left Vint Hill behind us. From there we'd be going to Fort Oglethorpe for overseas training.

Academics were needed as well as clerical staff, and in Britain, too, recruiting became urgent. Once again universities were trawled, but while there were many undergraduates studying European languages, there were virtually no Japanese speakers. The search therefore targeted those with an aptitude for the Classical tongues, on the basis that they had already demonstrated skill in mastering difficult languages. Alan Stripp was at Cambridge in the middle of the war and had already been accepted by the Air Force. One day, however, his destiny took a sudden turn:

In October 1942 I went up to Christ's College, Cambridge, for a year because I was too young to be called up for the RAF. One day in the spring of 1943 I went to my tutor to have my Greek composition marked. He sat in his comfortable chair like a well-fed pussy cat, and said, 'Oh, by the way, before we begin, would you like to learn Japanese? They are very short of people who can translate it.' I nearly fell through the chair, but managed to say, 'What would I have to do?' He replied, 'You'll have to have an interview. If you're accepted you'll train for six months in this country and then probably go out to the Far East in the army. I thought this sounded interesting and replied, 'I'm prepared to try anything once.' So I had an interview with Colonel Tiltman from the War Office department MI8. He asked me if I played chess, and I said I didn't; or did crossword puzzles, and I said I did; or could read music, and I said 'Reasonably;' and other questions which at the time seemed odd, but which later I understood. He said that I would hear from him, and I told him about the Air Force offer, but he said 'Don't bother about that.' So I started my summer holiday.

Half way through, on a day when I was sunbathing in the garden, a telegram arrived telling me to report to the Inter-Services Special Intelligence School at Bedford on the last day of August. So began the hardest six months' work of my life. There were thirty of us in the class, who had all done Greek and Latin at Oxford and Cambridge and so they thought we could tackle Japanese.

Stripp described the training given to candidates and the particular difficulties that this language involved:

On the first day we were issued with two Japanese–English dictionaries, one in English letters and one for characters. The Japanese do not normally write with letters as Europeans do, but with pictures called 'characters'. Every character can be pronounced in two ways, one Chinese (where the characters were invented) and one Japanese. A Japanese book starts at the back because they write from right to left and from top to bottom. If you are going to send a message by radio you cannot use characters and so you have to use what the Japanese call 'kana'; these are fifty syllables, each of which has a Morse equivalent, and they can be written down in English letters. [On the subject of Japanese code books:] If they wanted to send a message containing 'air special wireless unit' (kookuu tokushu musentai), all they sent was '0700.' The person at the other end looked up the number in his book. We, of course, did not have the book (at least not normally) and so we had to break the code without it.

The Bedford School was a remarkable, and very English, piece of improvisation. It was the invention of Colonel John Tiltman, an expert code-breaker who had been working at Bletchley Park since 1939. After Pearl Harbor he was asked to recruit men who knew written Japanese and found about a dozen, mostly at the School of Oriental and African Studies (part of the University of London). The School said it might be possible to train people in two years but not less. That was no good for Tiltman who was in a hurry, and he turned to Captain Oswald Tuck, a retired naval officer who had studied Japanese on his own initiative and was eventually appointed Assistant to the Naval Attaché in Tokyo. On 21st December 1941 Tiltman asked Tuck to conduct the first six-month course for twenty-two men and one woman, most of whom were classical scholars from Oxford and Cambridge. Tuck, who had never taught anyone Japanese, commented in his diary 'the idea sounded impossible but was worth trying'. He tried, provided all the text books himself, five in number, and was brilliantly successful – at the age of sixty-five.

We finished on the 9th February 1944 when we were told that twelve of us were going to be sent to Australia as quickly as possible because the need was urgent. Apparently Britain and America between them could find fewer than forty people who were competent in the language. My name was among the twelve.

Radio operators who were destined for the Pacific often began their training in Britain but continued it en route, bringing their skill to a pitch of perfection during a lengthy stopover in the Middle East. RC Grindlay attended one of the signals schools in the region. His was in the Biblical setting of Mount Carmel in Palestine:

> The training now started in earnest and mainly consisted of sending and receiving Morse code. Most of us were at the standard of 8/10 words per minute. It was pointed out to us that this was far too slow and that something in excess of 20 w.p.m. would be required for operational work.
>
> During the next six weeks we had Morse code send and receive lessons for at least six hours a day and most of us got up to the high twenties. A lot of emphasis was placed on reading through interference (i.e. static and other stations); this certainly proved somewhat difficult but practice makes perfect – or nearly.

There were establishments all over the East, as well as in England and the US, for dealing with Japanese codes. Stripp listed them:

> Decoding of Japanese traffic was carried out at Bletchley and at Arlington Hall in Virginia, where the 'really intractable problems' were dealt with. Then there were large US & British units at

Delhi, as well as other, smaller units elsewhere in India. There was a Sigint base at Anderson in Ceylon, one in Mauritius and one in Mombasa. They worked with US bases in Guam, Leyte etc. Chain of intercept stations that ran 'in a great arc from Melbourne, Canberra, Brisbane and Darwin through Ceylon to Calcutta and South China'.

He himself was posted to Brisbane, a city that would become familiar to a great many more codebreakers before the war ended. He discussed the work in which he was engaged, and outlined a number of important differences between the Japanese and German approaches to cryptography:

My section was 'Naval Air' (the Japanese did not have a separate air force, but their army and navy each controlled its own). Our task was to decode and translate messages picked up by wireless units which listened to Japanese aeroplanes, flying anywhere from Tokyo to Singapore, and to their bases, and sent messages to us in Brisbane. These told us a great deal about what the Japanese were doing and were intending to do, and [we] passed vital information immediately to the staff of General MacArthur who controlled all the American and Australian forces in the South West Pacific Area.

The Japanese approach to codes was quite unlike that of the Germans. Most of the important German messages for their three Services used the Enigma machine, with variations. The Germans were quite sure that it was unbreakable and unbroken, and remained so throughout the war. The Japanese, on the other hand, used a great variety of codes and ciphers. At any one time during the war at least fifty-five different systems were being used for army, navy and diplomatic messages, of which twenty-four naval and twenty-one army have been identified. This is all the more remarkable considering their love of tidy organisation.

There is a technical difference between a code and a cipher, though this is often blurred in many books: a code is a method of using groups of two or more letters or numbers to stand for words or phrases of a message; a cipher ... is a method of using letters or numbers to stand for the letters of a message, one at a time, or to change their order. All the work I did was with a code book which used a four-kana group to stand for a word or number, and a two-kana group to stand for a phrase, like 'estimated time of arrival'.

In all Japanese military, naval, air and diplomatic traffic, codes heavily outnumbered ciphers, a fact which is often obscured, partly because some writers do not distinguish clearly or correctly between codes and ciphers, and partly because the process of further concealing a code text is called re-ciphering. Japanese codes were generally based on numerals rather than on letters – though they used both – and were mostly reciphered for extra security. Letter codes were reserved for lower grade signals.

Captain Nave received messages from several wireless units. This was useful because if one version of a message contained gaps or faults another version might put these right. The greater the quantity of material available the better was the chance of breaking the code.

There were two great helps in this process. The first was being familiar with the shape of the message. Many messages were routine and followed the same pattern; for example, weather reports gave the place and time of origin, the general weather, the temperature, the amount of cloud, the wind direction and speed and perhaps the further outlook. In addition, the uncoded messages or 'traffic' from or to the aircraft might very well give a clue to one or several groups in a coded message.

The second were 'cribs', something which ought never to happen with well-trained wireless operators. A plane is flying, say, to Balikpapan, and sends its estimated time of arrival. The base replies, 'Sorry we do not have your code book 24; please send in 23.' The operator repeats the identical message in code 23, which the interceptors have already largely broken. So it is easy to read off all the groups in the new code 24. Code books were changed regularly and it was not always easy to supply copies of the new books on time to the more distant outposts. In January 1943 two New Zealand corvettes rammed a Japanese submarine off Guadalcanal and forced it to beach on an outlying reef. It was found to be carrying 200,000 'code books' (a term which may include other crypto materials), including,

apparently, JN25, one of the most important naval codes.
The Japanese changed some of it but left JN25 unchanged.

Stripp found that he and his colleagues, especially with enemy code books at their disposal, could think themselves into the mindset of their opponents and that fascination with his work could take over his off-duty hours:

> Each word in our messages was made up of four kana syllables, like KO FU TE SI which might stand for 'enemy,' together with some two syllable groups, like HI TO which might stand for 'expected time of arrival is ...'. Every evening I sent to Captain Nave a list of things I thought I had broken together with their meanings, and every morning I received back from him a list confirming them if they were right, correcting them if they were wrong, and giving me additional ones.
>
> Just to make matters worse the Japanese changed this particular code book about every twelve days, but our wireless operators were very canny. The most experienced of them knew the touch of the Japanese operators so well that they could tell which plane was transmitting even if it had just changed its call sign.
>
> After I had been there three months I was sent an actual code book which had been captured (I suppose from a crashed plane), and I spent a lot of my 'spare' time translating it into English. It gave one more of the feel of a Japanese message when one was familiar with the book from which it came.

As for all cryptanalysts, nothing made more interesting reading than captured enemy code books. Stripp was particularly delighted by:

> ... a wonderful find at Sio, west of Sattelberg, of some steel boxes in a water-filled pit. These contained many high-grade code books, which meant for the next months instant translation of all main-line messages with top-level information.

And went on to illustrate:

> Here is a typical actual message:
> SE NO SU sendan convoy

ME U TE no of
MU KU NO ichi position
TU RO HI R Rabaul
YA U TI kichi base
TO MO TI 32 32
TU RI NE 6 6
MO SI HE 50 50
YA SU KE shinro course
MU KA NU 355 355
TI HO SO sokuryoku speed
YA HO NA 8 8
Translation: Position of convoy: bearing 326 degrees, 50 miles,
from Rabaul base; course 355 degrees, speed 8 knots.

Despite the difficulties of dealing with a language, a culture and a mentality that were entirely different to those of Europeans, Americans or Australians, the codebreakers had quickly managed to get the measure of their enemy.

WOMEN AT WAR

In Australia, as in Britain and America, the field of cryptography was one in which women could make a valuable contribution. Those who were engaged for the work went through a process of selection and training similar to that experienced by their counterparts elsewhere. Patricia Penrose was a native of Melbourne, and was recruited through a family friend to work at a military camp within the city. She found herself engaged in highly secret work only a short bus-ride from home. She remembered the formalities of selection and induction. The women were advised by an officer:

> ... to forget what we saw in signals and never to even mention
> any Army matters when off shift. Then individually we
> were taken aside and, holding a Bible, took an oath not to
> divulge any information contained in any signal, nor to
> divulge the method or workings of any codes or ciphers that
> we learned. The punishment for doing so, under National
> Security Regulations, was a long prison sentence. Each of
> us signed our names to this as well as swearing to it.

Training then began in earnest:

Lieut Gange then asked us individually to spell out different words and military terms which were often used in signals. Our lectures and lessons were terribly interesting. Naturally, we could not take notes. We learned that certain codes and ciphers need a key, and for security reasons it was necessary to change this key every twenty-four hours. This was the minimum time it took enemy cryptographers to 'crack' even our highest grade ciphers. They had specially-trained personnel, just as the British had theirs at MI5 in England. By this time the enemy picked up several hundred or more enciphered radio messages in a day, so they had plenty of material on which to work. As there are certain consonants and vowels used time and again, the figures and groups which represented these were repeated more often.

She detailed the methods used to encrypt messages:

The recurrence of these groups of figures gave the enemy cryptographers their opportunity to 'break' enciphered messages and piece together the key for the day. The cipher books we were using were those used by the British in the 1914–18 war, so the whole of our security rested on the changing of the key each day. As short messages are easier to crack than lengthy ones, it was bad security for an officer to originate a message of only a few words. However, should we ever have such a message to encipher, we had to use padding. This was to follow a sequence but have absolutely nothing to do with the war, and should be so far removed from the original message that it couldn't possibly be deciphered and placed in with the original context. The War Office example was 'Mary had a little lamb' – message on – message off – 'whose fleece was white as snow'. Most signals originating in clear commenced: 'To - - ', followed by 'From - -', then sometimes 'For attention General So-and-so'. This meant that most signals leaving our headquarters gave as their origin: 'From Landforce Melbourne', and about 65% were addressed to 'Landops Brisbane'. The remaining 35% were addressed to Alice Springs, Darwin and other areas, which meant a constant recurring, year in, year out, of the same addresses. So it was essential to secrete this somewhere in the main context of the message. The person deciphering it was responsible for leaving out the padding, and replacing the address and message in correct order. When enciphering a message you would pencil-mark the original or clear version, showing where you inserted the address and padding. So your actual message would read something like this: 'Oh, I do like to be beside the seaside. Message begins Gen. Blamey and Gen. MacArthur to visit bases in South West Pacific Area (S.W.P.A.) Estimated time of departure 0900 hours 25 June repeat 0900 hours 25 June. Brackets on. To Landops Brisbane from Landforce Melbourne. Time of origin 0300 hours 24 June repeat 0300 hours 24 June. Brackets off. To check conditions morale and inspect camps. Make necessary arrangements. Carlyon message ends. How I do like to be beside the sea.'

The method of enclosing padding and address should never become stereotyped. As radio conditions were not always clear for reception and therefore a group of figures could be incorrectly received in Morse, this could leave you with one indecipherable word in a message. If the word was obviously 'and' or such like you could hazard a guess and mark with a query, but the missing word could be vital so, for this reason and to prevent delay in sending back to the office of origin for a repeat, figures and dates always had to be repeated, also NOT and MUST. These were high grade ciphers we were learning, the lower grade being used in the field, between commands and units, such as a Transposition Cipher whereby the first or second word in each sentence was transposed into another, or a Substitution Cipher where certain letters received in a message were substituted with quite different letters. This could be made a little harder with a double substitution, but such low grade ciphers had practically no security as far as the enemy was concerned.

Despite being separated by vast distances from scenes of fighting, the women had to follow rigorous security procedures regarding their code books:

Signals were to be enciphered and deciphered wherever possible behind locked doors. When not in use, the cipher books had to be locked in a safe. In the face of an enemy advancing or the possibility of a bombing attack, the cipher books were the cipher operator's first responsibility. He must guard them at all times with his life, risking all to burn them if necessary.

All these regulations referred to males, as to this time there had been few females handling these books. It was also laid down that officers only were to use them. However this was now to be relaxed and cipher operators could be NCOs to the level of sergeant. Should you take out a message commencing NODECO, short for No Decode, you were to call the officer on duty to decipher the remainder. This word was later changed to TOP SECRET. The priority of dealing with messages being MOST IMMEDIATE, IMMEDIATE, IMPORTANT and URGENT in that order, these being labelled accordingly with different brightly coloured tags.

THE INVALUABLE NAVAJO

Thousands of miles away, on the west coast of the USA, yet another group was training in 1942 for the Pacific war and they, too, would become involved in the transmission of coded signals. Their job, like that of Patricia Penrose, would be to send rather than decipher them. They were American Indians of the Navajo tribe, and the notion of using their own language, impenetrable to outsiders, for sending military messages was one of the war's great communications breakthroughs. They were to invent terms for a multitude of words that were otherwise difficult to disguise:

Terms for ships:

Battleship	Lo-tso	Whale
Aircraft carrier	Tsidi-ney-ye hi	Bird carrier
Submarine	Besh-lo	Iron fish
Destroyer	Ca-lo	Shark
Transport	Dineh-nay-ye-hi	Man carrier
Cruiser	Lo-tso-yazzie	Small whale

General vocabulary:

Airdrome	Nilchi-began	Air house
Armored	Besh-ye-ha-da-di-the	Iron protected
Artillery	Be-al-doh-tso-lani	Many big guns

Commanding officer	Hash-kay-gi-na-tah	War chief
Convoy	Tkal-kah-o-nel	Moving on water
Hospital	A-zey-tah-ba-hogan	Place of medicine
Report	Who-neh	Got words
Route	Gah-bih-tkeen	Rabbit trail

The notion of a code based on the language of an American Indian tribe was originated by Philip Johnston, an engineer employed by the city of Los Angeles, shortly after Pearl Harbor. Johnston, the son of a missionary, had grown up on a Navajo reservation and was fluent in the language. He was aware that security was seriously compromised by the lack of an unbreakable code and by the skill of Japanese decrypters, whose knowledge not only of English but of American slang, military jargon and even profanity enabled them to read and understand messages without difficulty. Large numbers of Japanese had been educated before the war at high schools and colleges in the United States. They therefore spoke English with authentic American accents, and knew as much about the country's culture as most natives. Johnston visited Camp Elliott, near San Diego, and asked the Area Signal Officer, Lieutenant Colonel JE Jones:

'Colonel, what would you think of a device that would assure you of complete secrecy when you send or receive messages on the battlefield?' Jones answered:
'In all the history of warfare, that has never been done. No code, no cipher is completely secure from enemy interception. We change our codes frequently for this reason.'

The colonel was persuaded to test the idea, though there was some initial scepticism. There were one or two precedents. In the previous war, the 141st US Infantry had used a small group of Choctaws to send orders by field telephone. The Canadian Army had also used Native Americans for signalling, but the difficulty had been that there were no words in their vocabulary for many of the terms necessary in military communication. Johnston's idea was that such terms could be *created* and Navajo trained in their use. Other Native American languages would have been equally suitable; it was simply his personal knowledge of this tribe that led him to suggest using theirs. One Navajo recruit, Keith Little, explained the advantage of using his tribal language:

It was a whole lot faster. The ordinary, conventional military code, in comparison ... if you match the two together, the Navajo code always beats them, for the simple reason that conventional code has to be changed, updated, maybe every day, two days, maybe every week.

The conventional code uses scrambled numbers and letters and it is scrambled – an ordinary message is written on a pad or a paper and given to an expert to scramble, to code. So when he's done he gives it to the radio operator and the radio operator sends it, and it is written down at the other end the way it is sent. And from there it goes to another expert and he unscrambles it. So there's time lost.

If a Navajo code-talker is really fluent with his code system he is given a message, it's sent, he looks at it, calls the receiver on the other side: 'Here's the message,' and the receiver will say, 'Go ahead and send it,' or something like that, and he encodes them as he is talking and the guy over there is decoding it as he's saying it. Maybe it comes through a minute or two minutes. Ordinary messages are never more than three minutes, and when you're doing that you're saving lives.

San Diego is one of the most important bases of the United States Marine Corps, and it may have been for that reason that Johnston approached this branch of the services. He was not to know that, in the war that had just begun for America, the Marines would not be deployed in the European theatre of operations at all. They would see extensive action in the Pacific, but would not face Hitler. As a result, the Navajo communications specialists recruited at his urging would be used only against the Japanese.

The scheme called for the enlistment of 200 Navajo into the Marines, though in the event only 30 were authorized as a cautious beginning. Recruiters visited schools on the Navajo reservations to find young men who showed the requisite intelligence. The tribe's population was not extensive; it was in the region of 50,000, spread throughout Arizona, New Mexico and California, and within this community there was only a small proportion with the level of high school education necessary to send or receive complex and vital messages. In addition to mental ability, candidates had to be able to meet the physical demands of the Corps, by tradition the toughest and most highly disciplined part of the United States Armed

Forces. Once a sufficient number had been recruited, they would have to undergo intensive, exhaustive training to prepare them for the fierce fighting of the Pacific theatre.

The first intake formed the 382nd platoon, USMC, and passed through 'Boot camp' at San Diego in 1942. Their background made them unfamiliar with any concept of 'spit-and-polish' military discipline, yet they adapted surprisingly well – and quickly – and were highly praised by their commanding officer for their cleanliness, order and skill in weapons-handling. They were described as 'excellent general duty Marines' and there was no question of any lowering of standards to add these valuable signallers to the Corps.

Once their general military training had been completed, they received further instruction as signallers, being taught semaphore and Morse. Only after this did they begin their important work: the developing of the code. After much labour they created a list of 211 frequently used military terms, as well as an alphabet for the spelling out of other words. The letters were mostly associated with the names of animals and plants; for instance, the code for D (*moasi* in Navajo) was the word for 'deer', that for Q (*ca-yeilth*) was the word for 'quiver', and Y (*tsah-as-zih*) the word for 'yucca'.

Keith Little remembered that keeping track of all these terms could be a challenge:

> That's the only way, you memorize it and you write it down. And you keep that in your mind because ... there's about over four hundred words by this time. The initial group made about 211 military words and about 26 military letters ...

Once the initial batch of recruits had been posted to active service in Guadalcanal, the success of the experiment began to be appreciated. Commanders in the field asked to be sent more Navajo signallers, and the Marine Corps arranged for the recruitment of another 200 men. The training programme became established, with a succession of classes passing through Camp Elliott, and Philip Johnston, though in his forties, was able to enlist in the corps as the course instructor. As the Pacific war expanded, involving ever larger numbers of men, the objective became the recruiting of 25 Navajo a month, with a view to making 82 available to each Marine division. This number could not be procured, and divisions had to make do with only seven or eight. Johnson suggested establishing a training centre in the Pacific at which both recent recruits and men already serving could attend courses and formulate additions to the code, since military terminology – such as the names for new types of tank and aircraft – was continually evolving. The centre was established in Hawaii and the code was extended, the number of words virtually doubling. Further terms were also added (the term for Britain was 'bounded by water' and for Germany 'iron hat').

The code had the advantage that, despite the lengthy and complex-sounding Navajo words, it made communication faster than any other system used by American forces. This speed was matched by the efficiency instilled in training. One graduate of the course, who took part in the fighting on Guadalcanal, later remembered some of the essentials that he and his comrades had been taught:

> One thing we learned in school was not to be on the air longer than was absolutely necessary. We had to be careful not to repeat words in a sentence – that is, if the message had to go through more than once, we tried to say it differently every time. We were also told not to use the same word too often in a sentence, and that we had to be accurate the first time! If a message has to be corrected or repeated too often, you are giving the enemy a better chance to locate you. On Guadalcanal we had to move our equipment in a hurry because the Japs started to shell the very spot where we were operating.

The Navajo were expected not only to 'soldier' as regular Marines but to be available at all times to send or receive signals. If a radio operator was sent a message prefaced by the words 'New Mexico' or 'Arizona', it meant that the nearest available Navajo had to be brought in to listen. In addition to radio and telephone communications, they had in theory to be able to work as 'runners', carrying messages by hand from one part of a battlefield to another. This need to dodge bullets during combat was one major reason why the Navajo recruits had to be fit. The work could be highly dangerous, and cost the lives of several of them. In practice, they were too valuable to be put at unnecessary risk. One who took part in several of the amphibious assaults on Japanese-held islands remembered that:

> Men in the first wave on the beach during an invasion barely have a chance to survive; the second wave has a little better chance, and chances are fair for the men in the third wave. On

Tarawa, they put me in the third wave to give me a better chance for survival. I was in the front lines a lot, but they would keep us where the action was only a half day – not longer than a full day – then send us back, keeping us involved, but trying to protect us in that they didn't want anything to happen to us. We couldn't be replaced like some of the men with general skills.

Though they did not think of themselves as in any sense an elite, at least one of their instructors (himself a member of the tribe) tried to instil this feeling in his students. He sought to ensure that they would keep their knowledge to themselves even under threat of death:

> I wanted those code talkers to guard their secrets with their lives. I thought of the idea of comparing them with the Japanese suicide pilots and the Nazi elite guards. If they were captured, they should guard the code with their lives! I would ask, 'Would you refuse to give away the secret of the code if you had a samurai sword at your throat? If the enemy would ask, "What is your word for A?" would you tell them? You begin to bleed; you begin to feel your own blood trickling down, with the cutting a little deeper. You WOULD lay down your life before you would tell, wouldn't you?'
>
> I would look them square in the eye and ask them to answer yes or no. I would say, 'Are you devoted that much? Are you willing to die for this secret method?'
>
> As an instructor in the field I ramrodded that. If, when I asked a question, a man would nod his head, I would say, 'No, I don't see a thing in your eye.' If it wasn't definite enough to suit me I would say 'I didn't quite hear you!' Then he'd say with emphasis 'Yes, sir!' I'd stay with it until I heard it loud and clear, and then I knew I could trust that man – just like the suicide pilots would give their lives when they made that last dive. Like the Nazi elite corps – no 'if' or 'maybe' about the way they did things, I wanted absolutely strict discipline – military discipline.

Fortunately this level of commitment did not prove necessary, for none of the code talkers ended up in Japanese captivity. Their presence in the front line, however, gave them occasional trouble with their own side. The physical resemblance between American Indians and Japanese was sufficiently close that, in the dark or in the confusion of battle, individual Navajo were arrested as Japanese spies. Their American uniforms and identification, as well as their knowledge of the language and culture, were merely seen as effective camouflage, and in one or two instances they were in danger of being shot until vouched for by their officers. One man remembered:

I had been on Guadalcanal for some time and was hungry for something like orange juice. The army usually had some, and a transport had just come in close to where we were waiting on the beach to leave the island. I walked over to the army supplies and started digging for orange juice when somebody put an iron in my back. I thought whoever it was was just kidding and kept on digging. He finally said, 'Get out of there, you damn Jap!' The sergeant standing there said, 'He has Marine Corps identification and speaks good English.' The man with the gun said, 'I don't care if he graduated from Ohio State. We're going to shoot him.' I finally mumbled, 'I'm from right down there,' but I couldn't see the direction because there was too much sweat running down into my eyes. Finally, they took me back to my outfit. I had 15 men around me, and the sergeant of the guard had a .45 cocked against my back all the way and I had my hands up all the way. When we got to the beach, they asked, 'Is this your man?' and of course got the answer, 'Yeah, that's our man. Hey – are you guys serious?' 'You're damn right we're serious,' they said, 'If you guys don't make a positive identification we're going to take him back.'

Finally the lieutenant came around and said, 'What's the matter?' 'Well, we caught this man over there in our yard and we think he's a Jap. If you don't identify him we're going to take him back over there and shoot him.'

After that they gave me a bodyguard. If I went to the head, he would come along behind me – this tall white man; I'd go swimming and he'd go swimming. They made him stick right by me.

A total of 420 Navajo communications specialists served in the Marine Corps between 1942 and 1945. One Marine officer, Major Howard Conner, declared: 'Were it not for the Navajos, the Marines would never have taken

Iwo Jima.'[26] The Japanese, who had broken other American codes without difficulty, never succeeded in interpreting their messages. In the view of a signals officer, Colonel Norman Goertz, the enemy's difficulty in understanding the language, compounded by a lack of technical equipment and time for analysis, contributed to the Allied victory. He wrote:

> My guess is that while the Japanese may have monitored their transmissions at one time or another, because the Navajos were used during periods of tactical engagement, the Japanese did not have either the time or facilities to identify the transmissions properly. Having had personal observation of the Japanese electronic equipment through the Iwo Jima campaign, I can speculate that, in the field, they did not have enough equipment to monitor our channels and record the transmissions for analysis.

The Navajo were so successful that it is only to be wondered why the other branches of the American government and armed forces did not make use of similar schemes, or why the Marines' experiment (which ended with the cessation of hostilities) was not continued into the postwar era. Their contribution had been vital and Keith Little reflected with satisfaction on the difference he and his colleagues had made:

> I have a real feeling that I was able to be a marine, and not knowing what I was going to do. All I was going to do was maybe carry a rifle or a machine-gun and shoot, but I ended up not using my weapon. My weapon was my language, and that language probably saved countless lives.

SEEDS OF DISASTER

Japan's territorial expansion had reached its limit in the spring of 1942, when it established a defensive perimeter that ran from Burma to northern New Guinea. This very success, however, carried the seeds of disaster, for an empire of this size meant stretching manpower and resources and could not be easily defended. At the same time, the United States had begun to hit back. The 'Doolittle Raid' on Tokyo on 18 April 1942, in which bombers had for the first time taken off from an aircraft carrier, had made it possible, also for the first time, to take the war into the enemy's camp.

The next month Japan received two further blows and from these it would not recover, for they would end its dominance of the region and begin the steady decline in its fortunes.

In April, Admiral Chester Nimitz, the American Commander-in-Chief Pacific, received intelligence from intercepted radio traffic that the Japanese fleet was on its way to capture Port Moresby in New Guinea – clearly a stepping-stone for an attack on Australia. Knowing exactly where to find the enemy ships, and knowing also the number of vessels and aircraft he could expect to encounter, Nimitz ambushed the Japanese in what became known as the Battle of the Coral Sea. This was the first naval engagement in history to be fought between two opponents whose ships were not even within sight of each other, for the actual combat took place between fighter aircraft launched from their respective flight decks. The advantage of surprise did not bring outright victory, for one American carrier was lost and another disabled. Nevertheless, the enemy was prevented from reaching its objective.

If the Coral Sea was the 'left hook' delivered by the US Navy, the Battle of Midway a few weeks later in June 1942 was the 'right hook'. This time the defeat of the Japanese was decisive. They lost four aircraft carriers, and with them any ability to dominate the Pacific. Once again success proved costly for the Americans, but the price was worth paying. After Midway, Japan was unable to threaten Hawaii, or the United States, again.

This battle was also a result of overheard Japanese radio traffic. Hugh Melinsky, who was a British cryptanalyst in the Pacific, explained that:

> Intercepted signals showed that a great Japanese fleet would move and try to capture Midway Island, known as the sentry for Hawaii itself. The instructions in the signal were 'to provoke action with the main American fleet and to destroy it piecemeal', and finally it disclosed that an attack on the Aleutian Islands would be made which was intended to draw off the Americans to the north. And leave the way open to Midway. As a result, Nimitz was able to avoid the trap of allowing his ships to be drawn off to the north. The Battle of Midway was to be the turning point in the Pacific.

The Midway Islands are north-west of Hawaii and are part of the same island chain. In 1942 they were America's westernmost outpost in the Pacific. That they might be a Japanese objective had been the conclusion of the US Navy's expert codebreaker, Lieutenant Commander Joseph Rochefort. An eccentric in the best traditions of Bletchley Park, Rochefort shared with the British 'boffins' an instinct for getting inside the mind of the enemy. He had been instrumental in breaking Japan's JN25 code, and it was he who had disclosed the Imperial Navy's plan to attack Port Moresby.

Rochefort was aware that Japanese code referred to places by groups of two letters, of which the first was A. AH was Pearl Harbor; AG was the site of a refuelling rendezvous for seaplanes. He decided that AF, a location that was featuring in messages with increasing frequency, was Midway. To put this notion to the test, it was arranged that a false message would be broadcast in 'clear' to say that the water-distillation plant at the naval base on Midway was out of action. Within 48 hours a Japanese signal was intercepted which announced that fresh water supplies at AF had run out.

The purpose of targeting this lonely American outpost would be to draw their Pacific Fleet into battle. Despite the pounding it had taken at Pearl Harbor, the US was still a formidable presence in the region, for by chance its aircraft carriers had not been in port on the morning of the attack. Admiral Yamamoto, the Japanese naval commander, sought to divide his enemy by staging a diversionary attack far to the north, and then destroying them in two actions. He had significant superiority in numbers, and had his plan succeeded it would have left America's west coast undefended. In the event, his opponents knew his intentions as well as his own subordinates did. Between 3 and 5 June 1942, the US lost one carrier and one destroyer. Japan lost four carriers, two cruisers and three destroyers. American air power was intact. Japan's was wiped out.

Though it would seldom exert such important influence on events, signals intelligence in the Pacific provided (as it did in the other theatres) a steady flow of highly useful information that often gave the Allies the edge, though – as always in the cryptanalysts' war – there were costly setbacks caused by an inability to decipher changes in codes. Hugh Melinksy recalled:

> In early 1942 1 Wireless Unit (Royal Australian Air Force) intercepted a message referring to the Japanese building an airstrip on an unknown island in the Solomons, spelled in Kana GA DA RU KA NA RU. This turned out to be Guadalcanal. (The Japanese language has no 'L' sound because they cannot hear any difference between 'R' and 'L'.) The US naval staff decided that it must be

recaptured before the airstrip was completed, and so US Marines landed there on 7th August. A ferocious struggle continued until December with heavy losses on both sides. The Allies lost four cruisers on 8th August partly because they were unable to decode a naval message about two Japanese cruiser divisions proceeding to Guadalcanal. The message was in JN25 code which changed periodically and it took us time to catch up with the alterations.

The codebreakers' greatest coup, other than the discovery of plans for the attack on Midway, was the ambush of Admiral Yamamoto. Eavesdroppers picked up the news that the admiral – to Allied minds perhaps the most notorious Japanese arch-villain – was to make a tour of inspection by air. There was considerable debate as to whether he could be shot down without compromising the source of this information, and only after lengthy debate did the attack go ahead. Alan Stripp told the story:

> In the first half of April 1943 Yamamoto ordered large scale attacks against Guadalcanal, Port Moresby and Milne Bay, and followed these up with a personal visit to his forward naval bases in the Bougainville-Solomons area. The Rabaul commander sent a message on the 13th giving the admiral's travel arrangements and this was picked up by 1 W.U. at Townsville, and also by the Americans in Honolulu. It was decoded almost entirely, and read:

> On 18th April C in C will visit RXZ [Ballale-Buin], R.. and RXP in accordance with the following schedule:
> Depart RR [Rabaul] at 0600 in medium attack plane escorted by 6 fighters.
> Arrive RXZ at 0800. Proceed by minesweeper to R.. arriving at 0840. (Have minesweeper ready). Depart R.. at 0945 and arrive RXZ at 1030.
> Depart RXZ at 1100 in medium attack plane. Arrive at RXP at 1110.
> Depart RXP at 1400 by medium attack plane and arrive RR 1540.
> In case of bad weather the trip will be postponed one day.

> The Americans weighed the risk that to use this information would be to blow the gaff and perhaps gain them the assassination of one man for the loss of great quantities of

tactical and strategic intelligence. The heavy personal item in their balance sheet was that they could not forgive him for the totally unexpected, unprovoked and devastating attack on Pearl Harbor, which was known to be his personal idea. It was also reckoned that his loss would depress Japanese morale, and that he was a ruthlessly efficient naval commander whom it would be hard to replace adequately.

On 18 April 1943 a flight of P38s, with long-range fuel tanks attached, set off from an airfield on Guadalcanal. At 0745 that morning they sighted their quarry: two bombers with an escort of fighters. Both bombers were shot down. Yamamoto's plane went down in jungle and the Admiral was killed. His chief of staff, Admiral Ugacki, was aboard the other bomber, which crashed in the sea, and he survived. The Japanese waited three days before announcing Yamamoto's death. To the immense relief of the Allies, the JN25 code was not changed. The operation was thus a complete success.

CODEBREAKERS AT WORK

Throughout the Pacific islands, administrative staff followed the fighting troops, setting up camps and 'offices' (usually in tents or dug-outs) to house the various support services upon which the armies depended. Alan Stripp described his British unit's arrangements:

> The operational part of the unit consisted of three large
> lorries with a canvas awning stretched between two of them.
> Under this I and four or five others worked at tables, with
> the wireless sets in one lorry and the Intelligence Officer in
> the other. The third lorry contained generators for providing
> the electricity. Airmen brought me messages which the
> operators had picked up listening to Japanese aeroplanes,
> and I did my best to decode and translate them. The other
> traffic consisted of all the other signals sent by the planes and
> their bases, and this was carefully examined and collected.

Irene Brion served with the American WAC in the recaptured territory of Hollandia in the Dutch East Indies. Her working environment was somewhat less primitive, but was still a challenge. She outlined the nature of her work:

The WAC area was on a partially levelled-off section of mountainside above the lake. The entrance to the burlap and wire-fenced compound faced the mess and rec halls, behind which a path led about fifteen feet to the tent area below. There were eighty tents, and two sets of showers and latrines. We were allowed to pick a tent. We decided to call our home 'Secret trash,' a term referring to waste papers that we used in our signal intelligence work.

We were ordered to report for duty in the advance echelon of SIS (Signal Intelligence Unit). SIS was a branch of Central Bureau (CB), an international bureau composed mainly of American and Australian signal intelligence units based in Brisbane, Australia. SIS, under the operational control of GHQ, was directed by Col. Abraham Sinkov. He was one of the three original disciples of the 'father' of SIS, the brilliant William S. Friedman, who was appointed by the army to found and organize the service in 1929.

Our office, one of three Quonset huts near the GHQ buildings, was ideally situated for work that required a quiet, relaxing atmosphere.

At that time, SIS, which included girls who had been trained before our arrival, was working on decoding one of the Japanese shipping codes. We were told that, in the haste of their departure from Midway, the Japanese hadn't burned the codebooks or thoroughly stirred the ashes, setting the stage for a valuable entry to be made into their code systems. [During training], we'd been thoroughly warned about the necessity of destroying all papers and scrap pieces that we'd been working on during the course of a shift, by burning them and carefully stirring the ashes. Despite the remote location of GHQ, this procedure was carried out every night, using a large oil drum that stood outside our hut.

It was our job to recover new values from messages to fill in gaps in the codebooks, then pass them, along with any pertinent information from the actual messages, to our superiors in signal intelligence. We'd been so well trained at Vint Hill [training camp in Virginia] that the transition was smooth despite the fact that we received little if any direction or supervision from our superiors. After preliminary explanations, we sat down at tables, spread out our papers, and went to work.

She outlined the structure of SIS:

We knew little about the organization of SIS, but it worked something like this. Signal radio intelligence would intercept messages that the Japanese transmitted in an enciphered four-figure code and send them along to traffic analysis, where call signals and dates of transmission would be identified and analyzed. Somewhere along the line, the key words used to encipher the four-figure code would be determined, and the messages would be passed along to our cryptanalytic section. At that time the Japanese were using exotic names for key words, which they changed every month.

Each of us, or each pair if two were working together, would copy on a large sheet of paper a number of messages that used the same key word. Decoding with known values, we'd run through the messages until they yielded a sufficient amount of plain text to make sense. From the text of a given message we could often assume values for the unknown code words and test them against the texts of other messages to assure validity. We'd work until we either completed the messages or determined a sufficient amount of text to extract information and add values to the codebook.

The messages usually followed a set pattern – the call sign of the transmitting station, sets of numbers informing the receiver which code to use, and other necessary information. The text of the message ignored one of the great sins for the transmitter – the necessity of avoiding repetitive phrases. Typically, they began with the name of the ship, the time of departure, the nature of the cargo, and the expected time of arrival. Most textual material was boring to us but often informative to our superiors in G-2, who were eager to get information concerning frequency, concentration, and types of supply movements. However, I remember a message that told of a ship carrying an interesting cargo – women. Were they geishas? Whoever they were, they didn't rate the status of passengers.

I loved the work. I would lose all track of time pursuing the meaning of the messages, and it was exciting when things began to fall into place. I'd take a breather and pass a note to Bell or Gemmy, usually containing a cartoon, a pun on a Japanese word, or a line from a pop song we'd been trying to recall. They did likewise. Despite those frustrating times when we struggled to come up with something that made sense, we all took great satisfaction in doing the job we were trained to do and making a tangible contribution to the war effort.

And, as might be expected, it wasn't always easy to stay healthy:

Our chief problem was 'jungle rot,' a term that covered a wide range of fungal infections. Sooner or later most of us got it, usually the mild variety that was treated with gentian violet. I got some between my fingers, which cleared up quickly, but Marge Wilhelm and Edith McCann's had cases that required hospitalisation. Marge broke out in sores all over her legs. Marge's was the most serious – the type that attacks the optic nerve and causes blindness – and she had to be shipped home. We learned later that she lost 90 per cent of her vision.

Patricia Penrose worked at home in Australia, but one of her tasks was to deal with messages from clandestine groups in the jungles of New Guinea. In a sense she felt she shared the danger of those at the other end of the radio link. On one occasion particularly she held her breath. She remembered:

Scattered throughout these islands were groups or parties of men attached to 'Z' Force. Each party being known by an individual name such as 'Lady Bird,' 'Lizard' etc. They were made up of Dutchmen, Englishmen, Filipinos, Japanese, Americans and Australians. All hand-picked personnel, many with a local knowledge of the islands and conditions, they were highly trained, equipped and surreptitiously landed at their destinations. It was necessary for us to learn American, Dutch and more English ciphers as groups from all these countries and Australia were combined in 'Z' Special Unit.

The job of the 'Z' Force parties was to radio back information about enemy movements as well as raiding and sabotaging enemy supplies, equipment or landing strips. Their work was hazardous, hiding out in caves, living on dehydrated rations and forced to work under cover. Not only were they in danger from Japanese troops, but they also risked betrayal by hostile local inhabitants. Working under these conditions it is little wonder that when we received their cryptograms they were often corrupt.

Rarely could we send for a repeat, so this would mean spending hours working out possible alternatives or solutions. I remember one signal sent from a party up a tree, their last line read: 'Japs are all around. Imperative you maintain strict radio silence.' Failure to do so on our part would have meant their easy detection and certain death. After several worrying days we were relieved to hear they were comparatively safe again.

Her own experience – working in an office, where rows of similarly uniformed young women sat at tables encrypting and decrypting – was more typical of the work of codebreakers, whether in Melbourne, Brisbane or Bletchley.

The Cipher Office was arranged with an officer at the head of the room. Next to him was a Warrant Officer who was Section Leader. The remainder of the cipher staff sat in twos, facing each other across tables.

Day shift commenced at 8 a.m. and finished at 4.30, evening shift concluded at 11 p.m. and night shift went until 8 a.m. The bulk of the traffic was dealt with during the day so two girls were rostered for this shift, if there was a big carry-over of work to the evening shift one would stay on duty a while to help the girl on evening shift. The night shift wasn't so busy, but it was very necessary to deal with incoming messages which could be vital. Shifts were rotated every six days at the end of which you had a 24 hour stand-down.[37]

... It was our job to faithfully encipher the cryptograms on the Type X machine. These signals were in turn passed to Staff Duties for retransmission to MI5 in London, where expert cryptographers worked at breaking enemy ciphers. [One of her colleagues] stayed at it for eight months before the strain became too great. Carrying out such exacting work on a loud and noisy machine in a confined space left her mentally and physically exhausted.

She remembered how the constant need for security could also become stressful:

> Arriving at the Cipher Office one morning I was given an unusual assignment. I had to take a book of key figure groups to a certain printer. He was to make a number of copies and, when the job was completed, I was to break the type, then return with the original and the type. I had strict instructions to keep the printer and his press under observation at all times. This was alright in theory but the man found it necessary to leave me on several occasions and obviously there were places I just couldn't follow him. So I sat with my eyes fixed on the press. As the hours went by, I became aware of a pressing necessity to leave also, but the call of duty proved greater than the call of nature and I crossed my legs and sat it out. Surely type was never broken so quickly as by my hands that day.

Some of her colleagues suffered even when asleep, as the pressure of their work invaded their subconscious:

> Early in the new year of 1944 the strain of high pressure shift work and camp conditions started to take its toll on the girls. Some of the morse operators became 'morse-happy,' often sitting up in bed, 'dit-dahing' in their sleep. Throughout each section girls were suffering with nervous disorders and a general lowering of resistance.

The job was not without its lighter moments, for domestic news as well as tactical and logistic messages were sent through their Morse keys. They often had to encrypt and pass on to men serving overseas the news that their wives had given birth. To save time, a formula was used by the operators for this purpose:

> They set up a pre-arranged signal for officers whose wives were expecting babies. This was the quickest and most direct method of notifying the fathers once they left the mainland. Should the baby be a girl, we sent: 'Bicycle arrived today.' If it was a boy, we added 'complete with tools'.

JAPAN IN RETREAT

The war was influenced by units like those Alan Stripp described because they pinpointed targets for Allied air forces. In spring 1944, said Stripp:

> The Japanese were withdrawing their main air bases westwards. Intercepts up to late March indicated that there were at least 310 aircraft parked on the Hollandia airfields, and on the 29th March the interceptors picked up a message from the air commander, Lt. Gen. Teramoto, directing the Hollandia base commander to evacuate his planes the next morning. The message was quickly enciphered again and flashed down to Brisbane. The next day, 150 [Allied] planes struck at midday destroying 25 planes; on the following day 138 attacked and destroyed a further 138; and on 3rd April a third raid by 310 aircraft completed the destruction of what planes remained. Aerial photographs revealed 288 wrecked aircraft littering the runways. The way was paved for the invasion of Hollandia.

The quality of specific intelligence enabled the Allies to repeat one of their most successful operations. Having done away with Admiral Yamamoto, they dispatched his successor in the same way:

> Wireless Units kept MacArthur's staff informed of enemy air plans, locations of airfields, movements of aircraft and types, details of bombing and reconnaissance missions, fuel stocks, air cover over convoys, and weather reports. On 3rd April (1944) a message reported that a flying-boat which had left Palau on 31st March failed to arrive at destination in the Philippines. Admiral Koga, C-in-C of the Combined Fleet lost in electric storm. His death was kept secret for more than a month.

Stripp described how the targets they indicated could be economic:

> Many successful sinkings were achieved in the second half of 1944, especially with those convoys plying from Japan to Singapore via Manila, and picking up vital oil from Borneo on the return trip. So valuable was this fuel that the Japanese even used battleships to escort their tankers.

They could also be what proved to be the first of the Kamikaze squadrons:

> An intercept of 3rd November 1944 disclosed the formation of a
> 'special attack unit' at Clark Field (Philippines) of twenty-two
> bombers and fighters, the first to be devoted to suicide bombing.

As Japan's resources were reduced by destruction or capture, its armies' desperation grew. Stripp recalled an act of deception that in turn called for the usual counter-deception – the pretence that an action was the result of chance encounter rather than codebreaking:

> By June 1945 the shortage of shipping in the East Indies area was
> so acute that the Japanese had decided to use a hospital ship,
> the *Tachibana Maru* 'for purposes other than those prescribed by
> the Geneva Convention.' The ship was renamed the *Hirose Maru*
> and bore floodlit crosses twenty feet high. It was to carry 1500
> troops and 150 tons of stores and munitions from Tual in the
> Kri Islands to Surabaya in Java. In case the vessel was stopped
> and searched, the troops were issued with hospital clothing, daily
> sickness reports were kept, and the regimental colours were sent
> by air so as not to give the game away.
>
> The messages arranging this deception, sent in May, were read,
> and the vessel was intercepted by two destroyers north of Timor.
> The search party found that cases marked 'medical supplies'
> contained ammunition, and the only wound among the patients
> was confessed to being the result of a packing-case being
> dropped on a thumb. In order to conceal the source of the
> information leading to the interception of the ship, its sighting
> had to be attributed to air reconnaissance, and – as always in
> such instances – a flight was especially arranged so that the
> enemy would not become suspicious.

A CHANGE OF FOCUS

By the spring of 1945, it was clear that Japan was as doomed as Germany. Its forces were in retreat everywhere and the 'Greater East Asia Co-prosperity Sphere' was almost all in Allied hands. Major defeats throughout Asia – at Midway, Kohima and Imphal, Leyte Gulf – left no doubt that its military power was spent. Japan itself was being devastated by relentless intensive bombing (the country's predominantly wooden housing meant that damage to property was greater than in Europe) as Anglo-American aircraft roamed virtually unchallenged. Japanese planes, frequently grounded by lack of fuel, were increasingly used by suicide pilots in a desperate attempt to trade the lives of a few untrained fliers for enemy ships. The militarist government, aware that invasion would come within months, had no intention of giving up, and intended to contest every landing. Like their allies in Europe, they were driven to fanaticism by the knowledge that they could expect no mercy. Here too there would be no negotiated surrender.

It seemed to many among the Allies that the biggest clash of the entire war was still to take place and the build-up for the invasion of Japan, which it was estimated could cost the lives of a million soldiers, had already begun. In the event, the atomic bomb was to make this operation unnecessary, but in the meantime the European war had ended at the beginning of May 1945 and vast resources were suddenly available for the Pacific. These included the cryptanalysts of the SLUs, who had followed Allied armies from North Africa to Italy and, in history's longest continuous advance, from Normandy to Berlin. While Bletchley stood down its German speakers, Japanese became the language of greatest importance. Japan was far from defeated and the conflict in the Far East was thought likely to last a further one to three years. It would be necessary to set up there the same infrastructure that had existed in Europe. Little by little, as their duties dwindled and they became available, the specialists were sent to Australia to consolidate an efficient organization before being spread through the myriad islands and archipelagos that made up the Pacific theatre.

When veterans of the European and Middle Eastern theatres arrived in Brisbane to prepare for what was expected to be a long and costly campaign against the Japanese home islands, they were struck immediately by the slow and easy-going pace at which their counterparts worked. While they found Australians charmingly hospitable and enjoyed what promised to be an active social life, they privately despaired of injecting a sense of urgency into the operations of the SLU. Another potential difficulty was the complete American dominance of the Pacific theatre, which meant that the codebreakers were working directly for the reputedly anti-British General Douglas MacArthur. It promised to be a challenging time. Squadron Leader SF Burley remembered:

I am afraid my first impressions on arrival were grim and I despaired for there seemed to be such a lack of enthusiasm. I was only interested in setting up all the arrangements for getting Ultra signals going and I had the impression that there was no hurry. Perhaps my only consolation was that the first echelon of the SLU would soon arrive and then we could get moving. At that time I had reluctantly come to the conclusion that as far as the Australian services and civilians were concerned the war was a long way away, which in fact was very true. It was a strange feeling to be located somewhere where after the hustle and bustle at home, where the order of the day was 'to keep moving, there was a war on,' now to find myself just waiting around. We had ideal offices, a whole floor at the Australian Mutual Providence Building in Queen Street, Brisbane. This had been part of General MacArthur's headquarters. My office was next to the American Intelligence and the whole lay-out was satisfactory. General MacArthur's attitude was very much anti-British and he really did not like the idea of us being around but despite this our relations with American units to whom Ultra was given were good and the material much appreciated.

Some experienced the discomforts of working in the jungle as well as in a Brisbane office block. The primitive shelters in which they sought privacy were all too familiar to veterans of the Middle East, Italy and Normandy, though the climate was more savage:

We were requested to set up Command Posts in Morotai, Lae and subsequently Labuan. These were under the command of Squadron Leader Parsons who had been in North Africa and Italy. Here we had problems for we had tented army headquarters and it was difficult to get what I wanted. The general idea it would seem in the minds of the Australian advance headquarters was that the SLU should be considered as part of the signal section which was totally unacceptable, but we were able to organise a separate area. Even so it was still pretty primitive and I found it necessary to brief all personnel on the security position and its problems and to make sure that a) the area allotted to the SLU was out of bounds to all other personnel, and b) in order to achieve this the Type X tents etc. should be enclosed by a further surround of hanging tent material to keep out anyone who became too nosey. It achieved its object and there were no incidents. Apart from all these problems the heat and the swamps didn't help to make life too easy. Transport found difficulty in the ever-present mud and so to overcome this problem palm trees were cut down by the army and laid to make a road.

Jack Poole was another old hand who expected to be in the Far East for a lengthy spell. He too worked in the Australian Mutual Providence Building in Brisbane, and felt that his unit was just getting into its stride when they found themselves redundant. For him, the war ended in spectacular, if convivial, circumstances:

This conspicuous semi-skyscraper in the centre of the city had been part of General MacArthur's headquarters. The SLU offices were on the 8th floor and commanded a magnificent panoramic view from the window of the cipher room. While the SLU staff already in occupation did most of the work those of us who arrived as reinforcements lost no time in acclimatising ourselves to this new field of Ultra. After the activities in the European campaign we found the set-up rather different but basically, of course, the system was the same. It was not many days before the remainder of the party with whom we had left the United Kingdom joined us and we were slotted into the duty-rosters of the A.M.P. Building. Our paramount task was to 'get the feel' of the type of material handled in the Pacific area in readiness for future operations. Life was relatively undemanding.[53]

... Things were moving behind the scenes that were calculated to affect us but in the meantime we enjoyed our work in the A.M.P. Building. Then came the day we were called together and Squadron Leader Yeudall explained that Flying Officer Reynolds was to take an SLU up to Manila. The list for the plane trip was read out and I found myself at the head of one of the parties. We packed our kit-bags in readiness for the signal to depart for the Philippines and decided to have a last fling in Brisbane. I and a couple of sergeants accepted an invitation to a dance at the RAF Recruits' Centre.

And then suddenly the world in which the codebreakers had lived for five long and eventful years came to an end. After the dropping of the atomic bomb on Hiroshima on 6 August 1945, the Japanese stopped fighting a few days later and would officially surrender on 2 September:

> As the nostalgia flowed there was a commotion on the dance floor. People stopped dancing and began to dash towards the hall door. An airman rushed into the Officers' Mess. 'It's all over!' he yelled exuberantly, 'The Japs have surrendered.' The atom bombs had obviously brought the Far Eastern hostilities to a precipitate end. But the officers at the dance were cautious and telephoned the *Brisbane Courier Mail* for confirmation of the news. Yes, said the news room, it was no rumour!
>
> The hectic celebrations continued next day and there was pandemonium in the centre of the city. For days the revelry was sustained and SLU boys played a conspicuous part, when not on duty, in the various events that were arranged. While all the shouting and the tumult was dying down, the SLU team was unwinding. The Manila trip was, of course, called off. Although I was glad that the war in the Far East was over I must admit to a feeling of slight disappointment in not getting up to the Philippines before the end came. It would have meant that I should have been at the scene of both the surrenders in World War II.

The swiftness of the Japanese capitulation took everyone by surprise and men who had barely unpacked, or had at least hardly acclimatized, found themselves ordered home for demobilization. There would be no further glory, or achievement, for the SLUs after all. Josh Reynolds ended his recollections with this fine tribute to all those who served in the Special Liaison Units:

> A small contingent of SLU marched in the victory parade in Brisbane. I think little has been said or even known about the work of the SLU organization in the Pacific. That it must, as in Europe, have proved invaluable was evident from the insistence of the main Australian and some American headquarters to have Ultra and to have it quickly. There is also no doubt our boys did a marvellous and most demanding job often under the most difficult conditions.

Squadron Leader SF Burley also remembered the final days of his service. With little time in which to adjust to changed conditions, his unit had to begin the process of closing down their office. He too paid tribute to his colleagues:

> The role of the SLUs was now coming to a close for although we were well advanced with the arrangements for echelons to be provided to forward elements of both air force and army commands ahead of those already provided, the atom bomb was dropped and the war in the Far East had come to its end.
>
> There was of course the formal closing down of stations and the mammoth task of collecting signals and other materials etc. for return to the UK. It was arranged that Squadron Leader Parsons was to be responsible for returning these by H.M. ship and having metal banded boxes made to take them. Parsons carried cover instructions that no one, repeat no one, could have access to the boxes and if there were any questions he should refer them to Group Captain Winterbotham. There were none asked and in due course the boxes arrived back. Here perhaps it was good to remember that our final signal to Bletchley Park saying we were closing down was not strictly in official parlance and we were delighted to receive back an acknowledgement in the same light-hearted tone – 'Well done oh true and faithful servants, thanks a lot,' or some such words. We at least appreciated that Bletchley Park had a sense of humour.

And Josh Reynolds concluded:

> May I sum up the vital part of my life in the SLU. A unique allied inter-service operation by few people, mostly enthusiastic amateurs with relatively low ranks who distributed vital, accurate information on enemy intentions to Allied political and military leaders and decision-makers on an almost worldwide basis. It was a quick, economical service which operated for five and a half years, 24 hours a day, 7 days a week, and all this time there was no breach of security. Security both technical and operational of the whole operation was paramount. The SLUs were never found wanting.

CHRONOLOGY

1642   Calculating machine invented by Blaise Pascal, a 19-year-old Frenchman. It is never built.

1693   Another, similar machine designed by the German Gottfried Leibniz.

1801   French textile manufacturer Jacques Jacquard invents 'operation cards,' an ancestor of the computer programme.

1821   Charles Babbage, a Cambridge mathematics professor, invents the 'difference engine' – a series of calculating machines connected to work in unison, and based on Leibniz' principles.

1834   Analytical engine also developed by Babbage. This is the fundamental concept of a computer with a programme and memory.

1890s   American Herman Hollerith uses Jacquard's card system to automate the analysis of US census returns. He later founds IBM.
Bazeries enciphering machine is invented by a French army officer.
Enciphering machines equipped with keyboards.

1914   British Naval Intelligence begins intercepting German signals traffic, establishing Britain's most efficient decrypting service of World War I. Its greatest triumph, in 1917, is the interception of the 'Zimmerman Telegram' from Germany's Foreign Minister to her ambassador in Mexico, offering incentives for Mexican alliance with the Central Powers. This causes widespread anti-German feeling in the US.

1918   Enigma invented in Germany for use in banks and other businesses.

1921   Washington Naval Conference. Japan is persuaded by the US and Britain to maintain a navy smaller than theirs. Anglo-American negotiators take a firm stance because decryption of a diplomatic message has shown Japan willing to compromise.

1923   Enigma displayed at the International Postal Union's congress in Berne.

1926   German Navy begins to use Enigma, followed by German Army in 1928.

1929   Polish Intelligence begins analysis of Enigma after a machine is accidentally sent to Warsaw from Germany.
US 'Black Chamber' – decrypting department – closed down. Yardley, the American decrypter of the Japanese telegram in 1921, writes a book, *The American Black Chamber*, about his experiences. It causes outrage in Japan and leads to the building of a powerful fleet. In 1934 Japan withdraws from the 1921 Naval Agreement.

1930   Japanese Government begins using Enigma.

1931   Japanese invasion of Manchuria, the unofficial beginning of World War II.

1932   Hans Thilo Schmidt, a German civil servant, begins selling Enigma secrets to France.

1933   Forschungsamt, or Research Office, established in Germany as signals intelligence unit, and attached to Luftwaffe.
Polish cryptographer Marian Rejewski discovers the wiring layout for Enigma.

1936   German operators begin changing Enigma's wheel-order monthly, then daily.
Z1 computer designed and built in Berlin by Konrad Zuse. It is followed by the Z2 and Z3. The latter is believed to be the first electronic computer ever built.

1937   Polish mechanic with experience of work in a German Enigma factory is smuggled to France to build a replica.

        December Large-scale Japanese invasion of China.

1938   Bletchley Park, Bedfordshire, is bought by a mysterious naval officer and work begins on the relocation of the Government Code and Cipher School.

        September Munich Agreement. Britain and France allow Germany to occupy and dismember Czechoslovakia.

1939   **August** Hitler-Stalin pact divides Poland.
      September Hitler invades Poland. Britain and France declare war on Germany.
      October Sinking of *HMS Royal Oak* in Scapa Flow by Gunther Prien.

1940   **March** The first of Turing's Bombes becomes operational at Bletchley.
      April/May 'Phoney War' ends with German invasion of Scandinavia and Western Europe.
      Winston Churchill, a keen supporter of the work at Bletchley Park, becomes Prime Minister
      and Britain's war leader.
      August Battle of Britain. German Luftwaffe attempts to destroy numerically inferior RAF.
      Radar, and Enigma, warn defenders of enemy strength and intentions, making possible
      effective, and successful response. 'Blitz' – intensive bombing campaign against British cities,
      begins and lasts throughout winter.

1941   US Intelligence breaks Japanese cipher.
      March Battle of Cape Matapan.
      May German trawler *Munchen* captured with Enigma settings on board. U-110 boarded in
      Atlantic. Vital codebooks and equipment seized.
      June *Bismarck* sunk.
      June Hitler's forces invade Russia, bringing the Soviet Union into the conflict on the side of the Allies.
      December Japanese attack on Pearl Harbor brings about war between the United States and
      Japan. Hitler declares war on America.

1942   **January** Germans break US military cipher in Cairo and obtain detailed knowledge of Allied plans.
      February Japanese capture Singapore, a key stage in their rapid conquest of much of East Asia.
      June Battles of Leyte Gulf and Midway. US Navy defeats enemy carrier-force and ends Japanese
      dominance of the Pacific.
      August US landings on Guadalcanal begin the slow and costly task of driving enemy forces
      from islands and territories throughout the Pacific.
      October Battle at El Alamein, Egypt, ends Axis hopes of conquering North Africa.
      November Operation Torch, Allied landings in North Africa.

1943   Extremely heavy U-boat losses (47 boats) convince Admiral Donitz that the Battle of the
      Atlantic cannot be won. Submarine fleet withdrawn from north Atlantic.
      January Surrounded German 6th Army surrenders at Stalingrad. Its defeat signals turning-point
      in the war against Hitler.
      February Chindits, commanded by Orde Wingate, become operational in Burma.
      April Ambush and killing of Admiral Yamamoto after decrypted messages reveal the time and
      route of a plane journey he is making over the Pacific.
      July Allied landings in Sicily. The arrival of enemy forces on Italian soil leads to the dismissal of
      Mussolini, the forming of a new Government and, in September, the surrender of Italy, which
      then joins the Allies.

1944   Development of 'Colossus,' the world's first programmable computer, at Bletchley.
      January Hitler's 'V weapons' – guided missiles – begin a second Blitz on England.
      June Allied invasion of Normandy brings the war onto the European mainland.
      July Plot to assassinate Hitler by senior officers. Among those imprisoned in subsequent
      retaliation is Admiral Canaris, former head of the Abwehr, the German secret service. He is
      executed in early 1945.
      August Allied landings in south of France.
      December Ardennes offensive. German forces make spirited attack in Belgium and
      Luxembourg, taking by surprise Allied forces whose decrypters had failed to notice that this
      action was imminent.

1945   **January** Death in captivity of Noor Inayat Khan, SOE agent.
      March Allied forces cross the Rhine.
      European war ends in May after suicide of Hitler the previous month. War against Japan ends
      in August following the dropping of atomic bombs on Hiroshima and Nagasaki.

BIBLIOGRAPHY AND SOURCES

Page numbers in *italic* refer to material that is originally quoted in the author's source.

Anonymous (Introduction by Denis Rigden) (2001) *SOE Syllabus*, Richmond: Public Record Office 28, 173

Barrett, Neil (2006) *The Binary Revolution*, London: Weidenfeld & Nicholson 44

Beevor, Antony (1991) *Crete: The Battle and the Resistance*, London: John Murray 136, *139*

Boyd, Carl (1988) 'Significance of Magic and the Japanese Ambassador to Berlin', *Intelligence and National Security*, Vol III, No.1, Jan 1988 *215–8*

Brion, Irene (1997) *Lady GI: A Woman's War in the South Pacific*, California: Presidio Press 245, 266, 268

Butters, Lindsey (2001) *Bletchley Park: Home of Station X*, Andover: Pitkin, 2001 *73*

Copeland, Jack B (ed) (2004) *The Essential Turing*, Oxford: Clarendon Press *39*

Davison, RB (1968) *A Guide to the Computer*, London: Longman 43

Dunlop, Richard (1979) *Behind Japanese Lines: With the OSS in Burma*, Chicago: Rand McNally 203, 207

Fleming, Peter (1957) *Invasion 1940*, London: Rupert Hart-Davis 98–9

Foot, MRD (1966) *History of the Second World War: SOE in France*, London: HMSO 164, *180*, 182, 190, 192

Good, IJ (1980) 'Pioneering Work on Computers at Bletchley', in N Metropolis et al (eds), *A History of Computing in the Twentieth Century*, London: Academic Press 32, 33, 44, 48, 52, 53, 66, 72, 73, 74, 75, 104

Hazelhoff, Erik (1980) *Soldier of Orange*, New York: Holland Heritage Society 164–5, 168

Hill, Marion (2004) *Bletchley Park People*, Stroud: Sutton *46, 52, 56, 59, 65, 74*, 153, *208, 209, 210, 224, 237*

Hinsley, FH (Harry) (1993) *Codebreakers: The Inside Story of Bletchley Park*, Oxford: Oxford University Press 55, 66

Hodgson, Lynn-Philip (2000) *Inside-Camp X*, New York: Mosaic Press *182*

Hoy, Hugh Cleveland (1932) *40 O.B. or How the War Was Won*, London: Hutchinson & Co. 10, 18, 19

Kahn, David (1978) *Hitler's Spies*, London: Hodder & Stoughton *15, 16, 141–2*, 193

Konstram, A and JM Showell (2003) *7ʰ U-boat Flotilla*, Hersham: Ian Allen 108

Kressman-Taylor, Katherine (2002) *Address Unknown*, London: Souvenir Press 12

Library of Congress Veterans' History Project 256-7

Lycett, Andrew (1995) *Ian Fleming, The Man Behind James Bond*, Nashville: Turner Publishing 106

Marks, Leo (1998) *Between Silk and Cyanide*, London: Harper Collins 55, 174, 175–8

Melinsky, Hugh (1998) *A Codebreaker's Tale*, Norfolk: Lark's Press 262, 264, 271

MoD (Navy) (1989) *German Naval History. The U-boat War*, London: HMSO 126

Page, Gwendoline (ed) (2003) *They Listened in Secret*, Wymondham: George Reeve 83

Paul, Doris A (1973) *The Navajo Code Talkers*, Philadelphia: Dorrance & Co. 255, 258-61

Pimlott, John (ed) (1994) *Rommel in His Own Words*, London: Greenhill Books 144

Pitt, Barrie (1981) *Churchill and the Generals*, London: Sidgwick & Jackson 141

Roskill, Capt SW (1954) *The War At Sea*, Vol. 1, London: HMSO, cited in Peter Fleming (1957) *Invasion 1940*, London: Rupert Hart-Davis 99

Ryan, Cornelius (1960) *The Longest Day*, London: Victor Gollancz 196

Smith, Michael (2004) *Station X: The Codebreakers of Bletchley Park*, London: Pan 20, 71, 94, 105, 210, 214

Smyth, Bt. VC, MC, Brigadier the Right Hon. Sir John (1968) *The Story of the George Cross*, London: Arthur Barker 123

Stafford, David (1986) *Camp X*, Harmondsworth: Viking 181

Stripp, Alan (1989) *Codebreaker in the Far East*, London: Frank Cass 209, 213, 240, 246-7, 248, 250-1, 265, 271, 272

Sunday Times, 5 June 1949 174, 190

Tyler Moore, D and M Waller (1962) *Cloak & Cipher*, London: George C. Harrap & Co. 23, 239, 243

Welchman, Gordan (1982) *The Hut Six Story*, London: Allen Lane 29, 40, 41, 54, 212

West, Nigel (1992) *Secret War*, London: Coronet Books 182

Winterbotham, FW (1975) *The Ultra Secret*, London: Futura 9, 16, 31, 36, *37*, 68, 87-9, 94-6, 128, 139, 141, 142, 144, 145, 154, 156, 159-60, 163, 214, 223-4, 238

Zabecki, David T (ed) (1999) *World War II in Europe: An Encyclopedia*, New York and London: Garland 53

IMPERIAL WAR MUSEUM
Department of Documents:

Addey, Miss L 05/62/1 160

Ashbee, Felicity 97/34/1 48, 58, 59, 64

Baker, Mrs D 91/4/1 84-6

Balme, Lt Cdr DE 02/2/1 101, 107, 110, 120-2

Brailsford, Sgt Frank [quoted by Sqn Ldr SF Burley, 78/74/1] 134, 235

Burley, Sqn Ldr SF 78/74/1 146, 148-9, 151, 222, 274, 275, 277

Carman, SM 'Memories of a Wren' 03/43/1 60

Churchill, Winston [quoted by DE Balme, 02/2/1] 101

Clark, Mrs FE Misc 190 (2827) 46, 49, 73, 76, 236; (2927) 56

Darling, Lt GP 05/63/1 13

Drury, RJ 99/42/1 78

Fairrie, CJ 04/2/1 112, 119

France, S 82/27/1 111

Gibbs, D 86/29/1 201, 204-6

Grindlay, RC 96/12/1 197-9, 247

Harding, Mrs A 05/67/1 49, 60, 63, 66, 75, 77, 79, 81, 92, 214

Holliday, Mrs LP Misc 190 (2927) 63

Howard, Mrs J 02/26/1 219, 225

Howard, Capt JN [quoted by Sqn Ldr SF Burley, 78/74/1] 163

Jackson, Sgt Douglas [quoted by Sqn Ldr SF Burley, 78/74/1] 220, 227

Jenks, RT 92/37/1 24, 25, 131-3

Kempson, CW 'Sunshine and Sabotage' [quoted by Capt. CA Watney, 03/25/1] 14 , 185

Kitching RNVR, Lt CT 86/11/1 116

Kup, Mrs EM 88/2/1 81, 91

Lamont, Sqn Ldr John [quoted by Sqn Ldr SF Burley, 78/74/1] 150, 155

Leeney, RA 06/22/1 202, 204

Longe, Major DE 03/54/1 166, 171-2

McCaffery, John 'No Pipes or Drums' 05/77/1 157

Marshall, Eric 94/32/1 108-9

Mellor, Sgt Jack [quoted by Sqn Ldr SF Burley, 78/74/1] 136, 221, 228

Monckton, Capt. E 35/29/1 113-4

Narey, Capt. Peter 78/74/1 227

Openshaw, Mrs EJE 88/3/1 17

Partridge, Mrs Barbara L Misc 190 (2827) 77

Poole, Flight Sgt Jack [quoted by Sqn Ldr SF Burley, 78/74/1] 56, 226, 229, 230-1, 235, 275-6

Rance, Mrs HB 96/4/1 69, 71

Rattray (Penrose), Patricia 'You'll Be Sorry' 94/27/1 211, 251-4, 269-70

Reece, Sqn Ldr OB [quoted by SF Burley, 78/74/1] 133, 145-7, 152, 233

Reynolds, Flt Lt NE ('Josh') [quoted by Sqn Ldr SF Burley, 78/74/1] 135, 163, 276, 277

Spencer (Luke), Doreen Gertrude 'My Road to Bletchley Park' 03/9/1 61, 62, 183, 235, 237

Spickett, Alfred 87/2/1 11

Tack, GH 95/34/1 206

Thompson, Sqn Ldr AL [quoted by Sqn Ldr SF Burley, 78/74/1] 143, 147, 148, 161-2

Ward, Margaret Misc 190, (2827) 58, 76

Waterhouse, Cynthia 'Bombe Surprise!' 97/34/1 51, 57, 69, 72

Watney, Capt. CA 03/25/1 166-7, 169-71, 186-9, 193

INDEX

Abwehr 9, 27, 99
Addey, Miss L: on convoy
   organization 160
Admiralty 19
   Bletchley ignored 103
   ciphers changed 99, 110
   Germans break codes 99, 100, 110
Adolf Hitler Line 159
Air Ministry 96-7
Alanbrooke, Field Marshal 162
Albania 129
Alexander, Field Marshal Harold 72,
   132, 146, 150, 153, 157, 159, 162
Alexander, Hugh 29, 53
Algeria 129, 145, 146
Allies
   Commonwealth troops 129, 136,
      140
   Eighth Army 140, 141, 152
   Fourteenth Army 204-5
   Germany entered 233
   North African victory 152-3
   victory in Italy 157-63
Amazon, HMS 112, 118
Anderson, Gen. 145, 148, 149-50
Anzio, Battle of 157, 158, 159
Ardennes 230-1
Ark Royal, HMS 124
Arlington Hall 214, 247
Arnim, Achim von 145
Ashbee, Felicity
   on Bletchley backgrounds 48
   on Bletchley induction 59
   as Clerk Special Duties 58
   flair for languages 58
   worrying room-mate 63-4
Athena 103, 118
Atlantic, Battle of 100-27
Atlantic Wall 223
ATS (Auxiliary Territorial Service) 52
Aubretia, HMS 112, 116, 118, 120
Auchinleck, Field Marshal 140-1, 142
Australia 248, 251-4, 273-5
Austria 47
Austro-Hungarian Army 24

Babbage, Charles 42, 44
Badoglio, Marshal Pietro 156
Baker, Mrs Daphne
   as enemy's target 86
   listens for German R/T 84-5
   on 'Y' station life 83-4
Baker-Cresswell, Joe 119
Balkans 128, 129, 157, 196-8
Balme, Lt.-Com. DE
   on Atlantic 'tonnage war' 107
   on boarding of *U110* 119-22
   on Britain's import need 101
   on convoy escort 110
Barratt, Air Vice Marshal 132
Barrett, Neil: on Universal Turing

Machine 44
Bazeries, Commandant 29
BBC
   coded messages 13-15, 190-2,
      194-5
   spreading of stories 51
Bedell Smith, Gen. 146
Beevor, Anthony: *Crete: The Battle and
   the Resistance* 136-9
Begue, Georges 191
Belgium 22, 80, 164, 228
Berlin 90, 233
Birmingham, HMS 115
Bismarck 17, 72, 124
Bletchley Park 16, 97
   acquisition of 46-7
   appearance/amenities 46-7, 50,
      63, 65, 75-7, 209
   expansion of 208-9
   invasion procedures 92-4
   message source disguised 82
   morale-boosting 72-3, 124
   post-war wind-down 236-7
   secrecy of 18, 48, 51-2, 55-7
   signal overload 218-19
   staff billets 51, 59, 62-4
   staff procurement 48-51, 82
   strict regulations 64-5
   tasks and skills 57-62
   US uniforms appear 214
   see also codebreakers; codebreaking;
      SLUs (Special Liaison Units)
'Blitz' 90, 95-7
Blitzkrieg 80
Bradley, Gen. 155
Brailsford, Sgt. Frank
   demobilization 235
   on SLU training 133-4
   V-1s 'ignored' 226
Brion, Irene
   cryptography classes 244-5
   on 'jungle rot' 268
   Pacific environment 265-6
   on SIS structure 267-8
Britain
   'Blitz' 90, 95-7
   German naval agreement 102
   German spies in 97-9
   Germany's invasion plans 86-8, 94
   import dependence 100-1
   invasion fears 91-4, 107, 129
Britain, Battle of 89-97
Broadway, USS 112, 117-19, 120
Brown, Tommy 123
Buckmaster, Col. Maurice 170
Bulge, Battle of 230
Bulldog, HMS 112, 116-22
'Bureau IV' 26
Burley, Sqn. Ldr. SF
   Australians' 'lack of enthusiasm'
      274

closing down office 277
   Eisenhower and Ultra 150-1
   on high-ranking support 147
   'most secret...intelligence' 148
   security in jungle 274-5
   as SLU in Algiers 145
   'SLU...unobtrusive' 149
   USAAF posting 221-2
   'What, a REAL earl?' 222
Burma 13, 243
Burma Defence Army 199
Bushey Park 220-1

Caesar, Julius 27, 28
Caesar Line 159
Cairo 140
Cambridge University 52-3
Campbell, Corporal 197
Canada 93-4, 180-2
Canaris, Admiral 9, 27, 194
Cape Matapan 129-30
Carman, SM: Bletchley or 'the
   kitchens' 60
Casablanca 146
CB (Central Bureau) 266
Ceylon (Sri Lanka) 243
Chapuis, Henri 167
Chiang Kai Shek 133
China 243
Church, Alonzo 44
Churchill, Winston 17, 50, 66, 72,
   81, 87, 90, 93, 95, 132, 213
   on Battle of Atlantic 101, 107
   Berlin entry wish 232
   Cassino prediction 158-9
   demands on Montgomery 142
   gives SOE order 169
   hastens Overlord 224
   kindness to SLU 161-2
   on 'U-boat peril' 101
   uses SLU channels 153-4
   Vichy fleet order 129
ciphers
   breaking technique 29
   definitions of 28, 248-9
Clark, Mrs FE
   Bletchley backgrounds 49
   Bletchley hostel life 62-3
   mysterious Bletchley 56
   'thrilled' to be at Bletchley 46
Clark, Gen. Mark 157, 159, 160
code breakers
   eccentricity of 55, 73-4
   'first to know' 152-3, 235
   qualities needed 28-9
   recruitment 28-9, 46-7, 53-5,
      245-6
   women as 19, 251-4
code breaking 10
   the art of 27-9
   'Banburismus' 104-5

'cribs' 249
German Naval codes 79, 100,
    104-6
  Italian section 130
  Japanese section 273
  Luftwaffe code 67, 90, 95-6
  organizing 'pinches' 105-7, 114-23
  pre-D-Day pressures 220-1
  U-boat messages read 116, 122
  workings of 'Hut 8' 104-5
codebreaking machines
  the 'Bombe' 66-70, 104
  early examples 29-30
  Type-X 134-5, 210-11, 225, 229,
    269
  see also Enigma
codes
  definitions 27, 28, 248
  early use of 18
  German variations 16
  Hydra 122, 124
  Japanese 212-14, 240, 244-5,
    247-51, 263, 267
  a misunderstanding 13
  Navajo tribe 254-8
  Offizier code 122
  personal codes 12-13
  'Shark' 124, 125
  Triton 125
  US Black Code 141-2
Colman, John 54
computers
  Colossus 45, 65, 70-1
  early development 8, 41-5
Conner, Major Howard: on Navajos
  260-1
convoys 101-2, 110-14, 125
Cooper, Josh 153
Coral Sea, Battle of 242, 262
Cory, Gen. Sir George 171
Coventry 96-7
Crawford, George 54, 219
Crete, Battle of 136-9
cryptography *see* codebreaking
Cunningham, Admiral Andrew
  129-30, 132, 146, 147
Curwain, Eric: on SOE trainees 181-2
Cyprus 128
Cyrenaica 129
Czechoslovakia 11, 26, 78

D-Day
  BBC assistance 15
  Bletchley contribution 224-5
  first landings 224
  German knowledge of 193-5, 222
  preparing for 219-27
  radio traffic before 192-3
Darling, Lt. GP, RN: coded message
  to parents 12-13
Davies, Gwen: 'half...were absolutely
  mad' 73
Davison, RB: on electronic
  computing 43

Dawnay, Col. 149, 150
Denmark 79, 88, 164
Denning, Major 200
Denniston, Cdr. Alistair 20, 36
Deuxième Bureau 34
Deveze, François 167
Dewey, Thomas E. 241
Dodecanese 128
Dönitz, Admiral Karl
  and Allied success 125
  concedes defeat 126-7
  'Rescue no one' 108
'Doolittle Raid' 261
Dourlein, Sgt. Pieter 184
Dover 83-4
Drury, RJ: Admiralty code example
  78
Dunkirk evacuation 80-1, 84, 86
Dunlop, Richard
  captured Japanese pilot 206-7
  Kachin women's strength 202-3
  Kachins' electronic talent 203
Dutch East Indies 243

Edinburgh, HMS 115-16
EDVAC 44
Egypt 128, 129
Einstein, Albert 44
Eisenhower, Gen. Dwight 146,
  150-1, 153, 232-3
  Pacific operation of 243
  on the resistance 164
  victory address 234
El Alamein 140, 142
Elizabeth, Queen Consort 93
Elwell, Charles: Germans know their
  names 184
Empire Starling 112-13
Enigma
  'abstracted' from Poland 35-7
  appearance 32, 36
  Bombas 34-5
  German development of 16, 31,
    32, 33, 34, 39-40
  Japanese use of 240
  Polish contribution 8, 33-5
  recovery from U-boat 121, 122
  typical message 211-12
  workings of 32-3, 37-9
Esmond 112
Ethiopia 128, 136
Ewing, Sir Alfred 19

Fairrie, CJ
  on boarding of *U110* 116-19
  U-boat encounter 111-12
Fasson, Lt. Francis 123
Fellers, Col. Bonner 141, 142
Figl, Gen. Andreas 24, 27
First United States Army Group
  15-16, 22, 223, 224
Fleming, Ian
  code book 'pinching' 106-7
  as SOE trainee 182

Fleming, Peter: *Invasion 1940* 97-9
Flowers, Tommy 71
Foot, MRD
  BBC coded messages 191-2
  'elementary...mistake' 189-90
  SOE agent's bad luck 182
  SOE agents' personal code 192
Foreign Office 45
Forschungsamt 26, 27
Foss, Hugh 32
France 22
  Allied agents in 185-7
  Cassino victory 159
  and Enigma 8, 37
  first BEF arrival 78
  resistance 14-15, 165, 187, 189-90
  surrenders to Germany 81, 107,
    164
  Vichy Government 129
France, S: U-boats' 'destructive
  chorus' 111
Freikorps 25-6
French Forces of the Interior 195
Freyberg, Gen. Bernard 136, 137, 139
Friedman, William S 266

Gamble, Lt.-Col. 202
General Post Office 20, 25
George VI, king 93
German Admiralty 21
German Army (*Heer*)
  6th Army 217
  Afrika Korps 140, 142, 143, 152
  Bletchley decodes messages 81
  Enigma machines of 32, 104
German Intelligence
  Allied plans obtained 141-2
  Englandspiel 183-5
German Naval Intelligence (*B-Dienst*)
  78, 103
German Navy (*Kriegsmarine*)
  code books obtained 20-2,
    105-6, 114-23
  codes broken 79, 100
  Enigma machines of 32, 100, 104
  Norwegian invasion codes
    broken 79
  see also U-boats
Germany
  Allies enter 233
  defeat in Italy 157-62
  doubts creep in 215-16
  final surrender 127, 234, 235
  invasion of Poland 8, 80, 86
  North African defeat 140-53
  overruns Scandinavia 79
  western campaign success
    80-1, 164
  WWI cryptography 24
Gestapo 183, 185
Gibbs, D
  Burmese diet 203-4
  'messages by runner' 202
  parachuting into Burma 199-200

radio power problems 204
recycled parachutes 203
requests supply drop 200–1
safeguarding the codes 204–5
Gibraltar 128, 143, 146
Gibson, Flt. Lt. 134
Gill, EWB: 'orderly Teutonic mind' 20
Glorious, HMS 103
Goering, Hermann 26, 87, 88, 95
Goertz, Col. Norman: on Navajo
  signallers 261
Good, IJ
  April Fooled 73
  Bletchley 'need to know' 51
  chess and Bletchley 53
  Colossus' features 71
  Enigma banking history 32
  on make-up of department 48
  on morale-boosting 72
  preparing 'Bombe' jobs 104
  'scientists...on...Reserve List' 47–8
  Shaun Wylie's talents 74–5
  'Turing...first class...runner' 74
  on Turing's behaviour 73–4
  Universal Turing Machine 43–4
  work could reach Churchill 65–6
  workings of Enigma 33
Gore-Browne, Lt.-Col. 135, 227
Gort, Field Marshal 9, 132
Gothic Line 160
Government Code and Cipher School
  (GC&CS) 16, 24, 45
  Enigma rejected 32
  recruitment 28–9
  single 'piece of...jigsaw' 17
  see also Bletchley Park
Graff, Henry: on Oshima's messages
  215
Grazier, Colin 123
Greece 107, 128–9, 136
Grey, Nigel de 208
Grindlay, RC
  arranges air support 198
  'attached to a group' 197
  Balkans parachute drop 196–7
  on OSS 'efficiency' 197–8
  trains in Palestine 247
Guadalcanal 258, 265
Gubbins, Brig. Colin 171
Gustav Line 157

Haines, Capt. 116
Hall, Admiral Sir Reginald
  'North Belgian Front' hoax 22
  and Room 40 O.B. 19, 20–3
  'Zimmermann telegram' 23
Halsey, Admiral 242
Hanslope Park 50
Harding, Mrs Ann
  accepted for Bletchley 59
  billet 'not nice' 59
  Bletchley evacuation procedures
  93
  Bletchley invasion preparations 92

colleagues 'very grand' 49
'fascinated' by Bletchley 66
learns of Norway invasion 79
'sister...turned up next door' 63
strange 'young men' mystery 214
tears of French officers 81
on Turing's arithmetic 74
Hazelhoff, Erik
  'choice of...every Hollander' 165
  Holland 'engulfed' by war 164
  on Holland's lack of cover 167–8
Hepburn Kana 245
Hermes, HMS 243
Heydrich, Reinhard 168
Hill, Marion: Bletchley 'a...conveyor
  belt' 210
Hinsley, Harry
  code book seizure plan 114
  on Hut 3 initiation 55
  on Hut 3 layout 65
  on ships saved by codebreaking 127
  warning to Admiralty ignored 103
Hirose Maru 272
Hiroshima 236, 276
Hitler, Adolf 15, 103, 108, 215
  on Allied information 141
  annexes Austria 47
  bombing of Britain 90, 95
  Britain refuses peace 86
  on Britain's supply routes 100
  Calais landing belief 223–4
  final strike hopes 230
  generals criticize 216
  Italian campaign of 154, 157, 160
  plans invasion of Britain 86–7
  refusal to face defeat 208
  reliance on intelligence 26–7
  seizes Sudetenland 47
  sends Rommel to N. Africa 140
  suicide of 235
  unsafe signals of 223
Hollerith, Herman 43
Holliday, Mrs LP: 'billeted in Bletchley
  town' 63
Home Guard 93, 97
Hong Kong 243
Hood, HMS 17
Hooper, Leonard 153
Housman, John 171–2
Howard, Capt. JN: Enigma 'innards'
  prize 163
Howard, Mrs J
  Bletchley and D-Day 224–5
  solves signal chaos 218–19
Hoy, Hugh Cleland
  Germany's cables severed 19
  secrecy at 40 O.B 18–19
  start of 40 O.B. 18
  'The ether was open' 10
  'Huff-Duff' equipment 124–5

Imphal and Kohima, Battle of 238,
  272
Iraq 128

Italy 16, 140, 142
  Allied landings 157
  armistice 156, 161
  driven out of N. Africa 128–30
  planes shot down 153
  resistance 165
  Sicily lost 155–6
Jackson, Sgt. Douglas
  in Patton's section 227
  as SLU codebreaker 220
Jacquard, Joseph 42, 43
Japan 163, 199, 205–7, 212–13
  anti-American feeling 239
  atom bomb dropped 236
  Britain/America naval treaty 238–9
  code book finds 249–50, 266
  defensive perimeter of 261, 272
  early WWII victories 243
  as information source 215–18
  invades Manchuria 240
  retreat of 271–3
  surrender of 235, 276
  WWI link to Allies 238
Java Sea, Battle of 243
Jenks, RT
  'Russian traffic' intercepted 24
  on SCU duties 131
  SLU workings described 131–2
  on variety of SLU postings 132–3
  on War Office radio network 25
  on 'Y' Section formation 24–5
Jeschonnek, General Hans 124
Jodl, Gen. 234
Johnston, Philip 255, 257–8
Jones, Lt.-Col. JE 255
Juin, Gen. 159

Kahn, David
  on agents' personal codes 192
  on Rommel's Allied information
  142
Kajihara, Tokashi 245
Kempson, CW
  Allied agents in France 185
  BBC aids resistance 14
Kesselring, Gen. 128, 154, 159–61,
  162
Khan, Noor Inayat 189–90
Kitching, Colin: capturing *München*'s
  code book 115–16
Knox, Dillwyn ('Dilly') 32, 35
Koch, Col. Oscar W 155, 227
Koga, Admiral 271
Korea 240
Kreschmer, Otto 124
Kressman-Taylor, Katherine: *Address
  Unknown* 11–12
Kup, Mrs Edith
  on French surrender 81
  instinct for enemy aircraft 91
  monitors Battle of Britain 90–1
Kursk 217

Lagarde, Jean 167

Lamont, John
  Alexander 'delighted' 150
  Anderson's annoyance 149–50
  Patton 'mighty pleased' with SLU
    155
Leibniz, Gottfried 42
Lemp, Fritz-Julius 118
Leney, RA
  radio problems in Burma 201
  swollen arm and Morse 201–2
Leonardo da Vinci 41, 42
Lewin, Ronald: Cambridge and
    Bletchley 53
Lewis, Major 200
Libya 128
Little, Keith
  learning a code 257
  'My weapon was my language' 261
  using Navajo code 255–6
London 90, 165, 166, 167
Long, Wing Commander 133, 135
Longe, Major DE
  on French resistance 166
  joining the SOE 171
  on SOE training 171–2
'Lord Haw-Haw': Bletchley
  speculation 50–1
Lovelace, Ada 42–3, 44
Luftwaffe
  basic code of 96
  Battle of Britain 89–97
  Bletchley breaks code 67, 90, 95 6
  intelligence gathering 26–7
  Sea Lion plans 88, 89
Luxembourg 80, 228
Lycett, Andrew: Ian Fleming's code
  book plan 106

MacArthur, Gen. Douglas 248, 271,
    273, 274
McCaffery, John
  Milan bombings audience 156
  SOE agent aids Italian peace 156–7
McCann, Edith 268
McClellan, Insp. George 181
Macdonald, Sqd. Ldr. 133
Magdeburg 20–1
'Magic' information 214–15
Maginot Line 78, 79, 80
Malaya 243
Malta 128, 141
Manchester, HMS 115
Manchuria 240
Maquis 14, 165, 185, 187, 192–3,
    195
Marks, Leo
  on Bletchley selection 54
  captured agents' security 176–8
  as codebreaking teacher 173–4
  coders' versatility 175
  'poems for...codes' 175–6
  on SOE code department 175
Marshall, Eric
  a Coder's life at sea 109

'Coders...were...welcome' 109
'heavily weighted code books'
    108–9
life on Atlantic ship 108
Marshall, Gen. George C
  on Pearl Harbor 241–2
  on US cryptography 241–3
Marshall, Lt.-Com. Leslie ('Freddie'):
  on 'Y' stations 82–3
Masters, Major 54
Mauborgne, Major Joseph 30
Meade, Sir Stewart G: 'admiration'
  for codebreakers 235–6
Mediterranean 123, 128–30
Melinsky, Hugh
  costly missed message 263–4
  Japanese Midway signals 262
Mellor, Sgt. Jack
  after the war 228
  codebreaking at Bushey Park 220–1
  on SLU interview 135–6
Menzies, Gen. Stewart 67
Merchant Navy 11, 101–3
Mexico 23
Meyer, Lt.-Col. Hellmuth 193–5
MI6 47, 82
Midway, Battle of 238, 242, 262–3,
    266, 272
Milner, Fred 202
Milner-Barry, Stuart 28–9, 53
Monckton, Capt. Eric
  actions after torpedoeing 112–13
  as U-boat prisoner 113–14
  U-boat's Enigma messages 114
Monte Cassino, Battle of 157, 158–9
Montgomery, Field Marshal Bernard
    132, 142, 143, 152
Morocco 129
Morse Code 15, 20, 60–1, 108, 110,
    183, 191, 270
Mountbatten, Admiral 132, 238
München 114–16
Mussolini, Benito 128–9, 156

Narey, Peter: Normandy volunteer
    227
National Socialist Party (Nazis) 11,
    26–7
Navajo tribe 254–61
Naval Intelligence 19, 22
Nave, Capt. 249, 250
Nelson, Sgt. 245
Nestor, HMS 116
Netherlands 80, 164–5, 167–8
  agents compromised 183–5
  liberated 228
Neumann, John von 44
New Guinea 243
Newman, MHA 43–4, 70–1
Nimitz, Admiral Chester 238, 262
North Africa 128, 140, 152–3
Norway 79, 88, 127, 164, 165

O'Connor, Gen. Richard 129

Oeser, Sqd.-Ldr. 218–19
OIC (Operational Intelligence
  Centre) 103
'one-time pad' 30–1, 131, 145, 210
Openshaw, Mrs EJE: Cipher Officer's
  war view 17
Operation Anvil 228
Operation Crusader 140
Operation Husky 153–5
Operation Overlord 127, 158, 222–3
Operation Sea Lion 87–90, 94
Oran 146
Oshima, Horishi
  on criticism of Hitler 216
  on Hitler's request 216
  as intelligence source 214–16, 242
  on Soviet recovery 217–18
OSS (Office of Strategic Services)
  13, 197–8
Owen, Major 197, 198
Oxford University 52–3

Pacific, war in 238–77
Palestine 128
Paris 228, 230
Parsons, Sqn. Ldr. 274, 277
Pascal, Blaise 42
Patton, Gen. 145, 155, 220, 223,
    227
Pearl Harbor 126, 141, 181, 240–2
Penrose, Patricia
  cipher office routine 269
  encryption methods 252–3
  new baby messages 270
  security procedures 253–4
  on security watch 270
  strain took its toll 270
  swearing on Bible 251
  training starts 252
  on Type-X machines 210–11
  on 'Z' Force parties 268–9
Peric, Bob 197–8
Petard, HMS 123
Philippines 243
'phoney war' 78–9, 83
Picard, Raymond 166–7, 188
Pitt, Barrie: Rommel's access to
  Allied secrets 141
Poland
  Enigma contribution 8, 33–5
  German invasion of 8, 26–7, 78,
    80, 86
Poole, Jack
  at German surrender 234
  on Bletchley secrecy 55–6
  busy but enthusiastic 226
  D-Day signals surge 225
  'German paratroopers' alarm 230–1
  German prisoners in Reims 233
  Japan surrenders 276
  Paris bombing signal 230
  ready for Manila 275
  SLU life in caravan 229–30
  SLU and V-2s 225–6

Prien, Günther 103, 124
Prince of Wales, HMS 243

radar 27, 85, 90, 124
radio *see* wireless
Raeder, Grand Admiral 126
RAF Coastal Command 126
Ramsay, Admiral Sir Bertram 84, 132
Rance, Mrs HB
  cleaning and tea-making 69
  operating the 'Bombe' 69–70
Reece, Sqd. Ldr. Oliver
  attached to Eisenhower 232
  'fascinating' Russians 233
  'panoramic view of...war' 152
  radio silence in Gibraltar 145
  recruited into SLU 133
  welcomed by 'top brass' 151–2
  well-treated by Americans 232
Reichling, Sgt. Walter 195
Rejewski, Marian 34
Rennie, Lt. 200
Repulse, HMS 243
resistance 14–15, 164–8
  active service perils 182–90
  air 'drops' 187–8
  BBC messages to 14–15, 190–2
  Lysander pilots' instructions 186
  see also SOE (Special Operations
    Executive)
Reynolds, Josh 275
  cipher training 134–5
  selected for SLU 134
  SLU tribute 276
  on SLUs' move east 163
  'SLUs...never found wanting' 277
Richter, Allen 203
Rochefort, Lt. Com. Joseph 263
Rochester 112
Rome 158, 159
Rommel, Field Marshal Erwin 72, 128
  El Alamein defeat 142
  heads army in Italy 157
  on lack of supplies 144
  receives Allied plans 141–2
  Ultra stops supplies 143
Room 40 (O.B.) 18–23
Roosevelt, Franklin 241
Roskill, Capt. W: German
  intelligence-gathering 99
Royal Air Force 78, 154
  Battle of Britain 89–97
  enemy R/T monitored 90–1
  Goering's plans 87, 89, 95
  Italian planes shot down 153
  long-range aircraft 124
  Luftwaffe's plans known 95–6
Royal Navy 19, 87–8
  code books captured 114–23
  defeats Italians at Taranto 129–30
  dropping agents off 184
  evacuation from Crete 139
  German intelligence-gathering 99
  Germany blockaded 101

Rommel's convoys sunk 143
Vichy fleet shelled 129
  'weighted code books' 108–9
Royal Oak, HMS 103, 124
RSA (Reich Security Service) 27
RSS (Radio Security Service) 25
Rundstedt, Karl 223
Russia 20–1
  see also Soviet Union
Russian Revolution 24
Ryan, Cornelius: Germans hear
  D-Day plans 193–5

SA (*Sturmabteilung*) 26
Scandinavia 14
Schapper, Gottfried 26
Scharnhorst 103
Schepke, Karl 124
'Schlieffen Plan' 80
Schmidt, Hans Thilo 32, 34, 35
SCU (Special Communications Unit)
  131, 145
'secret wars' 10–11
Senyard, Phoebe: Bletchley
  evacuation plans 93–4
SHAEF 233, 234
Sicily 128, 153–5
Sidi Barrani 129
Sinclair, Sir Hugh 47
Singapore 243
Sinkov, Col. Abraham 266
SIS (Signal Intelligence Unit) 266,
  267–8
Skorzeny, Otto 230
Slessor, Sir John: on Enigma
  'abstraction' 37
Slim, Field Marshal 132, 204, 238
SLUs (Special Liaison Units) 16, 17
  annoyance of aides 221
  in eastern Mediterranean 145–52
  final move to Pacific 273–6
  formation and duties 130–3
  getting ready for Europe 225–7
  and Italian campaign 153–5, 160
  life after D-Day 228–37
  and Operation Torch 145
  recruitment 133–6
  transfers to Normandy 227
  UK postings before D-Day 220–2
Smyth, Sir John 123
SOE (Special Operations Executive)
  55
  in the Balkans 196–8
  BBC messages of 190–2
  in Burma 199–207
  Camp X training school 180–2
  codes and ciphers 172–80, 183,
    192
  dangers for agents 182–4, 189–90
  procedures to observe 178–80
  setting up 168–72
Somali, HMS 115, 116
Somaliland 128, 136
Soviet Union

enters WWII 101
  Germany's rearguard action 127
  Hitler's attack plans 88–9
  Japanese pact 217
  soaring morale 217–18
  unbreakable code 24
Spaatz, Gen. 145, 225, 226, 228–9,
  233
  SLU commendation 231, 234–5
Spain 102
Speer, Albert 215
Spencer, Doreen
  cinemas and Stratford 76
  contact with agents 183
  German surrender news 235
  'I learned Scottish dancing' 76
  impressions of Bletchley 61–2
  Japan surrender ends job 236
  learned 'touch typing at speed' 61
  Morse Code skill 60–1
  'no mention of Bletchley' 61
  pantomime Principal Boy 236–7
Spickett, Alfred: enemy torpedoes
  sabotaged 11
spies 97–9, 240
SS (*Schutzstaffel*) 27, 39–40
Stalingrad 216, 217
Station X *see* Bletchley Park
Sterbity, GR 43
Stillwell, Gen.: on Burma conditions
  199
Stonehouse, Brian 182
Stripp, Alan
  Admiral Koga eliminated 271
  Allied targets provided 271
  Bletchley's expansion 208–9
  'discipline...hardly existed' 213
  'hospital ship' intercepted 272
  impressed by Bletchley 212–13
  Japanese codebreaking bases 247–8
  Japanese vs German approach
    248–9
  on learning Japanese 246–7
  many Japanese codes 240
  oil as target 271
  Pacific codebreaking 265
  recruited for Bletchley 245–6
  'spare' time practice 250
  on suicide squadron 272
  typical message 250–1
  on Yamamoto attack 264–5
Suez Canal 128, 136

Tachibana Maru 272
Tack, GH: codes/radios captured
  205–6
Taylor, Alfred: on SOE training
  school 181
Tedder, Air Chief Marshal 146, 151
telegraph 19, 20
Teramoto, Lieutenant General 271
Thailand 243
Thompson, Sqd. Ldr. AL
  Churchill's kindness 161–2

Eisenhower 'glad to get...
information' 146
German planes intercepted 143
I 'was completely independent' 148
'kept on a...low rank' 146
on 'life...in the mountains' 146-7
on SLU secrecy 147
worried by Victor Emmanuel 161
Thompson, Jean: Bletchley was 'Nut
House' 46
Tickell, Jerrard
on agent 'Madeleine' 189
women as agents 174-5
Tiltman, Col. John 209, 245-6, 246-7
Tirpitz 72
Tobruk 140
Tripoli 128
Troward, Capt. 203
Tuck, Capt. Oswald 246-7
Tulloch, Lt.-Col. 200-1
Tunis 152, 153
Turing, Alan 106
attached to Foreign Office 45
and Colossus 71
designs the 'Bombe' 66
eccentric behaviour 73-4
on Enigma workings 37-9
'I never did...arithmetic' 74
marksmanship training 92, 93
plans for Bletchley 50
sets up 'Hut 8' 104
and Universal Turing Machine 43-4
Twinn, Peter 92
on 'Banburismus' 105
and German naval cipher 104
whole message never decoded 100

U-47 103, 124
U-110 116-22
U-163 113-14
UC-44 (U-boat) 21
U-boats 21, 23, 100-4
Allies fight back 124-7
as Atlantic threat 107-14
'milk cow' refuelling 122
production increases 124
Royal Navy boardings 116-23
snorkels introduced 127
Type VIIC 102-3
'wolf packs' 110-11, 125
Ubbink, Lt. Johan 184
Ugacki, Admiral 265
Ultra information 17, 35, 87, 88-9,
95, 131
and defence of Crete 136-9
messages to Crete 137-9
and Rommel 140-5
United States 11
Black Code broken 141-2
cryptographers in 214-15, 218,
241-3
destroyers for Britain 107
joins WWI 23, 102
joins WWII 101, 125, 214

own decrypting centre 214
radio music ban 13
as U-boat target 125-6
Ultra shared 17
United States Army
First Army 152
Third Army 220
United States Intelligence
codebreaking successes 241-3
Japanese cipher broken 240
Pearl Harbor missed 240-1
United States Marine Corps 255-61
United States Navy
Atlantic escort duties 126
'Liberty ships' 126
United States WAC 265, 266
US Tactical Air Force 226, 228
USAAF (US Army Air Force) 187-8,
221-2
USSTAF 230, 231

V-1 rockets ('Doodlebugs') 224
V-2 rockets 224-6
Verdun 22
Victor Emmanuel III, king of Italy
156, 161
Vint Hill Farms 244-5, 266

WAAF (Women's Auxiliary Air
Force) 52
Ward, Margaret: 'joined Bletchley...
by chance' 57-8
Waterhouse, Cynthia
billet was a stable 51
on Bletchley shift-work 68-9
on keeping up morale 72
not 'clear who was in charge' 57
operating the 'Bombe' 68
Watney, Capt. CA
on Allied parachute mission 187
canisters fly tricolour 188
Churchill sets up SOE 169
getting SOE recruits 169-70
Maquis before D-Day 192-3
organizing agent 'drops' 185-6, 187
setting up resistance 166-7
on SOE 'schools' 170-1
undercover occupations 166
US canister drop in France 187-8
Wavell, Field Marshal Archibald
140, 142
Webb, Air Marshal Sir William 145
Welchman, Gordon
German 'radio nets' 40-1
how Germans used Enigma 39-40
'I...recruited friends' 28-9
recruiting for Bletchley 53-4
typical Enigma message 211-12
Whaddon Hall 50
Wilhelm, Marge 268
Winterbotham, Group Capt. FW
Churchill's Cassino news 158-9
Clark squanders chance 159
on Enigma 'mock-up' 35-6

Enigma obtained 36
'First Army Group' hoax 223
Gen. Spaatz commends 234-5
German Sea Lion 'confusion' 94
German signal numbers 16
Goering's 'Operation Eagle' 95
on Hitler and Overlord 223
'insight into...[German] minds'
213-14
intercepts Sea Lion signals 87-9
learns of Luftwaffe plans 88-9
on 'one-time pad' 30-1
on the 'Bombe' 67
Patton aided by ULTRA 155
'put the pressure on' 147, 221
on RAF-Luftwaffe encounter 95-6
sets up SLUs 130, 131, 134-5
SLU and Italian campaign 153-4,
162-3
'SLUs were...old hands' 154
Ultra denied Rommel's supplies
143-4
on Ultra and Mediterranean 128
on Ultra and N. Africa 140, 142,
144-5
Ultra and Pacific war 238
Ultra's value in Crete 139
on V-2 threat 224
The Ultra Secret 10, 238
wireless
commercial radio messages 13-15,
190-2, 194-5
First Army Group hoax 15-16
German 'radio nets' 40-1
radio listening posts 20
SOE radio operators 196-207
traffic before D-Day 192-5
War Office network 25
World War I 18-24, 101-2, 108
Wright, Pat: on 'noisy' Type-X
machines 210
WRNS (Women's Royal Naval
Service) 17, 52
Wylie, Shaun 75

'Y' section 24-5, 82-6
Yamamoto, Admiral 263, 264-5
Yardley, Col. Herbert 238-9
The American Black Chamber 239
Yeudall, Sqd. Ldr. 275
Yosuke, Matsuoka: on Russian
morale 217

Zimmermann, Arthur: Mexican
alliance offer 23
'Zimmermann Telegram' 22-3, 208
Zuse, Konrad 43
Zygalski, Henryk 35

ACKNOWLEDGMENTS

As is always the case, my wife Sarah has been absolutely invaluable, and no thanks could ever be sufficient in view of her support and assistance. I am also grateful to my dear friend Mrs Nora Relingh for valuable information about the Resistance in occupied Europe. In the Imperial War Museum's Department of Documents I have put Emma Golding to a good deal of trouble, and I much appreciate her efforts. I also thank Rod Bailey, an authority on SOE, for advice. Eileen Simon, of the Veterans' History Project at the Library of Congress in Washington DC, has been extremely helpful, as she has on previous occasions. The VHP, set up comparatively recently, is becoming widely known as an invaluable source for historians, and I feel privileged to have had access to it. I have received – as I always do – extremely helpful guidance from Ruth Binney and from Neil Baber. I would also like to acknowledge the help of Ame Verso, Emily Pitcher, Tracey Woodward, Steve Newman and Debbie Jackson. Finally, I wish to thank the many heroes and heroines of the codebreakers' war who gave permission for their remarkable stories to be repeated here. Any errors are, of course, mine alone.

PICTURE CREDITS

1 Bletchley Park house ©Bletchley Park Trust; 2 Enigma machine ©James King-Holmes/Bletchley Park Trust/Science Photo Library; 3 Alan Turing ©The Art Archive; 4 Bombe machine ©Bletchley Park Trust; 5 Colossus with Wren operators ©Bletchley Park Trust; 6 Hut at Bletchley Park ©Bletchley Park Trust; 7 Hut 3 at Bletchley Park ©Bletchley Park Trust/Science & Society Picture Library; 8 Wrens at Bletchley Park ©Bletchley Park Trust; 9 Code breaking at Bletchley Park ©Bletchley Park Trust/Science & Society Picture Library; 10 Code breaking at Bletchley Park ©Bletchley Park Trust/Science & Society Picture Library; 11 War Office Signal Office ©Bletchley Park Trust; 12 Battle of Britain WAAF at control ©Topfoto; 13 Radio room of U-boat ©The Art Archive/ E.C.P.A., Ivry, France; 14 U-boat refuelling ©The Art Archive; 15 U-110 before capture ©The Imperial War Museum docs 04/2/1 The Papers of C.J. Fairrie; 16 Enigma machines in use ©Bildarchiv Preußischer Kulturbesitz, Berlin; 17 Enigma machines in the field ©Bildarchiv Preußischer Kulturbesitz, Berlin/Photo: E.Bauer; 18 General Guderian with enigma ©The Art Archive; 19 French resistance workers ©Roger-Viollet/Topfoto; 20 French agent using radio ©Keystone/Camera Press, London; 21 Suitcase radio ©The Robert Hunt Library; 22 BBC broadcast Cody Images; 23 Royal navy coders ©The Imperial War Museum/A7599; 24 Japanese code book ©Bletchley Park Trust; 25 Chindit operations, Burma ©The Imperial War Museum/IND2292; 26 Supplies dropped by air, Burma ©The Imperial War Museum/CBI35851; 27 Troops pick up supplies, Burma ©The Imperial War Museum/CBI27443; 28 Navajo Indian Code Talkers ©National Archives/Corbis; 29 Navajo Indian Code Talkers ©Bettmann/Corbis. UK/US COVER front: Enigma machine ©James King-Holmes/Bletchley Park Trust/Science Photo Library. UK/US COVER back: U-505 Courtesy of Uboatarchive.net/Capt. Jerry Mason, USN (Ret.)